POETRY

INTERNATIONAL

22/23

2017

THE SAN DIEGO STATE UNIVERSITY PRESS

Map of the *Southern Colonies* is projected in the greatest Part from Actual Surveys, in others from Journals, as laid down by Persons perfectly knowing in the Topography of the respective Countries, by Messrs. COLLET, DUNBIBEN, COOK, DE BRAHM, and others, The Coasts of *East and West Florida*, and the *Gulf of Florida*, are adjusted by the very curious Nautical Surveys of Engineer ROMANS. This Map will be found to have a very particular Degree of Geographical and Topographical Merit———As the Lakes *Champlain* and *George* form the Main Pass between the Maritime Colonies and *Canada* we have added, as an Appendix to this Collection, a particular Map of these Parts done from Actual Survey.

LIST of the MAPS.

Poetry International

is published annually at

San Diego State University
The Department of English
and Comparative Literature
5500 Campanile Drive
San Diego, CA 92182-6020

THE PUBLICATION OF THIS JOURNAL IS MADE POSSIBLE BY A GENEROUS GRANT
FROM THE

Edwin Watkins Foundation

e-mail: poetryintl@gmail.com
web site: http://poetryinternational.sdsu.edu

Single issues of Poetry International are
$20 for individuals and $25 for institutions.
Individual subscriptions: 2 years, $40; 3 years, $60
Institutional subscriptions: 2 years, $50; 3 years, $75

Cover design by Patricia Cué

Journal design by Garrett Bryant and Patricia Cué

Copy editor: Mary Rakow

Cover Image: Smith, Charles. *Picture of Organized Nature*, 1828.

ISBN-10: 1-938537-87-4
ISBN-13: 978-1-938537-87-5

SAN DIEGO STATE UNIVERSITY PRESS
PRINTED IN USA

Follow, poet, follow right
To the bottom of the night,
With your unconstraining voice
Still persuade us to rejoice.

With the farming of a verse
Make a vineyard of the curse,
Sing of human unsuccess
In a rapture of distress.

In the deserts of the heart
Let the healing fountain start,
In the prison of his days
Teach the free man how to praise.

—W. H. Auden

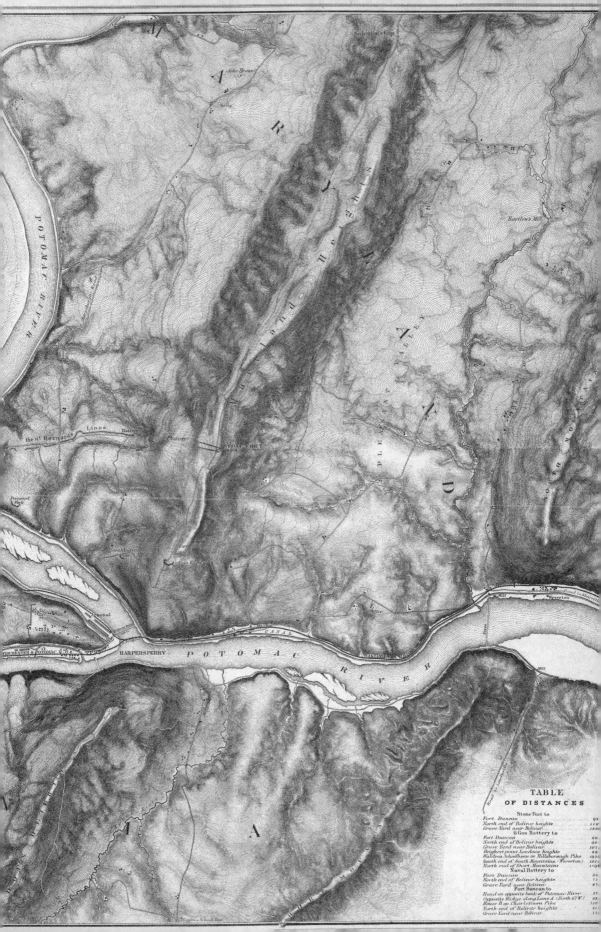

MARYLAND

John Brown

Salomon's Gap

Maryland Heights

Bartlow's Mill

POTOMAC RIVER

PLEASANT VALLEY

Gen.ˡ Barnard's Lines   Battery

Clutsey   STONE FORT

Prospect Rock

Naval Battery

Pontoon Br.

Weverton

Road to Knoxville

Mill

Miller

CANAL

WINCHESTER & POTOMAC R.R.

HARPERS FERRY   P O T O M A C   R I V E R   Mill

Canal

VIRGINIA

TABLE
OF DISTANCES

Stone Fort to
Fort Duncan 93
North end of Bolivar heights 110
Grave Yard near Bolivar 186
Gun Battery to
Fort Duncan 80
North end of Bolivar heights 90
Grave Yard near Bolivar 103
Heighest point Loudoun heights 88
Waldron Schoolhouse on Hillsborough Pike ... 1056
South end of South Mountains (Weverton) ... 1370
North end of Short Mountains 1100
Naval Battery to
Fort Duncan 85
North end of Bolivar heights 73
Grave Yard near Bolivar 83
Fort Duncan to
Road on opposite bank of Potomac River
Opposite Ridge along Lane A (North 67 W)
House B in Charlestown Pike
North end of Bolivar heights
Grave Yard near Bolivar

Contents

Poems

Edward Hirsch Portfolio

Valzhyna Mort Portfolio

Ishion Hutchinson Portfolio

Carol Frost Portfolio

Feature: Poetry from *Believer*

Edited with an Introduction
by Dominic Luxford

Li-Young Lee Portfolio

Malachi Black Portfolio

J. Hope Stein Portfolio: The Inventor's Last Breath

Feature: Poetry from Israel

David Gewanter Portfolio

Feature: Poetry from Bulgaria

Sandra Alcosser Portfolio

*

Mark McMorris Portfolio

*

Feature: Poetry from Sweden
Edited by Malena Mörling
and Jonas Ellerström

*

Maria Garcia Teutsch Portfolio

Kathleen Peirce Portfolio

*

Kerry Shawn Keys Portfolio

Symposium: On Kwame Dawes

Prose Poetry & Poetic Prose
Edited by Katie Farris

*

Sabrina Orah Mark Portfolio

*

Museum of Small Dark Things: 25 Poems by Georg Trakl
Translated by Jay Hopler

Nathalie Quintane Portfolio
Translated by Sylvain Gallais

Daniel Simon Chapbook

POEMS

VENUS KHOURY-GHATA

[Once she had a book]

Once she had a book
whose lines furled east to west like Siberian trains
Black smoke erupted from its pages when sentences tangled,
some hurtling into each other,
some conjoined, a small group that decided
to reach the word *end* before dark

He was an indoor book
fearful of winds that could fill him with sadness, with ill-spoken words
He recognized the woman by her smell: cumin and ink

She laughed with him
slept with him
her finger tapping in the darkness of his alphabet, paused in the same delirious
dream:

> A book in tatters walks down the village's only street
> the shoemaker adds a sole to the sentence that limps
> the blacksmith offers a horseshoe to avert the evil eye
> and the teacher teaches the first three letters

She had a second dream three nights before the great harvest:
> Her book sewn into a coffin waiting outside her door

Translated from the French by Cheney Crow

Catullus

LXX

My woman says there is no one
she would rather marry than me,
not even if Jupiter himself, god of the sky
and weather, were to court her.
But she says to her eager lover,
what a woman says while making love
should be written in wind and water.

Translated from the Latin by DiCarza

Katie Ford

A Spell

Take my lights, take my most and only opal,
take the thin call of bells I hear,
just. Take that thin lead,
wring out my water and drink
the wrung remains, take all that is nimble
and sun-up of day,
break my window to steal my eyes,
take their cotton, reap their fields;
as for my industry, it is yours.
I know in wishing not to bluff
so lay me on a threshing floor
and bleed me in the old, slow ways,
but do not take my child.

KATIE FORD

The Soul

It disappeared.
It reappeared
as chimney smoke
burning through carcasses
of swallows stilled,
and that it portrayed no will
was why I followed that smoke
with this pair of eyes.
It was that it didn't need
or require
my belief
that I leant upon it
as a tired worker
upon
a gate.

EDWARD HIRSCH

PORTFOLIO

After the Stroke

(William Meredith)

Suddenly he is standing at the bottom of a well
Trying to raise a broken arm in the darkness

It is curious

He keeps shouting louder and louder
But no one seems to hear him

All night singing rises and falls in his head

Where does music come from
And what is faith
Which does not desert him

He is a cello locked up in its black case

He is a church bell muffled in earth

God's Insomniacs

Those sleepless blurry-eyed mystics—
Cioran called them "God's Insomniacs"—
Mortified themselves
In the arid and obscure night.

They were spirituels, contemplatifs,
Voluptuous sufferers
Who could scarcely see the stars
Through the bitter light of their tears.

One of the saints never slept
More than two hours per night.
She stood up to pray
And nailed her hair to the wall.

One of the saints dipped her forehead
Into a candle, another tasted the flame.
She said it would start raining roses
After her death, though it never did.

Their austerities enthralled you,
One of the lonely agnostics
Lying awake at night and brooding
About the hole in your chest.

God and Me

The stars look like a broken belt
Glittering over the lakes and mountains

The moon looks like a tilted crown

Down here there's a whole lot of racket
In churches and bedrooms
Some good folks are speaking in tongues
And raising the rafters

I wonder if the Lord ever gets tired
Of so much flattery from the fundamentalists
He probably likes it better
Than all the complaints and entreaties

I'm standing up to listen
But he has nothing to say to the atheists

It would be nice to believe
That heaven is like a schoolyard
In which everyone gets chosen
Even the laggards

My friends are seekers and exiles
Who won't desert the stories

Me
I can't give him up
But I can't believe in him either
It's a one-sided relationship
I without Thou

He has whole galaxies to worry about
I don't suppose he gets too worked up
My puny self
Is more real to me
Than his immense non-being

I'm a tiny void with attributes
With my own little river of tears

But what is He
Who fills the world with trees and stars
And leaves us alone
With our wars and atrocities
Our deadly human nature
Our sad dominion over the fish and the fowl

Look
No one knows why
There is so much silence in the upper spheres
And so much suffering down here

The Almighty skipped over our houses

I Was Never Able to Pray

Wheel me down to the shore
Where the lighthouse was abandoned
And the moon tolls in the rafters

Let me hear the wind paging through the trees
And see the stars flaring out one by one
Like the forgotten faces of the dead

I was never able to pray
But let me inscribe my name
In the book of waves

Under a dome
Of a sky that never ends
And see my voice sail into the night

Prayers of an Unbeliever

Walk with me through the Old City at dusk

I want to see the Polish women scrubbing the stairs
And smell the cleanser burning off the stone

Let's wander over to Sienna and Sliska

In memory of the doctor in the attic
Who muttered the prayers of an unbeliever

While children slept in the orphanage downstairs

Look at the women throwing open
The windows and beating out the rugs

In a perpetual war on dust

...

There's nothing left here of August 6th 1942
It has all been disinfected

When 200 children marched

In a kind of tired trance
Like automatons

Through the hushed Warsaw streets

To the Umschlagplatz near the railway station
With chlorinated freight cars

...

Lord in whom I can't believe

I am going to walk through the Old City
And then lie down with my love

In this dirty world

Which is both the Song of Songs
And the Book of Lamentations

Troubadour Song

I woke this winter morning
    to the smell of the sea
and hummed a song for nothing,
    how nothing came to me.

I dreamed I mounted a horse
    along an empty beach
where we galloped far away
    'til I was out of reach.

We trotted past the lighthouse
    abandoned on the dunes
and paused by a small stable
    that was now in ruins.

I woke this winter morning
    to the smell of the sea
and made a song for nothing,
    how nothing came to me.

We rode to the starkest edge
    of nowhere, by the sea.
The horse was all that remained
    of what I'd longed to be.

We had somewhere deep to rest
    and nothing left to see,
and so the two of us walked
    into the cemetery.

I woke this winter morning
    to the smell of the sea
and sang a song for nothing,
    how nothing came to me.

Variations on a Psalm

When I was in distress, I sought the Lord; at night I stretched out
untiring hands, and I would not be comforted. (Psalm 77: 2)

And I would not be comforted
    When I was in distress
        I sought the Lord
I did not know why I did not believe

While I stretched out untiring hands
    And I would not be
        Comforted in my distress
I sought the Lord

 I would not pray
    I would not call on Him
        Stretched out with my untiring hands
And comforted I would not be

When I was in distress
    Without the Lord
        I stretched out tireless on the bed
My hands were sleepless in despair

And I would not be comforted
    In my distress
        I sought the Lord
I could not find Him

At night I stretched out untiring hands
    Like a penitent
        O Lord of disbelief
And I would not be comforted

David Tomas Martinez

Rebecca's Use

I was twenty-two and no longer news;

Pooh-butts and Gees creased to a cotton shank,
leaning on rusted fences and drooping stoops,
every part of Meadowbrook Apartments,
nodded or gave up the "P" as I passed.

And though I remember the ice cream
dripping down their youth,

the years also clicked up their wrists,

and the young boys I had know by name,
known by their embarrassing moments,
known by their relation of blood,
I now didn't know what they were called.

But I know what they are.

The boys in the "Brook
are a jagged apparatus in a jaw,
cutting until pushed out,
replaced by endless rows of teeth.

I made a necklace of these teeth

And a ring of Rebecca.

Nightly I snuck in her window
cold with beer,
hoping her father didn't hear.

Rebecca was still soft with youth

and I was hard with it,
without a sound we were
instruments of spring and clenched skin,
joint in our body's tool.

Rebecca still in the 'Brook—

belly six months big,
a boyfriend shot in the face,
a little sister all grown up
and staring at me—

pushed me
into the same bunk bed
I'd been hustled in and hid.

When she walked, I followed.
In her room, with precise

machine lust, we touched,
we tasted of lime and rust.

I sailed from Rebecca, the 'Brook,

stepping on the serrated edges of my pants,
leaving for a sea of dungarees and chevrons,

a Navy of brooms twirled before being used,
in everything being used.

Rachel Galvin

Village of Pulleys and Locomotion

I trail my suitcase along the platform,
the weight of the air's mechanism
at the small of my back. In the old country

a man would arrive from afar,
give each child a whistle, and parade them
through the village, whistling.

What is this fury of forms, boarding trains,
handing out whistles to children?
Dear spigot, dear filtering film of rubber,

if this world is the only world,
Anaximander will go on shaking his sieve,
persistently sifting with an ear to the ignition—

striker of matches, your scent of cloves, your fire
rides the circumference and a vortex gyrates at the center.
There is the vermiform signature: *you may eat*

of this tree. Now the glorious propinquity, now
the rupture. A village elder goes on debating
with his god. Who can tell if he receives a reply?

In the old stories, if you whistled,
the light would come to you
out of curiosity.

Valzhyna Mort

PORTFOLIO

Singer

A yoke of honey in a glass of cooling milk.
Bats playful like butterflies on power lines.
In all your stories blood hangs like braids

of drying onions. Our village is so small,
it doesn't have its own graveyard. Our souls,
are sapped in sour water of the bogs.

Men die in wars, their bodies their graves.
And women burn in fire. When midsummer
brings thunderstorms, we cannot sleep

because our house is a wooden sieve,
and crescent lightning cut off our hair.
The bogs ablaze, we sit all night in fear.

I always thought that your old trophy Singer
would hurry us away on its arched back.
I thought we'd hold on to its mane of threads

from loosened spools along Arabic spine,
same threads that were sown into my skirts,
my underthings, first bras. What smell

came from those threads you had so long,
sown in, pulled out, sown back into the clothes
that held together men who'd fall apart

undressed. Same threads between my legs!
I lash them, and the Singer gallops!

And sky hangs only the lightning's thread.
Like in that poem: on Berlin's Jaegerstrasse
Arian whores are wearing shirts ripped off
sliced chests of our girls. My Singer-Horsey,

why everything has to be like that poem?

Washday

Maria does her washing by the wall
so bare that you'd think she shaved it.

The window's open, any one can see.
Soap hisses. Air-raid warning rings
like a telephone from the future.
Her dress is nailed onto the laundry line.

From this gray garment, that is either guarding
or attacking the house, three yards of darkness
fall across the floorboards. She stands inside,
like on the bottom of a river, her heart an octopus.

Her hands so big, next to them, her head is a small o,
      (the neighbors squint)

stuffed hungrily with stubborn hair.

Crossword

A woman moves through dog-rose and juniper bushes
A pussy clean and folded between her legs.
Breasts like the tips of her festive shoes
shine silently in her heavy armoire.

One black bird, one cow, one horse.
The sea beats against the wall of the waterless.
She walks to a phone booth that waits
a fair distance from all three villages.

It's a game she could have heard on the radio:
a question, a number, an answer, a prize.
Her pussy reaches up and turns on the light in her womb.

From the rain, she says into the receiver,
we compiled white tables and chairs under a shed
into a crossword puzzle
and sat ourselves in the grid.

The receiver is silent. The bird flounces
like a burglar caught red-handed.
Her voice stumbles over her glands.

The body to be written in the last block –
I can suck his name out of any letter.

All three villages cover their faces with wind.

Factory of Tears

And once again according to the annual report
the highest productivity results were achieved
by the Factory of Tears.

While the Department of Transportation was breaking heels,
while the Department of Heart Affairs
was beating hysterically,
the Factory of Tears was working night shifts,
setting new records even on holidays.

While the Food Refinery Station
was trying to digest another catastrophe,
the Factory of Tears adopted a new economically advantageous
technology of recycling the wastes of past –
memories mostly.

The pictures of the employees of the year
were placed on the Wall of Tears.

I'm a recipient of workers' comp from the heroic Factory of Tears.
I have calluses on my eyes.
I have compound fractures on my cheeks.
I receive my wages with the product I manufacture.
And I'm happy with what I have.

Translated from the Belarusian by the author, Franz Wright and Elizabeth Oehlkers Wright

Belarusian I

Even our mothers have no idea how we were born,
how we spread their legs and crawled out into the world,
the way you crawl from the ruins after a bombing,
we couldn't tell which of us was a girl or a boy,
we gorged on dirt thinking it was bread.
And our future,
a gymnast on a thin thread of the horizon,
was performing there
at the highest pitch,
bitch.

we grew up in a country where
first your door is stroked with chalk
then at dark a chariot arrives
and no one sees you any more
but riding in those cars were neither
armed men nor
a wanderer with a scythe
this is how love loved to visit us
and snatch us veiled

Completely free only in public toilets
where for a little change nobody cared what we were doing,
we fought the summer heat, the winter snow.
When we discovered we ourselves were the language
and our tongues were removed, we started talking with
our eyes,
when our eyes were poked out, we talked with our hands,
when our hands were cut off, we conversed with our toes,
when we were shot in the legs, we nodded our head for yes
and shook our heads for no, and when they ate our heads
alive,
we crawled back into the bellies of our sleeping mothers
as if into bomb shelters
to be born again.

And there on the horizon the gymnast of our future
was leaping through the fiery hoop
of the sun.

Translated from the Belarusian by the author, Franz Wright and Elizabeth Oehlkers Wright

Belarusian II

Outside your borders,
they built a huge orphanage,
and you left us there, Belarus.
Maybe we were born without legs?
Maybe we worshipped the wrong gods?
Maybe we brought you misfortune?
Maybe we were deathly sick?
Maybe you were not able to feed us?
But couldn't we just beg for food?!
Maybe you never really wanted us,
but at first we also
didn't know how to love you.

Your language is so small
that it can't even speak yet,
but you, Belarus, are hysterical,
you are certain
that midwives mixed up the bundles.
What if you're feeding somebody else's baby?!
Letting another's language suck your own milk?!
A bluish language lying on the windowsill —
is it a language or last year's hoarfrost?
Is it hoarfrost or an icon's shadow?
Is it a shadow or just nothing?

It's not a language.
It doesn't have any system.

It is like death —sudden and unscrupulous,
like death you can never die from,
like death that brings the dead to life.

Language that makes you burn newborns,
language that makes a brother kill a brother,
language that nobody can hide from,
language that delivers men-freaks,
delivers women-beggars,

delivers headless beasts,
delivers toads with human voices.

This language does not exist!
It doesn't have any system!
It's impossible to talk to it —
it strikes you in the face at once!
Even on holidays
you won't decorate the city with it.
It can't be doctored up with either fireworks
or neon light.

Oh, come on, let this system kiss my
a c c o r d i o n

and my accordion,
when it stretches its bellows,
my accordion looks
like mountain peaks,
it eats from my hands,
it licks them and like a kid
won't get off
my lap
but time will come and it will
show its tra-ta-ta-ta!

Translated from the Belarusian by the author, Franz Wright and Elizabeth Oehlkers Wright

A Poem About White Apples

White apples, first apples of summer,
with skin as delicate as a baby's,
crisp like white winter snow.
Your smell won't let me sleep,
this is how dead men
haunt their murderers' dreams.
White apples,
this is how every July the earth
gets heavier under your weight.

And here only garbage smells like garbage.
And here only tears taste like salt.

We picked them
like shells in green ocean-gardens,
having just turned away from mothers' breasts,
we were learning
to get to the core of everything with our teeth.

So why are our teeth like cotton wool now?

White apples,
in black waters, the fishermen,
nursed by you, are drowning.

Translated from the Belarusian by the author, Franz Wright and Elizabeth Oehlkers Wright

Mocking Bird Hotel

A woman's hallelujah! washes the foot of Mocking Bird
Hill, her face eclipsed by her black mouth,
her eyes rolled up like workman's sleeves.
Stirred up, a fly speaks in the tongue of the hotel
doorbell, where, on the sun-ridden straw terrace
my salvation means less than praise
to a dumb child. Damned, blinded by ice cubes,
the fly surrenders its life into the waiter's clean hands.

Behind the kitchen of the Mocking Bird Hotel
a rooster repeats hallelujah! until it loses its head.
A man harvests the Family Tree before his forefathers'
features have a chance to ripen on their faces. Parakeets
watch him from the bare nerves of the garden. He harvests
before the worms that eat his father turn into demons.

Do not eat the fruit from your Family Tree. You have
eyes not to see them, hands not to pick them, teeth
not to bite them, tongue not to taste them even in speech.
The waiter slashes the table with our bill. We descend
Mocking Bird Hill without raising dust. Dogs,
their fur hanging like wet feathers off their backs,
piss yellow smoke without lifting a leg. Gulls
smash their heads between their wings.
Light lays the eggs of shadows under the shrubs.
Produce shacks stand empty like football gates.
What appeared blue from afar, turns green.
   I hold it all in, even my own urine.
But the mother of vowels slumps from my throat
like the queen of a havocked beehive.

Higher than hallelujah! rising like smoke over the hill,
I scream at the top of that green lung,
         why, in the Mocking Bird
Hell, do you value your blood over your sweat,
that bitterness over this salt, that wound over this
crystal? But often, to shed light on the darkness, light

isn't enough. Often what I need is even a darker
darkness. Like in those hours before the sun incriminates this
hotel, his two nostrils that illuminate our benighted bodies.

The Judgment Tale

Over the growing shadows fell the dead weight of light.

With a long bark mules metered the distance and turned back.
Dust rose like columns of unpaid debt.
Spit dried before it could reach the ground.

Then the thin-barked orange trees disowned their thick-skinned fruit.
Then mosquitoes spat out bad blood into the gutters and were gone.

Fish was opened like a two-page book,
its skeleton, caught aflame like an asp,
inscribed with fire along the bone lines,
then slapped on a stone face of a plate
next to a Coca-Cola bottle as cold as hell.

In the market fruit prices jumped up so high —
the seller women turned into hawks.

With a gibbous peacock brushing by their feet,
in the woods where each leaf hides a face,
                    and each trunk a spine,
                              and each tree a crime,
                                        where owls and angels,

a man and three women were contesting an apple.

The winner's body itself was an apple with skin chewed off.
Inside her breasts milk circled like a growling animal
locked behind two heavy nipples.

It was both day and night.
Her moon-white hand on the sun-gold fruit.
In her hair more stones than in a graveyard.

So

    I followed the woman as she ate

hoping if not for a bite
then at least
a spit in my direction.
But she left nothing of that apple.
Not even the memory of eating it

ever.

Psalm 18

I pray to the trees and language migrates down my legs like mute cattle.
I pray to the wooden meat that never left its roots.

I, too, am meat braided into a string of thought.
I pray to the trees:

luminescent in the dark garden
is the square star
of a window frame, my old bedroom.
Ghosts, my teachers!

In the branches of lindens – breathe, my ghosts,
(blood to my ears!),

in the lindens – cheekbones, elbows
of my dead – in these green mirrors.

*

How could it be that I'm from this Earth,
yet trees are also from this Earth?

A laundry line sagged under bedding among weightless trees,
yarrow and burdock, Bach's fugue, Bach's silence on our
clean wet sheets.

Fugue's Bach turns in the keyhole of the Earth.
Behind glass – portraits of the dead.

Close the curtains – motionless, they watch.
Open the curtains – they tremble.

Close the curtains – speechless, they watch.
Open the curtains – they whisper.

Trees, curtains – tremble.
On them
the dead wipe this prayer off their tongues.

*

At dusk, like eyesight, mint and dill
tense their smell. On a light curtain

wind polishes its bones.
Two beds along one wall,
where, head to head, we sleep.

The grave of memory, grave
upon grave of memory: a train of coffin-wagons,
head-first, rushes, head-first
rushes, rushes, train upon train
arrive into the earth.

At the next stop: my ghosts, come out, take a breath,
I would be waiting there. I would bring
fresh dogrose tea in our Chinese thermos.

Marie Marandola

How to Say I Love You

Practice:
on your mother
on your dog
on the friend at work
who knows how you like your coffee.

Notice how the words feel
in your mouth,
how they taste like something
you used to eat every day
then got sick of.
Hold them in your cheeks
until they are familiar again.

Wait for the right language
to present itself—it will.
One afternoon, he'll show you
a joke on the internet.
The punchline reads,
"I love you like trains."
And even if you don't quite get it,
laugh at its absurdity together.
Repeat it back to him then,
then again in a later conversation,
until it becomes part of your lexicon.

I love you like trains.
I love you like trains.
I love you like trains.

Then learn to love trains.

ISHION HUTCHINSON

PORTFOLIO

Fitzy and the Revolution

The rumour broke first in Duckenfield.
Fitzy dropped the shutters of his rum shop.
By the time it got to Dalvey there were three suicides.
The mechanic in Cheswick heard and gave his woman
a fine trashing; but, to her credit, she nearly scratched his heart
out his chest during the howl and leather smithing.

The betting shops and the whorehouse Daylights
at Golden Grove were empty; it was brutal
to see the women with their hands at their jaws on the terrace;
seeing them you know the rumour was not rumour,
the rumour was gospel: the canecutters did not get their salary.

Better to crucify Christ again.
Slaughter newborns, strike down the cattle,
but to make a man not have money in his pocket on a payday
Friday was abomination itself; worse canecutters,
who filed their spines against the sun, bringing down great walls of cane.

You'd shudder to see them, barebacked men, bent kissing
the earth, so to slash away the roots of the canes;
every year the same men, different cane, and when different men,
the same cane: the cane they cannot kill, living for this one day

of respite when they'd straighten themselves to pillars
and drop dollars on counters and act like Daylights is a suite
at the Ritz and the devastating beauty queens with their gaulin
fragile attention gave them forever to live in a tickle, the whetted
canepiece, this one day, forgotten in a whore's laugh.

Suddenly these men filled Hampton Court square
demanding the foreman's head.
They were thirsty for blood and for rum.
Fitzy stayed hidden in his shop behind the shutters.
He heard one man say it was not the foreman's head they should get,
that would not be wise.

The man continued: it must be fire for fire;
the factory must be burnt down.
But the men murmured. They were afraid.

Someone made a joke, they roared,
and soon they were saying fire can't buy rum,
they were roaring money, then rum, pounding Fitzy's shutter,
shouting his name for him to set them on fire.
They grew hoarse against the shutters.
The sun had taken all motion out of their voices.
Fitzy could hear them through the zinc,
like dogs about to die, cried-out children, that dry rustle
you hear after the crop is torched and the wind bristles the ashes.
No men were out there. Only a shirring noise.

That was when Fitzy opened the shutters.
Their red eyes in charcoal suits looked up at him,
and with an overseer's scorn, he nodded them in.

Punishment

All the dead eyes of the dead
on portraits behind her looked
down as she ate donuts off
a cloth napkin, her mouth
sugared. I saw myself possessed
by myself in her glasses' milky
lens that possessed the globe
on her desk, a Quaker gift the former
principal, dead but not yet
a portrait, left with Africa
spun towards us. She swallowed,
then asked why was I here.
I told her, for intimations.
She stopped mid-chew, surplice
of sugar danced at the down
curl of her lips. She said excuse me.
I continued: for immortality.
She looked with cow-out-of-pasture
concern, the others eyes' scalded
through me, the clock fell
silent though the second hand
wheeled around the white face.
For my freshness, she said,
you must be punished:
you must go out to the cemetery
by the chapel, write down
every last living name off
the tombstones before she arrived.
No problem, I knew the dead.
I was well off with their names.
But, she asked, a fresh donut
christened the napkin, if I am clear
why she has done this,
why she must punish me.
The portraits drew one breath.
I began: for my rejection
of things past,

because, for my life, the green graves
by the chapel puzzle me
and the sea outside our classroom,
those ships no one else sees,
humming, humming
their frail sails, join us,
though I don't know who us is.
She rose, utterly black;
I retreated, she filed
past the cabinet,
upset the globe;
I whirled out
the door; there
cliffs and clouds,
the dark manchineel
blinding the path
I bolted down,
hardly believing
my legs running
and leaping
above ground,
straight down
Hector's River
sea-road, flanked
by the hushed,
breaking sea.

After the Hurricane

After the hurricane walks a silence, deranged, white as the white helmets
of government surveyors looking into roofless

shacks, accessing stunned fowls, noting inquiries
into the logic of feathers, reversed, like gullies still retching; they scribble facts

about fallen cedars, spread out like dead generals on leaf
medallions; they draw tables to show the shore

has rearranged its idea of beauty for the resort
villas, miraculously not rattled by the hurricane's—

call it Cyclops—passage through the lives
of children and pigs, the one eye that unhooked

banjos from the hills, smashed them in Rio Valley;
they record how it howled off to that dark parish

St Thomas, stomping drunk with wire lashes and cramp,
paralyzing electric poles and coconut trees,

dishing discord among neighbours, exposed,
standing among their flattened, scattered lives for the first time.

It passed through Aunt May's head, upsetting
the furniture, left her chattering something,

a cross between a fowl and a child; they can't say
how it tore down her senses, no words, packing

their instruments, flies returning to genuflect
at their knees, on Aunt May's face, gone soft;

no words, except: *Don't fret*, driving off,
as if they had left better promises to come.

A March

Lesson of the day: Syria and Styria.
For Syria, read: *His conquering banner shook from Syria.*
And for Styria: Look at this harp of blood, mapping.

Now I am tuned. I am going to go above
my voice for the sake of the forest shaken
on the bitumen. You can see stars in the skulls,

winking, synapses, intermittent, on edge
of shriek – perhaps a cluster of fir, birches? –
Anyway. Don't get too hung up

on the terms; they have entropy
in common, bad for the public weal,
those obtuse centurions in the flare

of the bougainvillea, their patent-seeking
gift kindled. Divers speech. Cruelty.
Justice. Never mind, but do

pay attention to the skirmish – the white
panther that flitters up the pole –
its shade grows large on the ground.

Homage: Vallejo

Brailed up from birth, these obdurate, obituary corners
of second life the hospital light-ravened solstice

blessed with a caesarean and now we have a republic,
the bread-under-arm, water-bearer of the sea: Cetus, Christ.

After the blackbird I put on my herringbone jacket,
the feather hummed gargoyles bearing down buildings,

rain scowled down, *Vallejo* and *Vallejo* as I hurried
up Eager Street; Thursday, I remember the white stone

in the flask and wild asterisks hissing; Thursdays, falling
at noon, at Cathedral Street, blackbirds falling quietly at Biddle Street.

The Ark by "Scratch"

The genie says build a studio. I build
a studio from ash. I make it out of peril and slum
things. I alone when blood and bullet and all
Christ-fucking-'Merican-dollar politicians talk
the pressure down to nothing, when the equator's
confused and coke bubbles on tinfoil to cemented wreath.
I build it, a Congo drum, so hollowed through the future
pyramids up long before CDs spin away roots-men knocking
          down by the seaside,
like captives wheeling by the Kebar River. The genie says build
a studio, but don't take any fowl in it, just electric.
So I make it, my echo chamber with shock rooms of rainbow
King Arthur's sword keep in, and one for the Maccabees
alone, for covenant is bond between man and worm.
Next room is Stone Age, after that, Iron, and one I
named Freeze, for too much ice downtown in the brains
of all them crossing Duke Street, holy like parsons.
And in the circuit breaker, the red switch is for death
and the black switch is for death, and the master switch
is black and red, so if US, Russia, China, Israel talk
missiles talk, I talk that switch I call Melchezidek.
I build a closet for the waterfalls. One for the rivers.
Another for oceans. Next for secrets. The genie says build
a studio. I build it without gopher wood. Now, consider
the nest of bees in the cranium of the Gong, consider
the nest of wasps in the heart of the Bush Doctor,
consider the nest of locusts in the gut of the Black Heart Man,
I put them there, and the others that vibrate at the Feast of the Passover
          when the collie weed
is passed over the roast fish and cornbread. I Upsetter, I Django
on the black wax, the Super Ape, E.T., I cleared the wave.
Again, consider the burning bush in the ears of Kalonji
and the burning sword in the mouth of the Fireman and the burning pillar
          in the eyes
of the Gargamel, I put them there, to outlast earth as I navigate on one
of Saturn's rings, I mitre solid shadow setting fire to snow in my ark.
I credit not the genie but the coral rock: I man am stone.

I am perfect. Myself is a vanishing conch shell speeding round
a discothèque at the embassy of angels, skeletons ramble to checkout
my creation dub and sex is dub, stripped to the bone, and dub is the heart
breaking the torso to spring, olive-beaked, to be eaten up by sunlight.

Sibelius and Marley

History is dismantled music; slant,
bleak on gravel. One amasses silence,
another chastises silence with nettles,
stinging ferns. I oscillate in their jaws.

The whole gut listens. The ear winces
white nights in his talons: sinking mire.
He wails and a comet impales the sky
with the dual wink of a wasp's burning.

Music dismantles history; the flambeaux
inflame in his eyes with a locust plague,
a rough gauze bolting up his mouth unfolds,
so he lashes the air with ropes and roots

that converge on a dreadful zero,
a Golden Age. Somewhere, an old film.
Dusk soldiers on a cold, barren coast. There
I am a cenotaph of horns and stones.

The Night Autobiographies of Leopold Dice

Not another man to outtalk Leopold Dice;
all when the overproof rum dries up and flies
get brave enough to pitch and sleep on the dominoes,
putting more black eyes into the tiles, and moths
falling in the ice, now pure-so water, dust off
their wings catching gold in the bucket from the bulb
dropped from the ceiling in Coolieman's gambling
shop, Leopold Dice, spirited, measures out stories
all about himself in the peanie wallies' shir-shirring
and the tarpaulin's grunts when a breeze slaps it;
we do our best to look awake, rocking on wooden
stools, leaning on raw posts, the dark outside
and the walk back home in our heads, frightened
of duppy and thief together, and an owl's on-and-off
coarse screech in the manchineel, interfering
but not stopping Leopold Dice, who, in the prime
of another memory, stabs a finger out into the night
to tell us when he was Commissioner of Water—
we know it well—he was the first man to drive
an opened-back Morris up Stony Hill, long before
asphalt; a marine chariot, the piston butter smooth,
he lights a cigarette, exhales, a better ride Ezekiel
himself couldn't find to heaven; he loved how the Morris
sounded—soundless—when he drove those Sundays
through the bamboo road to Rio Grande, raft-men
spurring tourists down river shouted his name
across the water and he honked, the white people
smiled, but hardly two years passed and all the shocks
got loose and the engine started to slog like a battered
dray horse due to potholes and the merciless work
of making water pipes reach every single yard
bush and gully swallowed all over Portland,
the Morris, dead before any of us born, nearly broke
his pocket and spirit with all the trips to Bell Auto
Repairs, but what griped him most, to this day,
after all the miracles he had to perform to plant
the main pump down at Ransa Reservoir,

all in the name of his Party, not a drip came
to the taps, worse it was on the eve of election,
the wrench he used to strike the pump twice
echoed in his hand, the man the Ministry of Water
sent from Kingston, smiling in front of the crowd,
in suit and long rubber boots, stopped smiling
and started looking as if his mother just died,
a look that said there goes the votes, the look
that made Leopold Dice give up water, braps so,
for everybody knows, he stresses always at this point,
how ruthless politicians were then—worser than now,
for a hitman, then, was thruppence a piece, so he 'fly way'—
a term he grates his teeth on—to Miami, to pick fruits
in the glades, everyday wishing he had gone to Panama,
but Lord, everything was in Miami, the only tension
was America mad to drop nuclear on Cuba,
pigs even invaded a beach there, Leopold Dice stubs
his cigarette, but they were bayoneted by the Bloc,
yet the true tension, hotter than nations, was Isabel
Fernández García, herself Cuban, who he was pledging
out his soul-case to, she dredged all the money
he made in those swamps sinuated with mosquitoes
he was so afraid a snake or something wild would turn
him paraplegic; Isabel García, a real black widow,
Leopold Dice sucks his teeth remembering that life,
but concedes, as we expected, squinting, the heartache
she was causing forced him back, dreadlocked, nearly mad,
to his birth rock, now independent of Britain, rum
like leggo-beast in the roads, Leopold Dice laughs,
the owl screeches again, he remembers roaming,
hiccupping with his old water-bird friends, screaming
GOD BLESSED THE QUEEN AND THE QUEEN'S DRAWERS,
outwardly he was a lark, though the island was no longer
the green of his Party but orange of the Opposition,
and inside, where it mattered, he couldn't stand
those new aviator-wearing politicians with their orange
badges, orange flags, orange t-shirts, orange motorcades—

orange, the colour of the damn fruits he picked
so many bushels of in Florida, only the sun
left to be pulled down in one of those wicker buckets;
even now rind scent sickens him, anything citrus
does if it is not cut with rum, for rum was life
then, it covered him like a soutane, he draws
an invisible cloth down his body to show us
how it swam over him, always, this time of the night,
his voice slows, from somewhere a stillness
reaches for us, catches us, and we listen for the return,
his voice slower, a croak; his eyes twinkle when he says
the dice rolled his lucky number one night at a Bryan's
Bay beach session where he met the local baker, May,
selling her coconut drops, grater cakes, gizzardas,
potato puddings with hallelujah in the middle,
her ginger beer so strong it burned his throat for days,
purged him clean of wonder, rum, and other women,
and yes, he admits grounding his walking stick
he didn't really need, lifts himself up, they're not married,
after thirty something years under the same roof,
pissing in the same chamber, selling her bake goods
together; even still, Sweet May, whose real husband
not even God can make head or tail of his whereabouts,
was Leopold Dice's wife to the grizzle, May was salvation
own-self after America, he nods, one jaw glossy
in the bulb; then, finally, pocketing his pack
of Craven 'A' cigarettes, flaps on his felt, he repeats
the one phrase of true adjournment: Night, night;
walk good until tomorrow again, stepping into
the dark home, we too shuffling up, Coolieman
twisting the bulb off, we hear Leopold Dice shake
the kerosene oil in the soda bottle torch, strike
a match for the newspaper wick; the flame catches
as we walk out to the dark trees and hills of Port Antonio.

TOPOGRAPHIA DE LAVILLA DE MADRID.
DESCRITA POR DON PEDRO TEXEIRA
AÑO 1656

G. C. WALDREP

Caynham Camp

(1)

Through curtains, winter light. Late Mandelstam
open on the table. "Exile" means we are still in this life,
we are still in love with this life
where a fleet steams by in midnight Latin, new ghosts
for whom the heart crochets a new song. It's their birthday
and, like children, they know. Like children
they capture insects to pull off their wings,
tie threads to the fragile legs of honeybees and wasps.
It is cold where the children are, but so brightly lit.
I read Mandelstam in the morning. I am not abandoned.
At the supermarket it's all I can do
to point to the meat I want, pink jewel in its crystal case.

(2)

I photographed the hollies by the in-turned gate,
something regal, or as if the hill had developed lips, as if
the summit were working slowly
back towards a capacity for speech. My own tongue
a debt in it, a stud. I had barely spoken to anyone
in weeks, nodding to the waiter
at the dim French restaurant as if I were a foreigner.
I took a wrong turn in the medieval quarter
and found myself part of a procession, dark-clad, silent.
It was an accident, I wanted to say,
only to remember that once again I'd been cast
in the thief's role, which is why from every
house we passed I recognized an ancient, accusing glare.

(3)

The district opened on a grid of broken stone
punctuated by pasture; the larger mammals
shifted randomly, with the gentle Brownian motion
of hunger that has not yet reached despair, cannot imagine
that with some slight displacement of the body

every desire won't be met.
Then they were all around me, an encircling gravity.
I bowed, as only one fairly caught
in trespass may bow. I recognized the incised
language on the sentry trunks
and copied it carefully into the flesh of my eye
so that I could teach it to the offending light, which buzzed
drunkenly against my shins, my temples, my chest.

(4)

And then, as if in some half-forgotten children's tale,
I found myself an inheritor
of a tiny kingdom, misted with marsh gas
and briar's rank exhaust, depleted of its saints.
The people who lived there used the wounds of red grapes
as their currency. I met a few of them;
they made a small living as pipefitters, and they professed
never to have heard of me, or where I lived.
They claimed that if you dug under the ground
you'd find no evidence at all of any prior human settlement.

(5)

They trapped songbirds and sold them on the open market.
They gave nothing as alms. I liked a few of them,
mostly the women. Perhaps the problem
was that I did not, as I'd been taught, exit as I'd entered.
Now the season touches me
in a way that feels both more distant and less hindered,
days laundered not in war but in rumors
of war's creche, past and future. For days I slide letters
unopened across my kitchen table; when I finally
do open them I don't read them, merely leave them folded
like quiet hands in the matte lap of each torn envelope.

In the rose I waited for the sermon to break,
the last book close. I held a petal to the surface of my eye.

CAROL FROST

PORTFOLIO

Alias City

They were travelers, plotting river courses,
writing the Genesis of unknown people,
fugitives with a revolver in one hand, reins in another,
merchants among the olive trees, euphorbias, mimosas,
emissaries, deserters. Some knew the native tongues;
they called themselves by new names
in the eastern twilight, different parts of their soul
never having learned to live together.
Skies burned. Dust covered the palms
and minarets as they arrived by the incandescent shore
of our city, each with his own little dreams and disasters.
Some remained, never to be heard of again.
Some left with caravans, wearing native dress—ephemerids.
Where are they? What are they used to?
The only preserved interview—of an artist and explorer.
  Did he ever speak of his friends in X?
  Never. The only thing he liked in X was his sister.
  But did you know that he painted?
  Oh yes!—some fine things: stemware,
  a series of watercolors of Shoebills and Abdim's
      stork.

City of the Ridiculous

Ridiculous, we. All the long, bright days. Days
without death. Without without, the without. The suicide leap
       comic as sex—
hips and asses, sweat, rush.
All our acts become gestures of our acts. The litter of the
       years
has been, swept into another precinct.
A few steps ahead of us, death. And we are left
to ourselves without the means. To revenge,
to throw our bodies at ourselves. Be the voice
of besieging sorrow, we cannot.
Be the wintry sound as of cold spirals
of wind in empty lots, by which those given
a cot and a howl of greasy soup feel blessed.
It's not in us. A cry of art? Rid of ridiculous us.
The very air is rid of air. We play videos endlessly.
We daydream death in a forest, on a cliff
over the Sea of Japan. In Madrid, Alcala, 237—
the matador's gaiety and elegance in nearness
to the massive head, the natural beast, death.
In a suit of lights, with wanton thrusts
of hips, he fans death with a gory cape,
wrapped in fire, darkest, pivoting, fire,
at the last second or the second
honor's snuffed, ethos stilled, and death lives.

How Music Came into the City

From wild, half-peopled hills
I have brought to your streets
sixty-six birds, rare species
of hummingbird and frightened little finch
with their beaks sealed shut
so they would not be heard singing
until I arrived. I sewed them inside
my clothing, simple songs
past hearing for the days
when silent snow mocks stone
and loud voices voice
the wasted breath.
Already can you dream
the rubied merriment
when I open my coat
and unspool the ribbon
from their beaks;
and the heartbreak
when a sole bird falls earthward
as if from a golden tree?
Listen now for the key
of what has been—
a tiny magnitude pouring
myrrh and wind
onto the avenues,
rustle in the undertones.
It will take you back
to the hills and take
the hills away.

City with First Class Funerals

Angels are coming on vacation to our city—with the funeral
a wine feast, a beautiful corpse in brooch light,
mourners, their cathedral calm.
Er hat den 71er gekommen, the joke goes,
and all here can remember sweet spring chaos,
succulences in summer, the good fall like a woman
lying nakedly on a pelt,
and from north windows, years inevitably brought to their knees
like someone's son executed by a river.
The service is ending,
the representatives of the Union of Cemetery Singers have left
by the back door, and I think Grandmama, grown suspicious of
            strangers,
more appreciates the candelabras, lilies, red, red carnations,
and chrysanthemums festooning the caisson carrying her
to the family tomb. Her triumph was to be the reason
for all these flowers and the candles,
dark yellow and guttering, as if the wind was testing the
            certainties
to orient her in the grave an east wind.
What of her trysts and pricking conscience,
wrapped away in the god-awful mantilla?
Need we speak of them now?
Hush, the souls in the Namelos Friedhof
are whispering, trees in the urn grove rustle, an accordion
            starts,
he plays like an angel, and it all gets muddled.
Have we given coins to the undertaker?
The caskets are stacked? Then finally
Rudolph is where he wanted to lie, between Grandmama's mother
and Grandmama. The rains commence. Let the world
deride or pity. We hear you calling, lord of wind and flame.

Chickadee

For that I cannot know you, I keep you.
For that your reflection in a small mirror
turns your heart tender like mine,
and then you shriek.
For that you let me make small branches
of my fingers for you to climb,
I whistle your sayings.
For that I want a waking bird
in my throat, not colored feather-and-face
but entire. For that the hawk dives on you
and the sky shimmers through your doom.

For that you are caged, I feed you orange oil
seeds and dried papaya. You flute
whether the wire gate is closed or raised.
I clean your cage of offal,
I whistle your sayings
without knowing the meanings—
some tones as delicate as the taste
of poppy, some double-worlded.

What the Dove Sings

The mourning dove
wearing noon's aureole
coos from the rhododendron,
oo-waoh, shadow o-
ver what to do. Oh.
And the sad rhetoric spreads
through suburb and wood.
Those who hear
dove moan love no
querulous warbling more—
the going hence
about which is there no-
thing to do?
From no small rip in fate
the you you never shall be
more will be extracted.
Dove knows the rubric
and starts in, who,
who is next and soon?

Mole People

Leeches, slugs, flatworms, beetles, centipedes,
feral cats and dogs, and the cold flames
mole people in city tunnels awaken to.
Ignis fatus, luces del tesoro,
the stories tell, and who isn't a scavenger
of stories? For some the moles are lost
souls, for others hell's embers help
find their bearings. Below squander,
mole people make their lives, receding as night
recedes, advancing in pitch-black
along the lost stream beds, climbing the grates
and into metal dumpsters where
every necessity can be carried underground.
One moleman found a bookcase;
yet, I wonder if I were inside his head,
would I be reading as the moleman or as me?
The sensitivity of my hand
is six times poorer than the star
of the star-nosed mole, and to imagine
its tactile world, all my perception
must be as if my body were all finger and tongue.
But I have little desire to leave
the colorful and airy streets
and cannot imagine myself touching
an arm of the man whose coat is inside out.
The lights in the marshes, it is said,
will follow you but stand still if you stand.

Dog City

We have seen you following the scent—
heads like shovels, eyes stones,
and then heard you grrrrrrr
over the body, bedded then in an alley
or low corner. No reluctance in her young desire,
you say when yousay, yousay
You like it like this, don't you? You like it!
We remember the craven air,
semen on clothes, skin, and dirt,
moreso in our city, with its avenues,
high windows, courts, symphony halls.
The child is in darkness,
and we have gone into the cellar
where it is kept. For the sake of a return
to its happiness, how much happiness
would have to be leashed?
We go home with the paradox
that for the city to be what we think
and to live there,
some must be beaten, some raped.
We must know it
as we know Leda and Zeus, Philomena,
Procne, and the King of Thrace.
Dogs are in the streets in suits;
they run loose.

Song of the City at Night

Whatever hid the sun and moon inside a mountain
brought people there to found the night
where a city swans on river water
laving with light each passing wake,
mesmerizing a couple on the riverbrink.
They seem unaware what is myth
or real, taken up, as it were, by a swan's bill
and flown to a milkwater world
where it's possible to drink only the milk
and eat pearls. A gunshot, a siren
interrupts the quiet. Something is thrown
into the river, then the swan is mute.
To sing of this the swan would have to out-swan
itself, Sibelius out-Sibelius Sibelius.

Rumored City

Those who travel to this city hear long before
arriving the murmurs as of insects
in the wind that piles up the shadows
and moves the mornings into day.
Such curious stories, half-told,
reach them in winding sunlight,
float as on the surface of a lake trout rise to.

Is this what it is to be caught, to
have suspected not everything in the light
of day was genuine, nothing truly foretold,
but so badly to have wanted the day
and all one's hours lifted from shadow
and seen the feathered, bright insects
darting on the surface and leapt before

thinking? They were untroubled before
the rumor of the darting insect
held in the corner of their mouths. Shadows
bred, ugliness grew, they felt the day
slip into darkness. The story they'd been told
was a trap, light not sunlight,
after all, no place left to travel to.

Walled City

Their music was like music in other cities,
sway and pounding, jazz and chorus; their iniquities
no less and no greater when we read minutely
their religious texts. That I might have honey
and dates read one book, the other that existent
in all things, even non-living things such as stones,
glory was alive and not abstract. There was desire
and sexual pursuit, covetousness, lulls of speech,
oratory, false-smiling, whispering, bigotry.
So shut in, though they had their lives,
they looked for what might drop on them
from the skies. Death could. Hadn't the uncorruptible
been changed like to birds and other things?
They set upon the haters of their way of life,
inventors of evil, blood-minded, despicable.
They told them that they knew they could commit
things worthy of death and killed them.
Some avowed loyalty. Avowals of loyalty,
avowals of justice and revenge filled the air
above the place where the ATM blew up, seven dead.

Everyday City

When fate's hands tore the city in two,
a photographer stood in the middle
of the street and with no right to the view
looked in the bedrooms and toilets.
There was the basic box next to another
box, bristling with mirrors, colored dishes,
that somehow had the power
to make a life seem unique,
rooms in an imaginary encyclopedia
of everyday life, locked in the edges
of photos, on the screen of a video—
here a formica table, there. . . .
Who hasn't relished the idea
of walking without knocking into rooms
that aren't our own, to briefly live
someone else's life, to feel at home
and fascinated with the horsehair couch,
the closets with bed-sheets and smocks,
a grandfather's engraved pocket watch,
its paper-thin initials outlasting him
and us, perhaps. Why had it been left?
Not even the Wunderkammer Olberich
with its unicorn's horn (narwhal tusk),
mermaid's hand, chalices of coconut
and pink-polished conch with gold,
preserved Nile crocodile, lit parrots,
landscapes with seeping moon, saint's knuckles
in the end is more curious
than the building with empty daylight
of walls and windows torn open
and into which we could pour
our intense feeling for the everyday,
day in and day out, thinking
this is almost what I once was.

POETRY FROM *BELIEVER*

FEATURE

Edited with an Introduction by Dominic Luxford

DOMINIC LUXFORD

Introduction to Feature: Poetry from *Believer*

Since the *Believer* magazine began accepting poetry submissions in 2007, we've received tens of thousands of poems from around the country and across the globe, poems from doctors, inmates, teenagers, actors, registered prostitutes, priests—Nobel Laureates and the previously unpublished—and everyone in-between. From the beginning it has been our goal to choose work based solely on what we perceived to be the work's merit. Cover letters have always been optional, and no page on our website will describe "What We're Looking For," because we certainly haven't a clue.

With each submission, we have attempted to ignore everything we thought we knew about poetry and to allow the poet to tell us, freshly, what it is. Many of the best poems, today and in the past, come from poets who do what you "shouldn't" do—and do it extremely well. Our favorite poems have frequently been the most surprising—and often for surprising reasons. That which is new and original always surprises, even as it may tug at an uncanny sense of the familiar.

We also believe that to "judge" a poem is a necessary (and ridiculous) evil. So how is one to perform that act best? The questions we routinely ask ourselves when considering a submission are: Do I *actually* care about this poem? Would I want to share it with a friend? Do I find myself thinking about the poem later? There is also the sturdy 'curse test': After reading, for the first time, the poems we've ended up publishing, we've not-infrequently uttered "Holy @#$%," or some such indecency. There is no tricking the spontaneous inner self. As Emily Dickinson famously wrote:

"If I read a book and it makes my whole body so cold no fire can warm me I know *that* is poetry. If I feel physically as if the top of my head were taken off, I know *that* is poetry. These are the only way I know it. Is there any other way?"

Below are some of the poems that passed that test—poems that preoccupied us then, and continue to preoccupy us now.

A sincere thanks to *Poetry International* for inviting us to share some of these poems as a part of *PI*'s ongoing feature series of mini-anthologies from other publications. We hope you enjoy them.

Michael Dumanis

Autobiography

Attempted avoiding abysses, assorted
abrasions and apertures, abscesses.

At adolescence, acted absurd: acid,
amphetamines. Amorously aching

after an arguably arbitrary Abigail,
authored an awful aubade.

Always arabesquing after Abigails.
Am always afraid: an affliction?

Animals augur an avalanche. Animals
apprehend abattoirs. Am, as an animal,

anxious. Appendages always aflutter,
am an amazing accident: alive.

Attired as an apprentice aerialist,
addressed acrophobic audiences.

Aspiring, as an adult, after acolytes,
attracted an awestruck, angelic auteur.

After an asinine affair, an abortion.
After an asinine affair, Avowed Agnostic

approached, alone, an abbey's altarpiece,
asking Alleged Almighty about afterlife.

Ambled, adagio, around an arena.
Admired an ancient aqueduct. Ate aspic.

Adored and ate assorted animals.
Ascended an alp. Affected an accent.

Acquired an accountant, an abacus, assets.
Attempted atonal arpeggios.

Adam Zagajewski

Kings

I'm a student

Those were days when I walked around a little hungry,
a little dazed, and desire spoke to me
violently. A little lonely,
slightly happy, a bit the actor of myself,
I listened to music, the music was wild,
I admired the Renaissance palaces,
I visited our poor kings
at Wawel Castle and tried to comfort them
and stretched the truth; for all that, though, they
put fingers to their pale lips
and counseled silence. It was winter,
snow smothered the flowers and the voice
of destiny could not speak soon.
So it was. Woolen gloves. Amen.

Translated from the Polish by Clare Cavanagh

KAY RYAN

Fatal Flaw

The fatal flaw
works through
the body like
a needle, just
a stitch now
and then, again
and again missing
the heart. Most
people never bend
in the fatal way
at the fatal instant,
although they
harbor a needle
they shouldn't,
or, conversely,
some critical little
life-saving sliver
is absent.

XI CHUAN

A   00000

He never looks back, yet knows I am lurking.

He shouts: "Stop on the edge of the cliff, or your body won't withstand the anger."

He turns, sees the purple aura rising above me. He shakes his head, and the sun
    sinks into the trees.

He sees the devil's shadow behind me. (He must have witnessed Badanxin's smile,
    heard the azaleas sing.)

August, you must avoid crows. You must wake up early in September. You'll have
    a great future, he predicts, but mean spirits will block your path.

Another man appears in the lane and the stranger vanishes. I fidget. Could he be
    my fate?

We pass, brush shoulders; he'll catch me again in this maze of ruins.

A crow flies across August's forehead.

I close my eyes, and the crow sings, "Don't be afraid. Your body is not yours, it is
    a hotel for others."

Translated from the Chinese by Alex Lemon and Wang Ping

Yu Jian

96

A cold front is attacking the city
3 p.m. the sky is turning gray
Cold has gripped everything
Someone starts to be afraid of life
Someone loses interest in traveling
Someone pulls his coat tighter
but when a beautiful woman appears
even if it's just a glimpse of her back in the street
the controlling force loses its grip
life wants to live again
the traveler feels like taking off now
the Kunming man who hates cold weather
suddenly lets go of his collar
revealing his neck, pink from the cold

Translated from the Chinese by Ron Padgett and Wang Ping

Yusef Komunyakaa

Fata Morgana

I could see thatch boats. The sea
swayed against falling sky. Mongolian
horses crested hills, helmets edging the perimeter,
& I saw etched on the horizon scarab insignias.
The clangor of swords & armor echoed
& frightened scorpions into their holes,
& the question of zero clouded the brain.
I saw three faces of my death foretold.
I sat at a table overflowing with muscadine & quince,
but never knew a jealous husband poisoned the Shiraz.
I laughed at his old silly joke about Caligula
lounging in a bathhouse made of salt blocks.
I was on a lost ship near the equator,
& only a handful of us were still alive,
cannibal judgment in our eyes.
I came to a restful valley of goats & dragon lizards,
but only thought of sand spilling from my boots.
I witnessed the burning of heretics near an oasis,
& dreamt of gulls interrogating seahorses, cuttlefish,
& crabs crawling out of the white dunes.
I could see the queen of scapegoats
donning a mask as palms skirted the valley.
I was lost in a very old land, before Christ
& Mohammed, & when I opened my eyes
I could see women embracing a tribunal
of gasoline cans. I heard a scuttling
on the sea floor. I knew beforehand
what surrender would look like after
long victory parades & proclamations,
& could hear the sounds lovemaking
brought to the cave & headquarters.

Kathleen Ossip

On Giving Birth

That night
I was
full of
information.

TRACY K. SMITH

Field Guide

You were you, but now and then you'd change.
Sometimes your face was some or another his,
And when I stood facing it, your body flinched.
You wanted to be alone—left alone. You waded
Into streets dense with people: women wearing
Book bags, or wooden beads. Girls holding smoke
A moment behind red mouths then pushing it out,
Posing, not breathing it in. You smiled
Like a man who knows how to crack a safe.

When it got to the point where you were only
Him, I had to get out from under it. Sit up
And put my feet on the floor. Haven't I lived this
Enough times over? It's morning, but the light's still dark.
There's rain in the garden, and a dove repeating
Where? Are? You? It takes awhile, but a voice
Finally answers back. A long phrase. Over
And over. Urgently. Not tiring even after the dove
Seems to be appeased.

DEREK WALCOTT

No opera

No opera, no gilded columns, no wine-dark seats,
no Penelope scouring the stalls with delicate glasses,
no practised ecstasy from the tireless tenor, no sweets
and wine at no interval, no altos, no basses
and violins sobbing as one; no opera house,
no museum, no actual theatre, no civic center
—and what else? Only the huge doors of clouds
with the setting disc through which we leave and enter,
only the deafening parks with their jumping crowds,
and the thudding speakers. Only the Government
Buildings down by the wharf, and another cruise ship
big as the capital, all blue glass and cement.
No masterpieces in huge frames to worship,
on such banalities has life been spent
in brightness, and yet there are the days
when every street corner rounds itself into
a sunlit surprise, a painting or a phrase,
canoes drawn up by the market, the harbour's blue,
the barracks. So much to do still, all of it praise.

Zubair Ahmed

Hello, Brother

I pick up an earthworm
And you shoot it with a rifle.
Mom screams at us
But we don't listen.
She fed us expired milk this morning.
Sometimes in these Bengali summers
When dust sticks to our skins
And the crows shit on our heads
We bond like hydrocarbons,
Set mosquitoes on fire
And eat berries whose names we can't remember.
We ride our bikes like metal antelopes
Like drunken sparrows.
We play cricket under the monsoon clouds
And you bowl a perfect leg-spinner.
It starts to rain
So I shoot down a cloud.
We take it back to Mom
Who kisses our ears and pokes our eyes—
She does that.
We get ready for bed
With our usual battles,
And you fall asleep
Not knowing I slid the alarm clock
Under your pillow,
Set for 3:17 a.m.

Rae Armantrout

The Craft Talk

So that the best thing you could do, it seemed, was climb inside the machine that was language and feel what it wanted or was capable of doing at any point, steering only occasionally.

The best thing was to let language speak its piece while standing inside it—not like a knight in armor exactly, not like a mascot in a chicken suit.

The best thing was to create in the reader or listener an uncertainty as to where the voice she heard was coming from so as to frighten her a little.

Why should I want to frighten her?

Victoria Chang

[I once was a child am a child am someone's child not my mother's not]

I once was a child am a child am someone's child not my mother's not
my father's the boss gave us special treatment treatment for something

special a lollipop or a sticker glitter from the toy box the better we did
the better the prize one year everyone was fired everyone fired but me

one year my father lost his words to a stroke a stroke of bad luck stuck
his words used to be so many his words fired him let him go without

notice can they do that can she do that yes she can in this land she can
once we sang songs around a piano this land is your land this land is my land

someone always owns the land in this land someone who owns the land
owns the buildings on the land the people in the buildings unless an

earthquake sucks the land in like a long noodle

SAN FRANCISCO

SOPHIA KARTSONIS

Pessoa, Pessoa, Hall of Mirrors

Let's pinkie promise never to part
ourselves out just because we know
know what it means to be
many-ed as a hotel hallway.
Each corridor of us contains
a different guest, and as the case
may be, Fernando, Fernando,
it's hard to say who you are
when in your chest, there
is evidence of someone else's
aftershave, someone's cigar left burning
in the ashtray in another wing of you.
Nonetheless, you're my favorite octopod
and I'd run away with you, Baby

We could be in Sicily by Sunday,
some of ourselves wandering the city
before that early light gets all used-up
by others of us. Outside we greet
the crowd which is just you and me,
as I'm aware that you're aware
that mankind's just another mouth
saying: *there's nobody home*

I've been known to find myself
on a metro inside myself where one
or the other of I has already taken the last seat
and this ride, yet again, I stand, holding the strappy
thing that makes I feel like a side
of beef hanging jostled from the walls
while my city, I's city, smears
the windows and this I tries to stay upright

The train is preferable to a crowd
of 'I's packed into I's little automobile.
If one of us drives too fast in the rain
how many of us slide into us?

You're all about the stations between stations. You
you, every radio in every hotel, you,
in all the cities that are you, and you again

I'll give myself a heteronym, I,
the same as I's beloved's favorite poet, I,
every final couplet will read the same, I:
                How you like I now, Love?
                How do you like I now?

I've had some time to think it over and
I'd like to wash your back in Portuguese,
comb your hair in Spanish, address
your every eyelash by a petname

The sky is made of cardboard.
I adore corrugation: the ups and downs,
a sheet of cardboard's inner life:
zig-zag and heart monitor and some dark
honey eyes you've got there, Fern (may I call you
Fern?) casting your vertebraed
shadow in theatres everywhere

I loved me like God's greatest maniac,
until I kissed the magic from that top hat
and now there's nothing I can do but wait
for the previews to end. Therein likes the trouble
with leading men, Fernando, the screen darkens
and attitude gets thrown.

            Let's take a bus of us
to the drive-in movie starring you, co-starring
you, written, produced, edited by you:
my gaffer, my key grip, my best boy electric

You, me and Jesus, Baby, we're lousy with disciples.
Mine breathe down I's throat,

drag me around by the scruff of the neck
and when I ask whether it's bitch-love or cruelty
that motivates this mode of travel, they don't say

Here, there, everywhere you. And isn't that my poodle skirt?
Your laugh makes llamas cry. Little life, you won't wear
me again. Yet, once, we held ourselves up to each other
like lighters at a rock concert and then the swaying started
and all the little people in my head stood up and did the wave

KATHYRN NUERNBERGER

A Difficult Woman

I left the metaphor of myself I like best
in the rabbit warren and went to the office
to seem like the kind of person another person
might hire because it is a true fact that some
committee of persons hired me and this
because I pretended to be a Professionalism 4
once for an afternoon and that metaphor
was convincing enough to calcify over the flesh
of itself with a stiff-sleeved shirt and knee-length
skirt, and become the myself of myself now
who owes the office better than a Professionalism 3,
since the office is not the one who pretended
their way into this. The office is not the one
who didn't realize people really believe you are
how you pretend to be. The office is not
responsible for the fact I think curse words
bring flavor to any conversation and gossip
is a form of social capital essential to the building
of relationships because it makes a person
vulnerable and powerful with information
at the same time and forges a feeling, if not
the fact, of trust and authenticity. In pursuit
of Professionalism 4, I use a lot of smiley faces
and exclamation points in my discourse to iron
myself disarming. Professionalism 5 needs no
emoticons, for it is already ironed. I'm sorry
not sorry I left the metaphor of my uncomfortable
work clothes in the rabbit warren and decided
to wear jeans every day to every meeting
regardless of the pomp because no one asked
at the interview what I think about pomp.
I think pomp is maladaptive. That is
a Professionalism 2 sort of opinion to hold.
And anyway, I think pomp is fucking maladaptive.
I don't know why it is Professionalism 4
to keep that sort of opinion to ourselves.
I don't know why it is Professionalism 5

to love pomp. What if I fucking love pomp?
Would they have to create a box for 6?
Every little box is a warren and I try to stay inside,
but my haunches are itching springs and I want
to fuck over everything like it is May
and the oak leaves have just uncurled to the size
of squirrel ears. They billow more open, I think,
to try to hear the wind of all the discarded
metaphors for what I am and you are too.
The whole green lawn around the cinderblock
of our days is buzz and bloom for somebody to,
I want to say *Kick up a tempest of themselves*
getting fired, but really I just mean *Tell me something*
I don't already know and must swear never to repeat.

I'll Show You Mine if You Show Me Yours

In the coffee shop was a guy with a really nice bald head
and one of those sleek jackets with the zip-up neck
that look great with a pair of well-cut jeans, which
he also had. I confess, I was looking him up and down
like a woman who has been reading Rumi and also a tome
on the history of bear cults in Europe. I just turned 35,
just got a promotion, just discovered the male gaze,
by which I mean I gaze on men like some sort of man,
by which I mean I'm hungry for my own hunger.
I'm like a mountain, I sometimes think, and I'm afraid
mountain is a symptom of menopause. When I became
a gourd blossom of pregnancy, I didn't know what
was coming. I died on that table and then woke up
to a nurse putting a swaddled baby in my wind-battered
petals. I won't be taken off guard twice. I know the time
is coming when I'll grow a mustache and my calyx
will turn to sandpaper. I'll be a volcano for a while,
then a crater, then a little sack of dusty bones. It makes me
fear-mad, like a man with a power tool and a tree
that won't come down. It makes me good at sex and good
at finding a guitar screaming in the interstices of the FM
dial of the big fat car I drive down the rumble strip
eyeing the men in hard hats on machines building a highway
out of molten tar just beyond the line of wind-quivering
orange cones. My man of this morning, I traced my eyes
right down his runner's leg to the modest woman's pump
he was wearing, black with a chunky heel and a mary jane strap.
Like I used to wear before I got this feeling I needed boots
with brown laces. I used to keep mary jane vows of silence
everywhere I went. Now, when someone I work with
is giving a presentation, I ask the follow-up questions.
Sometimes the question is halfway out before I even notice
I'm the one talking. This afternoon I heard myself saying
to the woman who had just finished clicking her way
through a Powerpoint, "You're doing great at being
professionally objective, but doesn't it ever just piss you off?"
The subject was the agency of heroines in Shakespeare's
comedies and her thesis was Chastity. When I'm a mother

in my own kitchen I tell my daughter, "You get what you
get and you don't throw a fit." By which I mean "Apples
and peanut butter." Poets I admire have been known to say,
"First thought, best thought." To which I used to reply,
"If that worked I wouldn't need to write at all." If that
worked, I could just talk to people. I wonder if Whitman
ever walked out of some Manhattan pub shaking his head
at how hard it is to share a moment with another human being.
How you have to keep backing up to explain yourself
to your own fucking atoms. What I mean is, I was reading
an important tract on women's honor only yesterday
and the critic (she's a philosopher but for some reason
we don't call her a philosopher) was lamenting how women
have historically been expected to lie, to cheat, to keep
their secrets. No one expects us to be honorable, only chaste.
I'm asking you if we can tell the truth in front of a room full
of people, and if that truth might not be that even Shakespeare,
especially Shakespeare, doesn't know us at all. And also
what I mean is, isn't it too bad we never really talk to each other.
Like, for example, about how I've been thinking about women
who have sex with horses. Because of Rumi's poem about
just that. Because of the bear cults too. Because I feel I might
be turning into a centaur. Because I feel I might want
to be turned into a centaur. Because the last thing I want
is to give birth to a centaur. Wasn't there a maiden
in the forest who couldn't keep her hands off the ears
of some enchanted donkey? Was it her chastity in the face
of his bestiality we admire? Personally, I'm partial to the way
she strains against such honor. Because I don't know
how to talk to people, I guess. Because I'm lonely.
I want to touch this man on the shoulder and say, "I like
your shoes." But what I mean is, "I like what you are
telling me with your shoes." Or what I mean is, "I like
everything I know about you." But I don't say anything,
because I think what I can hear him asking is if he can be
allowed to pass unnoticed into the crowd of us. If that's
what you want, of course. I won't say another word. I'll be
quiet in my hope that I knew you as you wished to be known.

Rosanna Warren

Graffiti

Kitty Goes Kommando and the Goldman Rats — Phooey!
That blue scaffolding holds up the sky. Who did we think
we were padlocking in, or out? Give me that huge
looping black script no one can read, a secret glyph,
and just where someone has smashed the window, Jesus
the Way the Truth the Life and a dented aluminum frame.
He bent down, we know, and wrote something illegible on the ground.
A toothy black-and-white dinosaur gapes. I like the crack
in this wall of monsters where skylines topple and ogres
twiddle train tracks in their claws like pipe cleaners.
Down the long, semi-abandoned street in Queens
calligraphy gallops toward the shop displaying,
like guitar strings, seven different iron rods
for gates. Hole in the wall, rose sound-hole,
ribbed sounding board — always from fissures and gaps
melody strains as trains thunderclank across
the girdered overpass, a siren keens, and a solitary man
ambles past amputated acacias fisting out with leaves.

Rosanna Warren

A Way

The whole trick of this thing… is to get out of your own light.
          —*Marianne Faithfull*

She said she sangahreah very close to the mike
to change the space. And I changed the space
by striding down the Boulevard Raspail at dusk in tight jeans
until an Algerian engineer plucked the pen from my back pocket.
As if you're inside my head and you're hearing the song from in there.
He came from the desert, I came
from green suburbs. We understood
nothing of one another over glasses of metallic red wine.
I was playing Girl. He played
Man. Several plots were afoot, all
misfiring. One had to do with my skimpy black shirt
and light hair, his broad shoulders and hunger
after months on an oil rig. Another
was untranslatable. Apollinaire
burned his fingers on June's smoldering lyre
but I had lost my pen. The engineer
read only construction manuals. His room
was dim and narrow and no,
the story didn't slide that way though there are many ways
to throw oneself away.
One singer did it by living by a broken wall
until she shredded her voice but still she offered each song,
she said, like an Appalachian artifact.
Like trash along the riverbank chafing at the quay
plastic bottles a torn shirt fractured dolls
through which the current chortles an intimate tune.

LI-YOUNG LEE

PORTFOLIO

Just Time

It's just time, the book I read, the letter I write,
the window I look out of.

It's just a needle I thread,
a sleeve I keep trying to mend, the spool diminishing.

It's just time inside of time, the future inside
the seeds inside the pulp
of the apple I eat, skin and all, seeds and everything.

And the fruit rotting on the ground?
Time unraveling. And time
folded smaller and smaller.

And the fruit expected
overhead? Time appointed and appointing.

And when it's time, I'll hear the name
fire and air speak to each bowed head of grass.

And when it's time, I will remind myself:
All of the light is one, unanimous with the dark.

Every world is two: inside and outside.
Time is many: the voices of children in the playground
shouting out the stations of their games,
the specific gravity of my hands
setting the table at evening,
the names of the guests
on my mind, the names of the missing
become so many questions
arising at the year's revolving door.

In the meantime, the wind in the garden changes
from agent of a far end to vagrant
turning over the leaves, looking for a story.

Once upon a time,
we were lonely children in a river valley,
and teachers and schoolmates getting our names wrong
helped to keep us hidden, safe
to make the most faithful companions of god and death.
No wonder we were ruined
for any other company.
Now, as then, the one invents our games,
while the other spurs our delicious cries
by keeping every prize in jeopardy.

Then, and now, the wind
in the trees makes the sound
of the turning pages of our nights and days,
the shadows of birds intermittent,
causing restlessness in the living.

Hidden Hearing

God slips His portrait of me under His pillow.
Morning grows cloudy, the house darkens,
and I know what the rain at the sill is saying:

Be finished with resemblances. Your lamp
hides the light. A voice, being a voice and not the wind,
can't carry anything away. And yet,
it makes any land a place, a country of the air,
and laughter its seventh day.

Last night I dreamed of voices in a grove.
Ladders reaching from the ground into the branches.
I was mending my children's shirts,
worrying if the light would last
long enough for me to thread the needle.

Now I'm nodding with the trees in the wind,
counting seconds between the lightning and the thunder,
deaf to former things, unencumbered of things to come,
and leaving God to recoup
a human fate.

God snores, His sleep immense
and musty with the season's litter.

God rolls over in His sleep
and churns the sea-bed
to dislodge many buried keys.

Outside, a bird is telling time's green name.
It stops when I stop to listen,
and starts again as soon as I give up
holding my breath to hear it,
as though whole-hearted listening intrudes
where hearing ajar makes room for singing
so tender my attention snuffs it,
or else so brimming
my ear's least turning spills it.

God takes out again that likeness
he makes of me each day, now adding, now erasing,

and time is a black butterfly, pinned
while someone searches for its name in a book.

Folding a Five-Cornered Star So the Corners Meet

This sadness I feel tonight is not my sadness.

Maybe it's my father's.
For having never been prized by his father.
For having never profited by his son.

This loneliness is Nobody's. Nobody's lonely
because Nobody was never born
and will never die.

This gloom is Someone Else's.
Someone Else is gloomy
because he's always someone else.

For so many years, I answered to a name,
and I can't say who answered.

Mister Know Nothing? Brother Inconsolable?
Sister Every Secret Thing? Anybody? Somebody?

Somebody thinks:
With death for a bedfellow,
how could thinking be anything but restless?

Somebody thinks: *God, I turn my hand face down*
and You are You and I am me.

I turn my hand face up
and You are the I
and I am your Thee.

What happens when you turn your hand?

Lord, remember me.
I was born in the City of Victory,
on a street called Jalan Industri where,
each morning, the man selling rice cakes went by
pushing his cart, its little steamer whistling,

while at his waist, at the end of a red string,
a little brass bell
shivered into a fine, steady seizure.

This sleeplessness is not my sleeplessness.
It must be the stars' insomnia.
And I am their earthbound descendant.

Someone, Anyone, No one, me, and Someone Else.
Five in a bed, and none of us can sleep.
Five in one body, begotten, not made.
And the sorrow we bear together is none of ours.
Maybe it's Yours, God.
For living so near to your creatures.
For suffering so many incarnations unknown to Yourself.
For remaining strange to lovers and friends,
and then outliving them and all of their names for You.
For living sometimes for years without a name.
And all of Your spring times disheveled.
And all of Your winters one winter.

I Loved You Before I Was Born

I loved you before I was born.
It doesn't make sense, I know.

I saw your eyes before I had eyes to see.
And I've lived longing
for your every look ever since.
That longing entered time as this body.
And the longing grew as this body waxed.
And the longing grows as this body wanes.
That longing will outlive this body.

I loved you before I was born.
It makes no sense, I know.

Long before eternity, I caught a glimpse
of your neck and shoulders, your ankles and toes.
And I've been lonely for you from that instant.
That loneliness appeared on earth as this body.
And my share of time has been nothing
but your name outrunning my ever saying it clearly.
Your face fleeing my ever
kissing it firmly once on the mouth.

In longing, I am most myself, rapt,
my lamp mortal, my light hidden and singing.

I give you my blank heart.
Please write on it
what you wish.

AHREN WARNER

For

I will consider these kittens of Bercy, each a *servus*
       servorum
Dei, though none would stoop to serve
       nor
have any Lord before themselves.

True Epicureans, apostles of Dionysus;
       kittens
in togas, touting the grace with which they curve
       their bodies.
Each motion revelatory, a rapture, *un triomphe du Soi.*

Superego

Somewhere in a town
in which you've never been
my fist abuts your face.

Through a fine mist
you steal the flit
of your – now *my* – gait.

JUDITH VOLLMER

Hole in the Sky

The dead ascend to heaven through white holes
into blue and that is why Mary's robe
was blue, the priestdrone easy to believe until
she died
who fed & combed me
with the callused palm of her hand. When she died
I hid under the cellar steps
shredding the hem of her skirt,
it calmed me to see colors in the weave.
The sky sucked her up, Reverse Hell, it was icy
& lonely and the sucking tornado hole of it
took her from the other hole
no one stayed to see the dirt packed onto.
I was going up through the hole
I thought, sitting under the steps
& ceiling vents with all the other
houses along the old boulevards & alleybacks
facing the yellow rivers
and the huge rushes & mists furled
upward, escapes always up into the sky. I look
up and she's still alive to me
but not her
human world of steel buckets & sour boots & septic
fractures in the foundations & men
blowing their noses into their fingers.

Little Death

She will rip some hair from your head

Pluck pearls from your spine

She will open you

She will knock your teeth out

She scrapes at your sweet meats

Her own vulva gone rancid

And last she will drain your tender

Eye sockets   prancing with your eyes in her palm

With them she'll look around the universe

Seeing endless rings & spirals

For the first time

    Your tendons   your bones

    Sticks on the ground still working

    Themselves in their mother language

MALACHI BLACK

PORTFOLIO

Bildungsroman

As flies to wanton boys are we to the gods,
They kill us for their sport. (King Lear)

The only earth we knew
then was the earth
        we would outgrow—
the scuff of the screech owl
on parchment light,
        a yellow bulb
above the porch moths, an hour
there in the indistinct
        navy tablecloth
of night, running our hands
through it, rinsing our fingers
        as with lake water
in a winter without frost—
there in the weight of it,
        in the air between
pine needles and the rocks
sinking, even then, though
        imperceptibly,
into the tread of sucking mud,
we couldn't think of it,
        raised as we had been
once from the wet husks
of our mothers, lifted
        as by wind
and wound in bed sheets
warm as blood, we couldn't
        think of it—
if we had known, we could have
huddled, held ourselves
        and held each other,
we could have held each breath
until it clenched like granite
        to the riverbed
of lung—but there, unknown
to us, it was, as tenderly
        indefinite

as love, a death embedded
in the bright bead of each firefly
                              we cupped
out of the darkness with our palms
as soft as tongues, there
                              as our laughter
flapped above us like a swan—
it was, it was, it was, it was

Fragment from a Province Drawn in Dust

If there is water, it must come
from the skin. Mother, when

you spread our country across
the flat map of your hand, I saw

only your palm; I could not dream
even then. Now I squint, bent

like your finger in the wind-
driven sand, but still I cannot

dream: I see only your hand.

In Our Late Empire, Love

drops from upper air,
     like rain,
clinging brightly
     to the fresh-cut hair
of children
     and the infantry:
all hail
    the clicking heel, all will
regale
    the shrinking light
with grains
     of wedding rice, of salt,
of sands as fit
     a last brassy parade:
the marching band
      will soften
with its growing-distant
       drum,
the oscillating hand
      will stop
its waving
    soon enough, soon
enough;
    here now, the motorcade
hums
   gaily through the citizens'
applause
    and the children's eyes
bronze faintly
     with the glint
of far-off fireworks,
     or firebombs,
or falling evening stars.

Lines from the Throne of Old Ideas

Self: What is the substance of a mind?

Soul: Fireflies in a pickle jar.

Self: Is time a circle or a line?

Soul: Moth wings tapping on a drum.

Self: Am I the water or the fire?

Soul: Steam uprising from the soil.

Self: What, then, of the afterlife?

Soul: A coil of air, a curl.

Quarantine

Lauds

Somehow I am sturdier, more shore
than sea-spray as I thicken through
the bedroom door. I gleam of sickness.
You give me morning, Lord, as you
give earthquake to all architecture.
I can forget.
          You put that sugar
in the melon's breath, and it is wet
with what you are. (I, too, ferment.)
You rub the hum and simple warmth
of summer from afar into the hips
of insects and of everything.
I can forget.
          And like the sea,
one more machine without a memory,
I don't believe that you made me.

Prime

I don't believe that you made me
into this tremolo of hands,
this fever, this flat-footed dance
of tendons and the drapery

of skin along a skeleton.
I am that I am: a brittle
ribcage and the hummingbird
of breath that flickers in it.

Incrementally, I stand:
in me are eons and the cramp
of endless ancestry.

Sun is in the leaves again.
I think I see you in the wind
but then I think I see the wind.

Terce

But then I think I see the wind
as an intention, pressing us
with weather. All the pieces
of the air you've put together
somehow know just how to hold
the rain. They somehow know

to funnel and unfold, to swerve
the snow, to rake the beaches
and to slope the arcing seagull's wings.
As wind inside a shell: they know
you in themselves. I'll find you out;
I can know you as a hint in things.

I do. And through the window
I have known you as an opening.

Sext

I have known you as an opening
of curtains as a light blurts through
the sky. But this is afternoon
and afternoon is not the time

to hunt you with the hot globe
of a human eye. So I fluster
like a crooked broom in rounds
within the living room, and try
to lift an ear to you. I try.

I cut myself into a cave for you.
To be a trilling blindness
in the infinite vibration
of your murmuring July,
I cut myself into a cave for you.

None

I cut myself into a cave for you,
but you are quiet. You are shy:

an only child, you still hide
from blame and invitations

and you constantly deny
all suitors. I will not be

defied: you are the tongue
I plunge into this begging

razorblade so brightened
by my spiderweb of blood,

you are the one: you are
the venom in the serpent

I have tried not to become,
my Lord. You are the one.

Vespers

My Lord, you are the one:
your breath has blown away
       the visionary sun
and now suffocates the skyline
       with a dusk. If only once,
I wish that you could shudder
with my pulse,   double over
and convulse   on the stitches
in the skin that I slash wishes in.
       But, Lord, you are the gulf
between the hoped-for
         and the happening:
You've won.   So what is left for me
when what is left for me has come?

Compline

when what is left for me has come:
when what is left has left its wing
in something slumped against a door:
when what is left for me has come
to nothing ever after and before
this kingdom come to nothing:
when what has come is nothing more
than what was left and what was left
is nothing more than what has come
to nothing ever after and before:
if what is left is what is meant
for me and what is meant for me
is nothing come to nothing come
to this kingdom come to nothing:

Nocturne

To This Kingdom Come to Nothing:

I have itemized the night. I have held
within the livid tissue of my mouth
every particle of light and even now
I am a maze of radiation. I have felt
in each of my one hundred trillion cells
the rapturous, proud swell of darkling sounds
whose undulations break a body down
to sprays of elemental matter. As well
I have obtained a straightforward account
of the forces and conditions that propelled
the universe to burst from nothing else
and I can tell of every trembling genesis.

There is no end,

        What Has Come
            Will Come Again

Vigils

There is no end: what has come will come again
will come again: and then distend: and then
and then: and then again: there is no end

to origin and and: there is again
and born again: there is the forming and:
the midnight curling into morning and

the glory and again: there is no end:
there is the blessing in an and and an again:
the limitlessly yessing of began

begins incessantly again: and then
the infinite undressing of all when
there is the lifting everything again

the glowing endlessness and then
the floating endlessly again

Matins

The floating endlessly again:
the glowing and the growing back
again as I am as I can and I can stand.
I understand.
                    Though I am fashioned
in the haggard image of a man,
I am an atom of the aperture.

I am as a nerve inside a gland.

I understand. Though I am fashioned
as I am, I am a perch for the eternal
and a purse for what it lends.
I understand.
                    Though flakes of fire
overwhelm the fallen snow, though ice
caps melt, though oceans freeze or overflow,
somehow I am sturdier, more sure.

JACQUELYN POPE

Emphasis Mine

LOST declares the Highlander's Land of Lincoln plate,
now canting from a single rusted bolt. This I know,
for this I am: fish out of water, ever out
of sorts, foreign-born and foreign-hearted.
Stuck now, in the here-and-now, as the world turns
and turns away. Marking time in the lowest
of these low lands, in lots drawn and Chemlawned,
where the world spreads sprawled and blind, gorges
on blacktop. Its houses settle cheek-by-jowl, secured
by Rustic Wood and Heritage Plastic, needled
by evergreens, the roofs strafed by wind and jet fuel.
Here in the grasp of its grid of days, in seasons
detailed by dammed ice or peeling paint,
I go skidding past turns, out of true, tracked
through the muck of its weedrows and gumstick,
in the wrack of my failures of nerve.

DEVON BRANCA

19.

The son waits for his mother to finish
her conversation with the statue,
then the tree, then the town, then the dandelion
and all its seedpods on the ground.

When she is done,
he asks how to say hello.

Game length: It doesn't matter
what she says, as long as she speaks,
he will believe she said hello.

54.

1) Some days he wanted to be
the captain of a ship
inside a bottle.

2) To get an egg into a bottle,
start a fire inside the bottle
and place an egg on the bottle mouth.

Game length: To reverse 1 or 2,
start a fire outside the bottle, then use dotted lines
to calculate the distance from "here"
to "the dominant horizon."

CRAIG MORGAN TEICHER

The Hairdryer Cord Is All Tangled

You've stepped out of the shower,
dragged the towel up and down
your clean little self. Now

you've got to dry your hair, and quick.
Except there's this tangle. A clogged
artery? But nothing prevents you from

plugging it in—why won't you? *Does*
somebody love us all? Undo it,
or else who will, and when?

A time machine and God's eyes–that's what
you need. Does no one feel
the tectonic plates, magma, glaciers sliding?

You do, who've been anticipating death
since you were four. Your hair is still
so wet. Stop thinking! Your face

will stay that way like Gramma warned.
You'll catch your own swift undoing.
Untangle the cord, or the knots

will keep seething like a cracked oil pipe
snaking along the ocean floor.
This may be your one chance to stop

the fateful flap of the butterfly's wings.
Cities are shaking, sinking, singing.
The Earth is burning! Quick, untangle it!

Gnostic

I have a soul, I know it, have always
recognized it there within
me like a luminous ball in the dark

between my heart
and my liver, shifting
around under my ribs,
expressing itself sometimes

where my ribcage closes
just beneath the skin, a pushing
outward of something song-like, light-like
that could almost lift me
up and out of myself through myself

knowing everything I know and much more.
Fear—extreme fear—was part of it,
and something eons beyond
excitement, a certainty
that the body was only a beginning.

It was what I knew childhood
was for, to live close
to this, to sense it often, daily,
not to seek it—because

I was terrified of it, correctly—
but to accept it; it was
obvious, undeniable, like rain
or the hard floor of the house
if I tripped and fell.

I say this now, surely,
with a kind of nostalgia, with longing.
Life is much more literal
thirty years later. Transcendence
is mostly replacing one screen with another.
All light is fairly dim. There is nothing

to frighten me but death and debt.
And yet, that other, better terror
still rings—I hear it—between
and beneath these words.

Why else am I writing them?

Of Dog

He could never take such an animal for his own,
the neighbors' extraordinary Bernese
mountain dog, massive as a bear, but prone
to kindness, loving, eager to please
and be loved. He loves her already from afar.
A monstrosity tamed, she's all his heart fears
and covets, a beast to bound into his car.
They let her out for her nightly walk—he hears
her sniff and snuffle at the lawn edge.
She must smell him smoking now on his deck.
If only she'd come running through the hedge,
offer the soft depths of her warm neck,
her nose, to his hands. The light's so dim.
Let her bring her hot breath to comfort him.

*The Inventor's
Last Breath*

BY J. HOPE STEIN

PORTFOLIO

THE INVENTOR'S LAST BREATH

Ladies & Gentlemen The apparatus
you see before you
isn't quite a phonograph or telephone line to the dead
nor a movie screen to project their lives
It works more like a breathalyzer What is inhaled
is never quite What is exhaled is personality
Is words to your neighbors Is touching
your tongue to your nose Is blowing
out your candles Hiccups yawns & laughter

Ladies & Gentlemen The body
is the soul's model T
A factory of microscopic men tug the diaphragm
We breathe into stomach
not chest Ladies & Gentlemen
these are the principles that guide the machine
you see before you The Inventor's final secret
found by the great-great-granddaughter
of the mistress of the Inventor
Ladies & Gentleman if we were to voluntarily stop
breathing we would lose consciousness
& the tiny men would take over

Ladies & Gentlemen The test tube
you see before you
contains the Inventor's last breath A larva
in a jar since 1931 A soft vapor or vibration
at the cork's edge Not unlike
Galileo's middle finger
in a glass case still
pointing up The story of a man
can be told in a single breath A unique
chord struck by tiny starfish Tonight
we release the man into the machine
Ladies & Gentlemen All there is
to know about a man is in his breath

J. Hope Stein

March 5, 1878

To be close to something wild is to kill it—So I watch him from the bushes: He walks out the factory—His grey woolen eyes weaving sun—Lifts the bottle. A large amount of milk spills down his throat, chin, shirt, cheek. All the while he's walking in sunshine, like he owns it—The whole fucking street.   Like a man bent east for a late train—"It's good to be a little deaf while traveling."

INVENTION OF THE PHONOGRAPH
Mary

"If February is a little
will-you-ever-kiss-me?-goose,
April is a-will-you-kiss-me-circus.
But on a February afternoon, when you say, *goose*,
I can see your breath"—

& the Inventor says, "the motivation
for evolution is dollars & problems—
An ear is just a mouth
you can listen from. & Love,
love is the great goose
we make of each other."

[MARY]:

Sir?

[INVENTOR]:

Yes.

[MARY]:

I can always sense your presence.

[INVENTOR]:

What's that?

[MARY]:

I can feel when you're nearby.

[INVENTOR]:

What's that, girl? I can barely hear you … come closer.

[MARY]:

Without seeing you, I know in my nerves when you've entered
the room.

[INVENTOR]:

Half the time, I don't know myself when I've entered the room.

THE INVENTOR'S HYPOTHESIS

For the necklace with a tiny silver pony she misplaces on the floor of my factory—For I rescue the necklace from the floor of my factory and wait for her to disrobe and change into her street clothes. For when she sees me looking through the curtains that don't quite close.   For I give her the necklace and ask if there's a story behind the pony. She whispers *zebra not pony* and merry-go-rounds me like a ghost. Her hair, golden. For I levitate with my high plane of thought and summon her to keep returning to me. For touch is the only true correspondence of tiny men and I begin to sculpt her:

One I drum on her head.

Two I place my hand on her abdominals to possess her of her meridians.

Three I sandwich my weight to her bend & she can feel my monster.

Four She keeps saying zebra and keeps coming back.

Five I notice the chisels in her body.

Six I invite her to balance on one leg by clasping her foot to my inner thigh and she can feel my monster.

Seven We do seated poses to add suppleness to her knees, groin and ankles.

Eight We do reaching poses that make her blouse slide, exposing elements of her stomach. At first she struggles with one hand reaching. I have the factory hold these positions for a full minute. For she is swimming in golden hair.

Nine Sometimes she keeps on her necklace and in inverted positions, the zebra dangles to her lips. Sometimes she lets it slip inside her mouth.

Ten For it is the new moon—The disciples in the factory are wood-working with their eyes closed. For night is a dark open mouth & I have the mind to make a cocktail of her. I stand over her body, (for the fragrance of her swollen body in corpse pose) the room is dark, her eyes are closed—She must have summoned me with levitation. For sometimes you think about going right up to a rim of a volcano and having a glass of scotch. I bring her left pinky inside my mouth—

She does not change the pistol or compass of her electric breath. This girl does not make a single movement or noise in darkness surrounded by disciples with their eyes closed. We stay just like this for 4 minutes.

June 20, 1878

I watch Thomas slant green elements in a test tube—(What long perusal his edifying fingers make!)—There's a danger in a man who angles for a living.   He can grow stuck in his angle & lose his way.   I bring him a jar of nickel I extract myself from stone—Its powdered-particles sparkle in afternoon window light.   I will not be able to control what happens when we touch.

[MARY]:

Sir?

[INVENTOR]:

Yes, girl.

[MARY]:

Those are the same trousers you have been wearing since last
Thursday.

[INVENTOR]:

I can't hear you …

[MARY]:

Sometimes I get the feeling you use your hearing impairment as
an excuse to get closer—Look down my shirt.

[INVENTOR]:

Your voice—so quiet I will have to crawl inside your mouth.
What's your name, girl?

[MARY]:

Mary Stillwell

[INVENTOR]:

> How old are you?

[MARY]:

> 16.

[INVENTOR]:

> How long have you been working in my factory?

[MARY]:

> 18 months.

[INVENTOR]:

> What are we going to do about this?

[MARY]:

> Do about what?

[INVENTOR]:

> This marriage of ours.

J. Hope Stein

INVENTION OF THE TELEGRAPH

If I tap the insides
of your wrist -- .- .-. .-. -.-- / -- .
/ -- -.-- / .-.. .- -- -... (Marry me my lamb)
-- .- .-. .-. -.-- / -- . / -- -.-- / .-.. .- -- -...
(Marry me my lamb) -- .- .-. .-. -.-- / -- .
/ -- -.-- / .-.. .- -- -... (Marry me my lamb)

INVENTION OF LIGHT BULBS
Just Married

Husband is food. I mean good
or roof. Which husband? *Men,*
women and snowmen—Where…
is my underwear? Husband wakes me
with licking cheeks. I make pillow
of husband's shoulder & husband.

Sousing the dishes topless for husband:
I douse the mugs & bowls with warm
lemon froth & bubble; I sponge
our utensils: spoon, knife & prong,
for food we will eat next Tuesday
& Sunday & Tomorrow; I scrub
& bristle & muscle the pig-headed pans
with sporadic splash & suds to skin;
I rinse & fill & rinse & empty & fill & empty
& fill & empty to the music of water on twice the dishes.

Husband puts his face in a bowl of afternoon
cereal & we sing: *Where, where is my underwear?*
In the phenomenal
sock project, I watch husband place lone socks
across the kitchen table:
could be inside a pair of pants or suitcase.

In the earth of blankets,
I gladden husband
by the glow of candlelight through the sheets.
(Where is my underwear?) The sky
drools sweetly to the ear,
the purring animals in our bed.
Light snore, the seashore at night.

INVENTION OF MOTION PICTURES

INTERIOR INVENTOR'S LIBRARY:
Inarticulate squeaks —A mouse?
CAMERA REVEALS: The Inventor
standing in a grey button down shirt—
head pressed against
a wall of books—getting industrious
with something between his legs.
CLOSE UP: The Inventor inserts
his penis into a soapy test tube
(whistling Beethoven) 22 frames
per second. CUT TO: INTERIOR
LIVING ROOM FLOOR: OVERHEAD
Mary—a trail of white foam, little white caps,
leads down to her hips and hands.
She's listening to Beethoven.
CLOSE UP: Mary maneuvers a light bulb
covered in shaving cream like a rubbing
lamp—Music swells as it disappears into her pelvis.
[MARY]: There are as many ways of fucking
as disposing of the dead. But in our country,
when the filaments of two minds curl towards
each other—This, we call a kiss.

INVENTION OF LIGHT BULBS
Hand Massage

She rubs the factory from his palms.
Salutes each finger like an admiral—
Removes the ring
& begins on the bark
of his hands. It feels good
to him when it's off & she makes putty
from elbow to finger.
She slips the ring back on. (It feels good to him
when it's on) & how he finds himself by daylight.

INVENTION OF LIGHT BULBS
Chicken

An animal gives off a certain light, don't you
think? I'm talking to a woman cooking
chicken in 1846. We grow old, us
& the chicken. Inter-special love
is never easy. Talking doll/Talking
clock. *But how to cook boneless, skinless*
chicken? I'm talking to a girl in 1886.
Have you found your thoughts depend
on what's in hand and which hand?
And as much as war? The 20-year old
man beside her wears his cap low over
his eyes. His mouth is the dirt path
to meadow. His mind, a decomposing
mouse up ahead. *Cook 'til the water runs*
clear. I'm talking to a woman in 1990
pregnant & horny—An artist
with a talent for eye pencil & shadow.
On Monday she paints her lids red.
Her irises are the blue intestines of fire.
Husband dumps a pail of water on her face—
Smothers her with a blanket of mouth & muscle.
They make rain and grassy mud.
On Tuesday there is only blackness & thick
wet mascara with tiny lightening bolts
at the corner of her eyes and between
her eyes. Husband is hit by a hailstorm.
On Wednesday her clean wet lashes
are like a child who doesn't want to get out of the tub—
The back of his hand along skin.
His ring along skin & catching lip & skin.
Husband brings pieces of chicken
to her mouth. Sauce dripping jaw—
Chicken, there is only chicken.

INVENTION OF THE ELECTRIC CHAIR

"Let us agree, there are the things we can see
& the things we can't"
Husband pulls my coat—Splays it—
Over my lap (& the-now-what-are-we?)
Ouch!— I am sitting on someone's knuckles.
The persistent fist opens
under my skirt (& the-now-what-are-we?),
I begin to settle into its fingers.
Husband says, "This is what we call the electric chair."
I dampen in the lumbar
& recite the headlines of today:

WALT WHITMAN'S HEART WAS VERY LARGE
AND WAS THE ONLY ABSOLUTELY HEALTHY ORGAN.
THE BRAIN WEIGHED BUT FORTY-SIX OUNCES
THE BODY IN A CONSTANT STREAM AS IT LAY.

Husband & his machinists
form a semi-circle
at my hip & waist-—Arms up
in the now-what-are-we & my girdle—
This is what Husband calls, "assembly line."
I hold onto its nimbus,
& recite the headlines of today
as an ungovernable leg &
a negligent thigh
spasm to the now-what-are-we
& the now-what-are-we & the now-what-are-we
& their heads:

WALT WHITMAN'S HEART WAS VERY LARGE
AND WAS THE ONLY ABSOLUTELY HEALTHY ORGAN.
THE BRAIN WEIGHED BUT FORTY-SIX OUNCES
THE BODY IN A CONSTANT STREAM AS IT LAY.

In machine howl & machine yelp
there is no gathering of dust.

One must yell as an angry landlady
into the big-holed hinged jaw
monkey-mouth of history to be heard.
In short, I want something in my mouth.
Husband says, "This is what we call consumption"—
Hoists his finger up in the custom of me—
Feeds me an elixir (ice cream)
until my mouth freezes, my speech impedes
& I scream—Funny!—
Although we are surrounded by people constantly—
Me & the warm palm in my hosiery—
we are very much alone.

INVENTION OF LIGHT BULBS

Sometimes I can hear Husband turn his pages
faster than mine & I
become irritated—
& throw a book across the room—
An ember
in husband's eye that rounds his balls.

"Come here, sensitive, we are
both turning
because the mind is turning…"

Save it for the factory, Husband!
Only animal pantomime
& balloons, please.

Husband moves like an inchworm
across the carpet.
Does his best monkey.
Motions as if to offer a string connected
to something in sky
& I take it.

We act as two animals holding invisible balloons.

J. HOPE STEIN

December 13, 1903

Thomas says, "We are not ourselves- we are only a conglomerate of tiny men who work in the factory of our bodies. Thomas says, "Forgive me, Goose—These tiny men, in our final breaths: exit through the open windows of our mouths." Thomas closes my mouth with his fingers—I hold onto Thomas' wrist—His pulse is a tiny man walloping—

How can I forgive you? (if you won't say what it is that you have done?)

INVENTION OF THE STOCK TICKER

OVERHEAD: ZOOM OUT, CAMERA
REVEALS: Mary on a generous bearskin rug
as if she lives inside his belly,
her eyeglasses tossed to her side
at an earlier point —The Inventor taps
Mary's wrist -... .-. . .- - .... /
 .. ... / .-- .... .- - / -- .- -.- . ... / -- -.-- /
 -... --- -.. -.-- / .- .-.. .. ...- . / My breath
is what makes my body alive
 - -. -.. / .-- .... .- - /
 -- .- -.- . ... / -- -.-- / -... --- -.. -.-- /
 .- .-.. .. ...- . / .. ... / -.--.- ... .. .- .-. .--. .-. .. .. -.--.- /
 -.-- --- ..- & what makes my body alive
is (surprise) you.

INVENTION OF THE ELECTRIC CHAIR

I'm buried in a field overrun
by wild carrot

sun
a small high window

bit me red
my raw scalp

bleeds, they say
you don't have the liberty

to see the top of your own head
my body catches fire

*

I die in new store-bought clothes
my throat muscles

my breath begins
to ash

they say he wears a red carnation
my pistol sparks he catches my fire

*

"let no man hurt this man"—
the president says bleeding
dozens drag my body spitting
wanting to beat me dead
would do it again

the sun bit me red

*

"what kind of man shoots while shaking
hands?" I don't apologize every muscle
in full extension I didn't kill the man
eyes bulging I put a bullet in bankers
dealers car men presidents everywhere
who put the money in the money inside
the money heavy leather straps
& skull-burn would do it again
we are your inventions

*

what was america wearing
when you met her?

an unemployed steel worker
the first joint, blood

trickles the arm
of chair

a paid dollar for one
an empty pocket for another

right index finger curls
into flesh

eyes fix open
you can't see your own expressions

we are your inventions

*

bankers promoters
car men

stirring the sauce
of my madness

my shoes worn
through in waiting

the crowd took
punches at my head

*

I'm dead, no
I still

twitch a little I still
spittle, yes

my chest inflates
deflates

"let's try 2,000 volts"
something breaks

under my skin
would do it again

from my strapped mouth something oozes

trickles my face switches

on & off
the blood in my brain

burns to black powder
a field of wild carrot catches fire

[Flashback: 1847-1864]

INVENTOR LOSES HEARING AS
MOTHER READS WHITMAN

A Baby. No, a boy now.
A cool damp cloth. The lobes of your ears
fever on the front porch of my lap. You say
you can feel it in your throat. You say you like
when I read to you—*only the lull I like,*
the hum of your valved voice. The rash first
on your neck. Your skin turning wood & splinters.
You say you can feel it in your stomach.
.-.. --- .- ..-. / --- -. / - .... . / --. .-. .- ... ... /
 .-- .. - .... / -- . *loose the stop from your throat.*
You're vomiting now. Your fingertips.
Toes peel like raw garlic. Tongue is lobster.

You say you can feel it in your head—To *know*
the universe .. - ... . .-.. ..-. / .- ... / .- / .-. --- .- -..
as many roads .- ... /.-. --- .- -.. .-.-.- /
..-. --- -.. / - .-. .- ... . .-.. .. -. --. / ... --- ..- .-.. ...!
Can you hear me, baby? *I pursue you where no*
one else has .--. ..- .-. ... ..- . -.. / .-.- --- ..-
The soul travels. The body -.. --- . ... /
-. --- - *travel* .- ... / -- ..- -.-. .... / .- ... *the soul,*
- .... ./ -... --- -.. .-.- / .... .- ... / .--- ..- ... - /
.- ... / --. .-. . . .- - / .- / .-- --- .-. .-.- / .- ... / - .... . /
... --- ..- .-.. *and parts away at last.*

[END OF FLASHBACK]

LIGHT'S GOLDEN JUBILEE
The 50th anniversary of the light bulb—October 20-24, 1929

1.

The servants set silver and supper
for 500 pioneers of our age. (Boneless
squab in butter & Virginia ham
with mushrooms). The bankers.
The men who invented wealth.
The men who invented how you think.
The men in charge of machinery.
The broadcasters. Cable & socket men.
The king of ballyhoo. The presidents
of electricity and department stores.
The men who decided what you like
to eat. The steel men. The financers.
The patrons of the arts. The woman who
invented a way to see inside your bones.
The man who made you fly. The car man.
The new president on his first journey
from the capital. The sun, an electric bulb.

& The Inventor says, the happiest man is
the one who catches butterflies—The happiest
time in my life is when I was 12 years old.

& The Inventor drinks a glass of milk—
When I drink milk I get God he says.
My legs throb and swell. GOUT not GOD.
& The Inventor & Mary enter a banquet of partners & rivals.

2.

John D. Rockefeller & Charles Schwab
plant their warm-blooded cocks in a pair of squabs—
Rejoice in their puppet-selves,
then deflate into the gravy.

(We love what fools us into the gravy!)

Orville Wright whittles his wood by the paw,
makes true monument & insult to gravity—
All the questions puddle into one
& a great cream lagoons.

Herbert Hoover consults the policy-makers of his genitals
then makes gladsome meal
of the nibblets of an injured factory worker,
rejoices in his dainty country with solid
genitals & gravy, deflates, rejoices again
in presidential meekness & gravity.

Will Rogers sucks the cold cock of an ice sculpture—
In 6 years his plane will puddle to lagoon
but now he sings *Let's Go Flying*
into the oyster (what-is-it?) of night
& licks with a grateful tongue

... as mouths congratulate each other for the century.

3.

There is a wet & unsinkable
young woman in the coat room
contesting everybody's trousers—
Orville Wright grabs her by her most intricate lobes,
bites into her knobs like olives—Bends
back pink knees to sluice
what was mounting— She
looks like his marsupial
baby riding in his animal
pocket. He marvels at the aerodynamics:

That the room is a two-

hundred-lunged animal rejoicing in the harmonica
of its nation —Unifies
& unifies & unifies, blankets the globe in optimistic juices;
That the nation is flag-
rippling-drunk, harmful
& harmonious, embodies & embodies, re-embodies;
That the room is a shipwreck,
sunk heads within sunk heads, the candles begin
their slow motion
toppling; That the table is set;
That we rejoice in the mouth;
That we can be both roast & appetite; That the squab carcass
knows nothing of puppetry;
That life is a form of eating (death
is another); That the two candles
burning know
nothing of their inches.

4.

And the Inventor says,
the secret to my genius?—
The secret to my genius is
there's no such thing as man.
There is only work.
Man is microscopic starfish.
When man dies, the starfish move on,
swarm with new starfish to become cat or asparagus.
That is to say, your personality will not survive.
The secret to my genius?
I believe in pinheads—
Men who carry their brains in slings.
Men who invented slavery instead of motors.
There's no such thing as genius.
Thinking—there is only thinking.

5.

[All raise glasses]

Despite the countless triumphs of the human mind we still find ourselves Despite thecountless triumphs of the humanmind we still find ourselves Despite the countless triumphsof the human mind we stillfind ourselves Despite the countlesstriumphs of the human mind we still find ourselvesDespite the countless triumphs of the human mind we still find ourselves

[Inventor faints]

SCENES FROM THE BEDROOM

We are the dimwit or dog-dumb day
.................................the crap-morning
after the swig-swig night........................……
…………...In making music.....................……..
……it's not you………...……who says, remove
your clothes...................exposing the flesh
of the heel…………...that makes your dog dog
under tablecloth............or put your thumb in
......(baseball makes me sleepy)…….............
It's not you who grabs that woman's boob in the
elevator........................ant-stubborn..........
...................brain-wild......................…...……
tormented by the sound of snow……….…..…
……………something of fire deserves an exit…
It's not you.......just stood there..................
dumb-luck…...…..... as in penis...................
.Something of fire requires choking……………
…………. In the name of science..................……..
……….…….. something of man is always a guest
& rattles……………. & we........................…..
chew silence ...in the final breath.

[CLOSE UP: MARY
with a test tube captures
the Inventor's last breath]

THE INVENTOR'S LAST BREATH

Ladies & Gentlemen The Inventor's last breath
has been waiting A trillion tiny men A movie screen
to project your lives All there is
to know about a man is in his breath
Ladies & Gentlemen The body
is the soul's couch potato The soul is
the body's mooch The tiny voices that make
up a man Lovers ailments & turkey stew

Ladies & Gentlemen The breath goes
to the highest Machine goes to
the highest breath An opera repeated
in the pickle of man A sip of scotch
Ladies & Gentlemen The tiny current
at the pulse of the wrist begins & ends
in the breath of our meeting

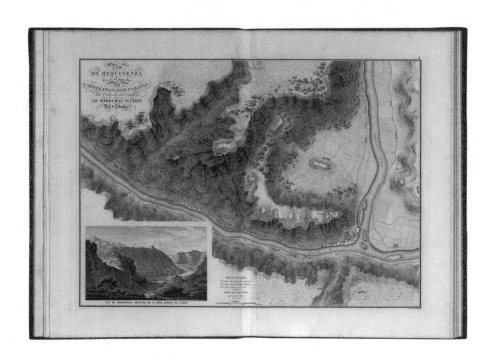

Mario Bojórquez

At the banks of the Delaware River Waterfront facing Camden and watching the lights of the Walt Whitman Bridge

One day you grew a beard
like a frostbitten river
and you turned to ice
ancient poet head of clouds

For all your screams that Mexico deserved to disappear
that the fate of your nation was large
so large it should exterminate the entire world

Some of your compatriots
believe in your words and tend your dream

—and today 150 years of your anger
the lightning of my tongue sings to you en libertad.

Old, old, old, viejo, viejo Walt
                       Whitman

(1847-1997)

Translated from the Spanish by Hari Alluri, Binh Nguyen and Jonathan Rodley

Guggenheim Museum

The unceasing spiral where the world goes
                                    below
The spiral unceasing where I go with me
                    to rise in myself
                            and return

For where I unceasing
                        spiral in my bones
Dextrous from what is mine
                                – around I
            twisting   in   myself

Unceasing where I
                only spiral
        breathless I
return

Where unceasing I spiral
                    —toward me in me

Translated from the Spanish by Hari Alluri, Binh Nguyen and Jonathan Rodley

Adam Day

Sentimental Remembrance

No one moves about
with a reluctance

to sneeze and belch
like she did,

nearly breastless
huntress, collecting

the little droppings
from my soul.

Commencer

Tonight I want everyone who passes,
except widowers and tweens. Not
the kids. Not your mom— she's no
looker. And not Dave or Jeff.
And no wild game, even if we are
in the South. That still leaves sheep. But
not the dead; they're all up and doing
things in poems. But maybe Ben.
He's had a hard life, and I could make it
easier. I'll be gentle, Ben. I promise.

POETRY FROM ISRAEL

FEATURE

Yudit Shahar

Fuck the Tomato

Fuck poetry fuck
to strip,
to daintify skin
to display in cold light
the pitifulness.

To sell tomatoes
in tony Tel Aviv,
to shine them one by one
in a white shirt
in the light,
to sell to the wealthy—
what do they care for poetry?
What do they care about a tomato,
a rotten one?
Fuck the tomato
fuck.

Translated from the Hebrew by Aviya Kushner

On the Day You Came

On the day you came to me I stripped off my clothes
and drew on my scars:
a Madonna lily, rare birds
and a lone brown dove.
The dove opened her mouth and said "Go"
but the lily rushed to burn the flesh
and the birds flew away and screamed,
rubbing their wings against each other,
raining on me and on my eyes
purple and gold feathers—
on the day you came to me.

Translated from the Hebrew by Aviya Kushner

DAN PAGIS

Testimony

No. No: they absolutely
were human: uniforms, boots.
How to explain. They were created in the image.
I was a shadow.
I had a different maker.
And he, in his grace, did not leave within me death.
I escaped to him, rose lightly, blue,
reconciled, I would say, apologetic:
smoke to unrestricted smoke
without body or equal.

Translated from the Hebrew by Carl Adamshick

Encounter

You meet a mirror and turn away too late.
How are you? Haven't changed? Goodbye. Goodbye, be well.
You meet, almost in hiding, with a bunch of old papers.
You survived, survived. What else will you tell them? You mixed up the years.
You wander in the veins, in the arteries to the beating heart and from it
to another beating. Even this name isn't yours.
Suddenly, in the closet, the photograph: you, you
with the bulged cheek bones, the surprised look.
Yes. Yes, the same bones. Now
you understand, you didn't even die. You denied for nothing.
What is the answer you won't accept, the question you can't ask?
You are ready, stand, hurry through the door,
down into the cellar and talk to the wall.

Translated from the Hebrew by Carl Adamshick

Twenty Years in the Valley

And after it all, I do not know,
each of us fell
into our own forgetfulness.
The road widened. We stay on the shoulder,
upside down in an armored car.
At noon, sometimes, I look
from his burned eyes. I could not remember
those tall trees.
Others pass by
forgetting a different war
with different dead. They are quicker than us.
But sometimes a wind comes down,
lifts the bouquet
that spun into the valley
and picks, petal by petal, saying:
They love. Yes. No. Yes.
A bit. No.
A lot.
No.
Too much.

Translated from the Hebrew by Carl Adamshick

Eli Eliahu

The repo men

They knocked on my door at noon (a misunderstanding
with the municipality about tax collection).
Came with pistols, pulled out papers.
Said this number of square meters,
that much accumulated debt, interest,
arrears. Saw books on the shelves,
the sofa, the table. The tall one asked
if I was a Ph.D. student. No, I said,
a poet. He saw my book on the table,
opened it and read aloud: "The world peels away
like a gigantic snakeskin." Nice, he said, the world
peels away. Really nice. They agreed to
split the debt into equal payments. From all
the books, they repossessed one line and left.

Translated from the Hebrew by Vivian Eden

On how I am like a pencil

I write one side and on the other I am erased.

**

Pain makes me sharper.

**

Concealed, thinner than thin, a silvery thread
of lead runs through me, innersecret.

**

Even if I break into a thousand times myself
there will still be an end that continues to
write.

**

I feel fingers
tightening on
my throat.

**

Where do they end?
Where do I
begin?

Translated from the Hebrew by Vivian Eden

Burial

My father rode ahead of us
a hundred meters ahead of us
we rode a hundred meters behind him
we kept our distance.

We buried him one meter
beneath our feet
a meter beneath our feet
beneath the fine sand.

Rabbi Natan would say:
"Press down,
press down tight."

That's how my father's life
beneath the ground began.

Translated from the Hebrew by Vivian Eden

Tal Nitzán

[The truth and I are flatmates]

The truth and I are flatmates.
Since I moved in before her
my room is larger than hers. Since
I sleep late and she wakes early
we share each day only
eight hours, half of them
darkness, half light.

Some mornings she
longs to wake me up,
hesitates at the edge of my room
while I fall dizzy from dream
to dream to dream, and her small
hand, clenched for a knock,
casts on my door
a trembling black bird
of a shadow.

Translated from the Hebrew by Jenny Minniti-Shippey and the author

It snowed again

Like fine ash from a fire
that spread in the sky while we slept.

Fluffy and clean on the roofs underneath my window,
mucky already from footprints on sidewalks.

In a world whose colors vanished
I see the black-fingered loneliness.

Small distant feet,
a twitch tires and freezes –

again she writes me as I watch the snow
and her hand trembles, not from the cold
and not from the lie.

Translated from the Hebrew by Sandra Alcosser, Ilya Kaminsky and the author

Nocturno

Night-drops in the grass, the moon
flattened and pale like a plot-canceled fable

the birds' cries more piercing and desperate
in the aftermath of rain, a piano hesitates a sonata

in a nearby house, and I am thrown back to love,
forcefully, without being asked.

Translated from the Hebrew by Katie Ford and the author

Hagit Grossman

Love Poem for a Cook from Florentine Street

I won't corner you into small spaces
I'll pull up a sofa wherever you want to rest your head
I now know how
When everyone else is out celebrating
You hide among the pots.

When everyone goes out into the streets
You enclose yourself into a narrow room
They are gorged, and you haven't rested since morning
Though there is a war on, the restaurant is full.

Translated from the Hebrew by Benjamin Balint

Aviya Kushner

The Grammar of God

אֱלֹהִים   בָּרָא   בְּרֵאשִׁית
elohim   ***bara***   ***Bereishit***
God   created   In/at the beginning

הַשָּׁמַיִם   אֵת
hashamayim   ***et***
the skies; the   [no English equivalent;
heavens   introduces a definite direct object]

הָאָרֶץ   וְאֵת
ha'aretz   ***ve'et***
the earth/land   and *et* [see *et* above]

הָיְתָה   וְהָאָרֶץ
hayta   ***V'ha'aretz***
was [feminine verb, past tense]   And the earth/land

וְחֹשֶׁךְ   תֹהוּ וָבֹהוּ
v'choshech   ***to'hu va'vo'hu***
and darkness   wild emptiness; void

[The phrase *to'hu va'vo'hu* appears only twice in the Bible; the other place is Jeremiah 4:23.]

תְהוֹם   פְּנֵי   עַל־
t'hom   ***p'nei***   ***al***
water; deep water   [the] face   on

["Face" in Hebrew is always plural; the same is true for "water" and "life."]

אֱלֹהִים   וְרוּחַ
elohim   ***veh'ruach***
[of] God   And the wind/spirit

הַמַּיִם   פְּנֵי   עַל   מְרַחֶפֶת
hamayim   *p'nei*   *al*   ***merachefet***
[of] the water   face   on   flutters/hovers

1 In the beginning God created the Heauen, and the Earth.
2 And the earth was without forme, and voyd, and darkenesse was
the face of the deepe: and the Spirit of God mooued vpon the
face of the waters.

Genesis 1:1–2, King James Bible (1611)

1 When God began to create heaven and earth—
2 the earth being unformed and void, with darkness over the
surface of the deep and a wind from God sweeping over the
water—

Jewish Publication Society Bible (1985)

1 At the beginning of God's creating
of the heavens and the earth,
2 when the earth was wild and waste,
darkness over the face of Ocean,
rushing-spirit of God hovering over the face of the waters—

Schocken Bible (*The Five Books of Moses*,
translated by Everett Fox, 1997)

1 In the beginning, when God created the universe,
2 the earth was formless and desolate. The raging ocean that
covered everything was engulfed in total darkness, and the Spirit of
God was moving over the water.

Good News Bible–Today's English Version,
American Bible Society (2001)

1 In the beginning God created the heavens and the earth.
2 And the earth was waste and empty, and darkness was on the face
of the deep, and the spirit of God was hovering over the face of the
waters.

Darby Bible (1890)

1 When God began to create heaven and earth,
2 and the earth then was welter and waste and darkness over the
deep and God's breath hovering over the waters,

Genesis: Translation and Commentary
(Translated by Robert Alter, 1997)

Creation

My family generally discusses the grammar of creation when I'm carrying at least thirty pounds of food. I've often walked into the dining room with a heavy platter of chicken and roasted potatoes just when my brother brings up the first line of Genesis, the opening of the world.

"It's a problem," my younger brother Davi says. "Every commentator knows it's a problem."

"It all comes down to how you read that one word," my mother says. "Do you read the verb in the first line as *bara*, in the past tense, so that it means 'in the beginning God *created*,' or do you read it as *bro*, a form of the infinitive, so that it reads 'in the beginning of God's *creating*'?"

Someone reaches for the asparagus.

"*Bereishit bara elohim et hashamayim ve'et ha'aretz*," Davi says. In the beginning God created the heavens and the earth. I can guess what he's thinking. If Genesis 1:1 says that God definitively created the heavens and the earth, over and done with—then why would line 2 go on about the time before the earth's creation, saying "and the earth was without form, and void" as if line 1 wasn't even there?

I survey the table, looking for an empty spot to put the platter down. For the moment, everyone seems focused on eating. There are eight of us: my three younger brothers, my younger sister, my mother and father, and my grandmother—my father's mother—who lived with us then, and remained for more than a decade. I'm nineteen, my next brother, Amiad, is seventeen and a half, and Davi is sixteen. My sister, Merav, is twelve, and our youngest brother, Daniel, is six.

"Maybe the beginning isn't exactly the beginning," Davi says.

The Shabbat candles flicker desperately, as if they know their stay on earth is limited to this meal, their lives as short as a conversation.

Here we are again, on the seventh day, discussing the Hebrew of the first day.

"I remember reading Ramban in the eighth grade," Davi continues, referring to the thirteenth-century commentator who lived in Christian Spain. "And what he said about the first line of the Bible. I thought it sounded a lot like evolution, what we were learning about in the afternoon."

"That's ridiculous!" my father suddenly screams. "Don't be absurd!"

"Why?" Davi says.

Davi ducks out of the way as I lift the platter over his head in an effort to reach the empty spot of table space directly in front of him. And he gives me a look that says, Isn't there anywhere else you can put this?

Well, no. It's the only spot. And this table is, sometimes, the only place on earth where I can fight with myself and my family and God and the opening lines of the Bible all at the same time.

"I'm just saying," Davi continues, "Ramban's idea that everything was there, just formless, but was given form later is very close to what Darwin says hundreds of years later. Don't you think it's similar?"

"I can't even listen to this," my mathematician father says. My father has spent years of his life studying physics, battling math, and immersing himself in the history of discovery. The idea that Ramban's rambling comment even approaches Darwin's achievement infuriates him. "This is science. The rabbis—that's absurd!"

Davi recites what Ramban says anyway.

I sigh and settle in for a long discussion. Ramban's commentary on Genesis 1:1 happens to extend for pages. Ramban, also known as Nachmanides, often writes long entries, and he goes all out about the very beginning of the Bible. First, he insists that the idea that God created the world is the core of belief. But eventually he moves into radical territory by trying to understand why there is so much text about creation after Genesis 1:1, from the making of man to the Garden of Eden scene to the near-destruction of the world and the saving of Noah. And that's when things get interesting.

Ramban argues that what God created in Genesis 1:1 was a formlessness, which God later changes into form. In the beginning, Ramban suggests, God created primordial matter that later became the various parts and inhabitants of the world.

"Well, what if line one isn't the real beginning, anyway?" someone interrupts.

When this conversation erupts again a decade later, while I am a graduate student at Iowa, twenty-nine years old and coming home for the holidays, I smile to realize at least this part of life has not changed.

As the discussion quickly moves to where the Bible should have started in the first place—Rashi, in his commentary on Genesis 1:1, quotes his father, Rabbi Yitzchak, who says the Torah should have begun with the first moment of nationhood, and not with creation—I think about how little of the rabbis' elaborate commentary could be elicited from the English translation. In the 1611 King James rendition of Genesis 1:1—In the beginning God created the heavens and the earth—there is no room for mystery. There is no room for puzzlement, no room for what prompted the rabbis' lengthy commentary.

Rashi reads Genesis 1:1 as a clause or a phrase connecting Genesis 1:1 and Genesis 1:2 into one long sentence. This reading is nothing like the King James Bible's two-sentence translation for Genesis 1:1–2, but it is pretty much how Genesis 1:1–2 comes across in the most recent Jewish Publication Society translation, published in 1985:

> When God began to create heaven and earth—the earth being unformed and void, with darkness over the face of the deep and a wind from God sweeping over the water—God said, "Let there be light" and there was light.

That "began to create" is close to what Rashi is trying to convey. Rashi believed that *bara*, the word frequently translated as "created" in Genesis 1:1; should be read as *bro*, meaning "the creation of" (in the beginning of the creation of), the argument my mother was referring to.

But how, exactly, does Rashi come to this conclusion, and why is it so confusing to begin with?

The answer is one of my mother's all-time favorite dinner topics: vowels.

In Hebrew, vowels—dots and dashes located above, beneath, and inside letters—frequently determine meaning. And Rashi claims that in Genesis 1:1, the vowels should have been rendered differently. This complaint isn't unreasonable. In the medieval era, and in our own, typos and human errors were not unheard-of phenomena. Then as now, they can be both irritating and critical, prompting irate letters to the editor—and pages of biblical commentary, which is pretty much what Rashi is doing in his commentary on Genesis 1:1.

Rashi, in the eleventh century, can argue that the vowels are wrong because he knows that written vowels were added to the text only in the eighth century, and before that, the reading of the text was passed along orally, from teacher to student, parent to child, perhaps around tables like the one we are eating at right now. Rashi uses his deep knowledge of the text, of all that comes after Genesis 1:1, to help him, just as a modern reader might use past experience to flag a typo. In this case, Rashi thinks there should have been a dot above the verb instead of lines beneath it. It is the verb, and more specifically the grammatical state of it, that determines a world of meaning.

It's not just recent Jewish translations that are defining the verb in Genesis 1:1 as a phrase, as Rashi did. Interestingly, the New Oxford Annotated Bible, New Revised Standard Edition, published in 2001, also combines Genesis 1:1 and 1:2. It reads:

In the beginning when God created the heavens and the earth, the earth was a formless void and darkness covered the face of the deep, while a wind from God swept over the waters.

I look over at my father, who is eating peacefully again. Maybe my father is simply too hungry to comment on evolution. In previous meals, he has said something like, "There is no way the rabbis knew about evolution. No way, or the entire history of science would be different!"

In the rare silence, I imagine the Shabbat meals of several hundred years ago, eaten by candlelight. When Ramban lived, evolution wasn't a dominant idea, though Aristotle had already suggested it. Perhaps the thirteenth-century concept of evolution was more like a few observations scribbled on a scientist's pad, like the calculations my father leaves around the house on yellow legal paper in his pursuit of a beautiful theory or what his field calls an "optimal experimental design."

I don't really know what "optimal experimental design" means, but to me what is optimal is the sight of work; I love seeing the start of creation. And I like that I can't even understand what I read in my father's neat handwriting. I see equations, x's and y's, the linearization of some polynomial—it doesn't matter. What is beautiful is the process of his thought, the fact that the questions go on, that my father is not troubled by not finding definite answers.

It's a little like some of the rambling moments in biblical commentary; what grips me is how the commentators get where they are going question by question, point by point, and how sometimes even the great Rashi writes *aineni yodeya*, which means, simply, "I don't know."

"All the commentators are interested in grammar," my mother says, moving the conversation back to her favorite subject while spearing a roasted potato. It is flavored with *chawaj*, a spice from the Arab world that finds its way into our chicken soup, too.

My youngest brother, Dani, and I try to look bored. My sister, Merav, who is seven years younger than I am, tries to focus on her plate, making her way through her vegetables with her usual efficiency. We have been listening to the grammar wars, the roar and explosion and finally the temporary calm, all our lives. But no amount of pleading can stop my mother from discussing grammar.

There is nothing more fascinating to my mother than the ways to look at an ancient word. For as long as I can remember, my mother has been trying to convince us that grammar is a universe, and that the tiniest parts of grammar tell a story. "It is impossible to read a word without its neighbors," my mother says to us. "You have to read the first line next to the rest."

The rest of us keep munching. Around us, the paintings on the dining room walls, all of them of Hebrew letters floating in the air, look on. They were once my grandfather's, painted by his rabbi and friend, a man as in love with the look of Hebrew letters as I have been with the conversation they create.

I grew up in Monsey, New York, a town twenty-five miles and a universe from Manhattan. Officially, Monsey is an unincorporated area, though a few years ago it was given a green-and-white sign on the highway. A few decades ago, Monsey was mostly farms and orchards, and there are still pear trees on the street where I grew up.

But in the Jewish world, Monsey is famous: it is sometimes called *ir hakodesh*, the holy city, the term usually reserved for Jerusalem, or *yerushalaim shel mata*, literally the Jerusalem of below, or the Jerusalem outside Israel. Monsey is home to thousands of rabbis, many students of the Torah, and important yeshivas—schools of Jewish higher learning. The word *yeshiva* comes from the verb *lashevet*, to sit, or to settle, and many scholars seem to settle in for years, decades, even lifetimes. Some of the yeshivas belong to large, well-known Chassidic sects, like the Satmar or the Viznitz, whose yeshiva has castle-like towers. Chassidim are adherents to a movement that began in the eighteenth century, with the Ba'al Shem Tov—whose name literally means "bearer of a good name"—a rabbi who promoted the idea that emotions matter more than scholarship. This radical concept meant that a devout shoemaker could hold the same status as an erudite rabbinical student.

In addition to the major Chassidic sects that are represented in Monsey, there are smaller sects, like the Stoliner, whose school is on a main road; other sects' schools are not that easy to find. On the block I grew up on, there are Gerer Chassidim and Belz Chassidim, and not far away is the Popov Rebbe, a man I have heard of but never seen. These rabbis are major presences in the lives of their followers, and in Monsey. But as soon as I leave Monsey for Manhattan, or Newark Airport, the importance of the Popov Rebbe suddenly recedes. Still, the Popov Rebbe managed to have an effect on me. I once heard a conversation between two people who were trying to buy a house as close to the Rebbe as possible. Years later, when I tried to live as close as possible to writers I admired, I finally understood that aspect of what makes Monsey tick: the desire to live close to great teachers, to great thinkers, to the rabbinical presence.

You can reach Monsey from Manhattan on the Chassidic bus. With a curtain down the middle separating male and female riders, this was the bus I took to get to high school, and I often rushed on Friday afternoons to catch the last bus before Shabbat started, when I, like many other Monsey residents, would no longer be able to travel. On the bus, Yiddish is spoken—the thousand-year-old language of exile that is mostly a mix of German and Hebrew. All my life I have heard scholars lament the death of Yiddish at the hands of the Nazis, but I heard plenty of it in the streets and on the bus I took every day to and from school. Inside my house, though, we spoke Hebrew. Hebrew will always be my first language, the one I think in when I am tired, the one in which I first read and absorbed the Bible, the language of my dreams. English, however, is the language of my daily life, the language I work in and converse in with friends. There will never be a time when these two languages, and the cultures they represent, ancient and modern, will not be in conversation with each other in my head.

In Monsey many people spend the entire week preparing for Shabbat. The schedule for the neighborhood was more or less as follows: Monday might be the day for dry cleaning; Tuesday for laundry; Wednesday for the purchase of meat and the removal of household clutter; Thursday, the purchase of fish and fresh vegetables, the dusting of furniture and the polishing of silver and the baking of challah bread; Friday for the cooking of all the food. Some families were even more organized and began on Sunday, with everything cooked and ready to go by Thursday night.

We were Orthodox, a "modern" family, and by the time I was in junior high school the rest of the block was Chassidic. The Orthodox have their own network of schools, kosher stores, and fundraisers, but the Chassidim were winning out on birth rate as well as Shabbat preparedness. Most of the Chassidim were ready for Shabbat by Friday morning. The women spent Friday sending the children out to collect charity for the less fortunate, showering, braiding and styling hair, and setting the table. Men went to the *mikvah*, the ritual bath. By late afternoon, the Polish maids were sent home. The workweek was over.

My family was different. Technically, the Hebrew word for people who are not Chassidim but who still keep the laws of the Torah is *mitnagdim*— objectors. In the summer, we swam in pools with men and women—"mixed swimming," it was called. Scandalous, as was mixed dancing. My father, rebel that he was, mowed the lawn with his shirt off. There were other differences, other ways of objecting, or merely looking different, which in Monsey counted.

Though there were five kids in our house, plus a grandmother for a decade, by comparison our family was small. In all the years, through all the mess of eight people, we never had a maid, unlike the Chassidic families on the block with ten kids or more. We were also last-minute Shabbat preparers, and we tried to shop and clean and cook on Friday, which made that day crazy busy, always. My mother really couldn't devote six days a week to cleaning and cooking, and I don't think she ever wanted to.

Though she stayed home and took care of all of us full time until I was thirteen, when she got a one-hour-a-day teaching job that paid for the bus I took to high school, she was always in school: graduate school, twenty-five miles and a universe away in Manhattan. To the other mothers of the block, whose life was the home, my mother's travels to learn probably made her seem like a resident of a far-off galaxy.

My mother drove, whereas the other women did not, though she learned to drive fairly late, when I was thirteen and she was pregnant with my youngest brother. During the week she did not cover her hair, and on Shabbat, she wore just a hat to shul, unlike the other married women, who wore wigs or kerchiefs called *ticheles*. And I'm sure the neighbors noticed her schedule: a light was always on in our house.

My mother had a life of the night. After everyone else went to sleep, she would sit at the dining room table with a large milkshake and several piles of dictionaries. She was reading Akkadian tablets—I know because I used to wake up at night and watch her, sitting in her nightgown with her very long hair pinned up, from the darkness of the kitchen. Piles of papers and pens before her, she'd talk to herself in some ancient language that she told me you could hear recorded at the Smithsonian Institution. From a room away, I heard the rhyme and rhythm of antiquity.

Sometimes, when I let her know I was awake by coming to the table, she would read me some Akkadian and translate it. She'd explain how it was so closely related to Hebrew and how it all rhymed. I thought that all mothers were like that—mothers in the daytime, and something secret between midnight and when everyone else woke up.

I still recall some of the Akkadian words: *imum*, mother, the word so like *ima*, the Hebrew word for mother. Then *abum*, the Akkadian word close to *abba*, the Aramaic—and modern Hebrew—word for father. *Kalbum*, dog, related to *kelev*, the Hebrew word.

The Akkadian stories were wild: tales of slaughter, of heads piled up. By the light of the dining room chandelier, my mother read me the Code of Hammurabi, a legal document dating from 1780 B.C.E. And she laughed, not because of the horrifying punishments, but because the ancient—and all of its grammar—brought her joy.

My mother never finished her Ph.D., at Columbia University and the Jewish Theological Seminary, on an aspect of ancient syntax and the Bible. Her mentor died, and with five children, she could not easily relocate to another university in some other city. But she did continue learning, and teaching, and she instilled her love of the Bible, of Hebrew, of ancient language, and of language overall, into every one of her children. Though we have all loved language in individual ways, and though some of us have rebelled against it in our own ways, and though we have very different careers in law, business, translation, politics, and writing, we all have a fascination—or in some cases even an obsession—with it.

My mother did manage to carve out a teaching career. She has taught Hebrew at SUNY Rockland for twenty years and still enjoys packed classes and devoted students, but she is no ordinary Hebrew teacher. She teaches what is rooted in Ugaritic, Phoenician, Akkadian, Aramaic—all the languages she loves. A person who tries to learn Hebrew grammar from my mother learns the structure of antiquity, the building blocks of the ancient world. And though my brothers, my sister, and I are all grown, and no longer living in the red house in the middle of the big hill, I know my mother is still there, up late at night, reading ancient writing. The geography of her night has never changed: she's at the dining room table, in the chair just under the chandelier. Her books and her notebooks are lined up in front of her. The refrigerator behind my mother is buzzing, and in the freezer there is ice cream. If I close my eyes, I can hear the slurp of my mother drinking a milkshake in the relative quiet of the night.

I read the King James Bible out loud, sitting in my screened porch overlooking the backyard. It is my favorite place in Iowa City, a green refuge that is impossible to imagine from the front of the house, which faces a main road. In the back, the big weepy trees lean down; grapes climb the wooden fence next to the lone blueberry bush, just in front of the spot where raspberries grow wild and numerous in spring. The only noise is from the occasional rabbit searching for something to munch. A dirt road is visible just beyond the wooden fence, where I sometimes see my neighbor the pastor walking to the bus.

This afternoon, my other neighbor is working industriously on his lawn, leaving mounds of cut grass everywhere. All throughout our neighborhood in Iowa City is the sweet smell of freshly removed grass. But I am also feeling industrious. The official text for my class is the Oxford Annotated Bible, but since the teacher repeatedly refers to the King James Version, I have decided to read that, too. And so I read aloud:

In the beginning God created the heavens and the earth.

I stop. There is a period at the end of the line.

A period!

All there is in the Hebrew is the *sof-pasuk*, two dots that come at the end of each verse, whether the verse is a sentence or a phrase, a statement or a question, a description or a command. The *sof-pasuk* reminds me of a line ending in poetry; all it indicates is that a line ends there. But a line ending in a poem is not a period.

Translating punctuation from the Hebrew Bible is a problem, since ancient Hebrew has periods, but no commas, semicolons, colons, exclamation marks, question marks, or quotation marks.

The King James Bible, on the other hand, has a lot of punctuation. It affects tense, sound, and sense, but it also makes everything read slower. Way slower. With a period at the end of the sentence, God is definitely done with creation, instead of breathlessly rushing on and possibly still continuing. Staring at that period, I realize that my reading is stalling for an obvious reason: the King James Version is taking me longer to read because it is longer.

I read Genesis 1 out loud in both Hebrew and English. The English definitely has more words and syllables, but it also has more stops and starts. The breath required after a period simply adds time to the reading experience. I decide to walk through the King James Bible the way I was taught to walk through the Torah: I scrutinize every letter, every line break, every dot, every possible path. I leave the house and pass neat lawn after neat lawn, old nicely painted home after old nicely painted home, until I get to a line of new condos and then the cornfields. Walking by the tall stalks at the end of the road, I begin to count.

First I count letters. Then I count syllables, then words. The idea of counting as part of reading has been ingrained in me since elementary school; it is a standard part of education in yeshivas, or Jewish schools. As a child, I was taught that every letter in the Torah has a numerical value. *Aleph*, or *a*, has a value of one; *bet*, or *b*, has a value of two. There is an entire system, called *gematria*, based on the math of words—their value in numerical form—and the meaning that that number might lead to.

I recite the opening lines of Genesis in translation until it's obvious: English takes longer in every way.

Someone is honking.

"Are you all right?"

"Yes," I say. "I'm just counting."

The driver hurries away, but I continue to recite as I walk, slower than before. "In the beginning" is one word in Hebrew: *bereishit*. It's three syllables, and six letters. English, on the other hand, insists on three words, five syllables, twelve letters just to get things going, just to convey the first word of the Bible. One, three, six, versus three, five, twelve. It's somewhere between double and triple the length.

It's such a basic difference between languages, but it's a huge one.

On the way back home, I test out poems and stories I have memorized, with and without a period. There is a big difference between stopping and not necessarily stopping at key moments. Even at street corners there are crucial options: green light, yellow light, red light, a choice between stop sign or none at all.

I sit in a coffee shop and email a dear poet friend for some outside-reader perspective on the first line of Genesis.

"What's the difference between a line ending and a period?" I type.

The answer comes in less than a minute. Poets have priorities.

"The first is the end of a line of poetry," he fires back, "and the second is the end of a sentence in a poem. How does that grab you?"

Well, if a line that ends with no punctuation means a poem, then Genesis 1:1 is the start of a poem.

Is that even possible? Should I read the opening of the world as a poem?

No. Genesis 1:1, I reassure myself, is not a poem, no matter how it ends. It's just melodious prose. I've already spent hundreds of hours of my life thinking about this verse, and now I'm supposed to reframe it as a poem? Well, that doesn't grab me well at all.

"Ridiculous," I say to myself. But then I dismiss my hasty rejection of the idea. The whole point of reading the English translation is to consider other options, to see the entire world again.

In the beginning God created the heavens and the earth.

What could be more poetic than that, the sky and land rolling out of nothingness? It's beautiful. My friend the talented poet is absolutely right. Yes. Poetry.

No. Prose, I insist back, regaining my senses, remembering the Hebrew. The line endings of verses one and two don't rhyme. They don't even have "slant rhyme," or similar-sounding endings that aren't exact rhymes but still give the listener some sense of pairing. They don't share any similar sounds, the way lines of ancient Hebrew poetry like the Psalms often do because masculine plurals generally rhyme with masculine plurals, while feminine plurals are another frequent source of rhyme. Instead, the opening of the world puts *aretz*, earth (singular), with *shamayim*, heaven (both singular and plural). They don't have a paired music, they don't echo each other.

But my friend makes me realize that line endings matter, and that I have to pay attention to them as I make my way through the translation. The way a line ends determines how the whole line is read, in both languages. And in Genesis 1, this is the beginning of the world: it's the line of all lines, the introduction of heaven and earth. If it is ever reasonable to obsess about a single dot on a page, this is the place.

That lone dot determines how a reader might see the world: present, past, future.

But maybe it's not the *look* of Genesis 1:1 and 1:2 that matters here, but the sound of it. In fact, all my life I have heard these lines, heard them more than seen them.

Maybe what matters is just how it sounds out loud.

I decide to try this theory out on my poet friend: he is a person who breathes words and their rhythms, who understands sound.

"Do you always indicate a line ending when you read it out loud?" I email, remembering that once, long ago, we sat through an entire class on the way Robert Frost worked with the sound of breath. Our teacher, in that class years ago in Boston, the great poet Derek Walcott, said that what distinguishes American poetry from poetry in other languages is the monosyllabic line, and that line requires that the writer figure out how to manipulate the act of breathing. Consider these two famous lines from Frost's "Death of the Hired Man," each word only one syllable:

Home is the place where, when you have to go there,

They have to take you in.

Even without the commas, it's clear that the speaker has to stop to breathe between "where" and "when" and between "there" and "they." The need to breathe is part of the music, and it also defines the meaning. It controls what is emphasized in this two-line span.

Frost, Walcott insisted, was a master of making breath, or the lack of it, part of his poetry. An example is Frost's opening line in the famous poem "Mending Wall":

Something there is that doesn't love a wall.

This classic line is built for an American speaker, with American intonations and patterns of breath. An American pronouncing this line would probably say: "Something there is" (breath, pause) and then recite "that doesn't love a wall" into one phrase, requiring no breath. That's because many Americans, speaking quickly—I remember Walcott demonstrating out of the side of his mouth to demonstrate—would connect "that" and "doesn't," so that the line would sound like:

Something there is thadoesn'tloveawall.

Frost understood how contractions in speech—like "doesn't"—help move one word into another, and the way some letters are swallowed by speakers of certain regions. He knew that "does not love a wall" would have an entirely different sound. Part of the power of Frost's line, I was taught, is the choice of the word "doesn't." "Doesn't love a wall" is one unit, one idea, one breath.

This is the stuff I know my poet friend obsesses over, so I am pretty sure he will be open to devoting time to the exact way the ending of Genesis 1:1 sounds in English.

What I want to know is whether, if Genesis 1 is read as a poem, he thinks readers will stop at the end of line 1, separating verse 1 and verse 2 into two discrete units and therefore two stand-alone ideas.

"Well, of course people stop at least a tad," he replies in his Texas idiom, "at least mentally, at line endings, even if they are enjambments."

Of course? Just a tad?

I like the idea of enjambment, which is the running over of a phrase in a poem from one line into the next. It fits exactly with the ideas of Rashi, who reads lines 1 and 2 of Genesis together as one sentence. Interestingly, the Jewish Publication Society translation from 1985 doesn't just connect lines 1 and 2, as Rashi does, but also connects them with line 3, rendering the first three lines of the Bible as one long sentence:

When God began to create heaven and earth—the earth being unformed and void, with darkness over the face of the deep and a wind from God sweeping over the water—God said, "Let there be light" and there was light.

Everett Fox also links verses 1, 2, and 3 in his translation, which sounds a little different. Fox is making a special—and impressive—effort to preserve some of the sound of the Hebrew. This can be heard in "wild and waste," which tries to mimic the Hebrew *tohu va'vohu*, two mysterious words that have similar sounds and echo against each other:

> 1:1 At the beginning of God's creating of the heavens and the
> earth,

> 1:2 when the earth was wild and waste, darkness over the face of
> Ocean, rushing-spirit of God
> hovering over the face of the waters

> 1:3 God said: Let there be light! And there was light

My friend wants to say more, now that we've opened the subject of how to read the space—or non-space—between Genesis 1:1 and Genesis 1:2.

"I've been thinking more about this," he writes. He tells me that capitalization is also something to consider, that it, too, affects the way we rest and stop.

"Oh, no," I say out loud, and then hastily cover my mouth in embarrassment.

My fellow coffee drinkers look away. In this coffee shop, plenty of other writers have made the mistake of reading their work out loud to themselves—or worse, talking to themselves. I plan my response to my friend. I'll tell him there's no capitalization in Hebrew, in Genesis 1 or elsewhere. Capitalization makes everything look confident, definite, just as the period does: Here, this is where it starts, this is where it ends. Capitalization helps close the door on doubt, just as the red letters in the Bible I recently bought try to make sure the reader knows exactly which phrases matter. It is one reason why the appearance of the Bible in Hebrew and English is dramatically different.

Later that night, unable to sleep, I write to my friend—"Genesis 1:1 is an open door."

He writes back: "Tell me more."

What should I tell him first, I wonder.

Genesis 1:1 is a microcosm of biblical Hebrew; it is ambiguous, rich, lyrical, evocative. But my friend and I are both in love with English, so I try to phrase it in terms of both languages. I try to think of how each language is built. Sentences in English tend to have a standard structure—subject, verb, object: but sometimes English, like most languages, is disobedient. A typically structured sentence in English might read, "Three girls walked into the store." But the classic John Updike story "A&P," written from the point of view of a young supermarket clerk, opens with the memorable sentence: "In walks these three girls in nothing but bathing suits." That puts the verb phrase first, and of course, it's not a grammatically perfect phrase—the girls are plural and should "walk," not "walks." There is also that famous and unforgettable opening line from Frost, which is also unusual in its word order: "Something there is that doesn't love a wall."

Hebrew is probably more flexible than English, especially biblical Hebrew: a sentence can begin with a subject, a verb, or an object. In the Hebrew Bible, a verb often appears before a noun; the common biblical phrase "and God said" is actually "and said God" in Hebrew, a construction not used in modern

Hebrew. For translators, this one seemingly small difference in sentence structure can create big problems, because once the order of a sentence is altered, the meaning can be up for grabs, too.

Besides this difference in sentence structure, there is the additional complicated issue of word structure. Hebrew is a Semitic language, and therefore its words come from trilateral—that is, three-letter—roots. These roots can have multiple manifestations—as verbs, nouns, and occasionally even as adjectives. These related words share a kernel of meaning, but it takes a somewhat knowledgeable reader to understand how a word functions grammatically in a particular passage. And that's not all. This root issue is exacerbated by the fact that the ancient text was not vocalized, or written out with vowels, until the eighth century. Furthermore, since the Bible was originally an oral composition according to many scholars, which was then copied and recopied by hand, human error—the tiniest slip of the hand—is certainly a possibility.

These three challenges—sentence structure, word structure, and centuries without an official version with all vowels included—led to errors of reading and translation. The infamous misreading of Moses as a creature with horns might be explained, in part, as an example of reading a verb as a noun. The Hebrew in Exodus 34:29 beautifully describes Moses' skin as beaming with light; but some translators seem to have read the noun *keren*, a synonym for both a ray of light and the horn of an animal, instead of the verb *karan*. The words *karan* and *keren* share the same three letters, and therefore the same root (*krn*), but the lines and dots beneath the letters make them completely different words.

The "horned Moses" passage has its roots in St. Jerome's fourth-century translation of the Hebrew Bible into Latin, which became the official translation of the Catholic Church. Jerome's Latin version reads *cornuta esset facies sua ex consortio sermonis Dei*—"this face was horned from conversation with the Lord." Some scholars, who seemed unaware of this error in translation, argued that "horned" was actually an expression of authority and power. In time, Jerome's "horned" probably led to massacre—both noun and verb.

I was constantly reminded of the tremendous importance of verbs and their role in our understanding as I traveled through Europe trying to learn about the lives of the biblical commentators and finding myself looking up at church window after church window. In Hebrew, Moses is beaming; in Christian Europe, Moses is devilish, horned like an animal. If Moses could be transformed in translation, so could God. If human joy could be changed—so, too, could expressions of divine approval, or even divine love.

KATE GALE

The Snakes In My Hair.

I wish I weren't so fat.
The snakes in my hair keep me up at night.

I wish I made more money.
I get raped and then snakes?

I want to be the center of someone's universe.
The cave is cold.

I want someone to lick me.
The walls are wet and slimy.

There is no burble in the wood.
I'm hungry.

I can't eat.
I'm on a diet.

All the men in the world are eating pizza, nachos, warm melted cheese sandwiches.
All the women in the world are eating celery, apples, nuts, radishes, heaps of lettuce.

I want a man to make my heart break into blossom.
Like the windows in a Japanese house in spring, pink and white petals of morning.

This morning.
I exited the cave.

Found a machete.
Severed the snakes.

I washed my body.
I anointed my head with oil.

Sure my cups run over.
Like I said, I need to go on a diet.

Don't put your hands around my waist.
Don't even try.

Try to cup my breasts. I dare you.
I walk through swarms of honeybees un-stung.

I smell of sweetness.
I eat thickets of blackberries all afternoon.

Have you ever wished to be transformed?
This is that story.

You can walk out of the cave, into the bright sunlight.
The curse was a story.

The light is a story.
The wings are a story.

Flight is a story.
Let there be light is a story.

Medusa In Love

You start off young and beautiful; things go wrong.
That's my life. That's any life.

My father used to say, smile when you come into a room.
When I come into a room and see men, I smile.

The suitors line up for me. Boys and men.
Never a fan of beards. Hairy men are a no.

Mother says, Don't act like that, they'll call you a bitch.
Like what? I say. Like a bitch, she says.

At parties, I dance. The doors of the world opening.
Windows too. I wonder who I will marry.

My smiling works on everyone, but eventually I have to choose.
When you're young, pretty, smiling, there is everyone to choose from.

Ask Ovid, ask anyone.
I was raped in the temple of Athena.

After rape, everything changes. What were you doing?
Did you struggle? Did you try to get away? What were you wearing?

Poseidon held me against the white columns in his monstrous hands.
He raped me on the floor of the temple.

If you get raped in church, it's hard to go back to church
and talk to God. It's obvious God doesn't listen to you.

I could hear children playing on the shore.
Sunlight poured through the white temple.

Everyone attended a party that night. My suitors were there.
Too bad, they said. They danced with the other girls.

Don't ask me what happened next. Athena's curse.
The years huddled dark. My hair turned a vile nest of vipers.

I grew hair everywhere. Women are not supposed to have hair
except on their heads and that head hair should be contained.

The men who had wanted to bed me, competed to shoot me
with arrows. Pierce me with swords. Throw spears. Knife throwing.

Throw bottles. Break glass. I absorbed all human rage.

I had not only my own snake, but many snakes.
Women cannot have plural snakes and the power to kill men.

O Perseus, you rescued me from torment.
I will be born again. I will have a new name.

DAN ROSENBERG

Bearing in Teeth My Invitation

halfway through the sycamore I am
in sight of the red temple aloft
    its blood gables and Star of David
clutch between branches   some new midrash
burbles like sap stabbed into the air

while I grip and hoist the stripping bark
each grope exfoliates   my path is
marked by yellow literate gashes
    what I climb is heavy bearing name

against me   some parasite   am I
within as always leaping distance
but such terrestrial dirt am I
    crawling the vertical respiring
shade   I hear the synagogue settle

for what flightless sacrifice am I
reaching upward to the double gates
    unfurled as if the wings of justice
were for me a thin water feature

I pass through with paper-tasseled fists
    the gnarled rabbis stumble their secret
language into what seems one long name
for a gentle god I can't buy   not
here   not nameless crawling upward I

DAVID GEWANTER

PORTFOLIO

English 1

FIRST,   We tied to each other
NEXT,   Coconuts for the swimming
THEN,   The Boat-Soldiers shoot
MEANWHILE,   Many dying
AND THEN,   We swam with dead People
LATER,   We get on the land
FINALLY,   We left our dead Friends.

What grade does this exercise deserve?
Homework folded like a handkerchief,
a little book of tears, burns, escape—

And still I mark the blasphemies
of punctuation, common speech;
the English tune will help them live.

Rickety Hmong boy, flirting simply
with the loud girl from Managua—
I taught him how to ask her out,

taught her how to say no, nicely;
my accent and suburban decorums
are tidy and authoritative as

the checks I make for right answers,
the rosy golf-clubs on the page.
By next year they'll talk their way

out of trouble instead of smiling
as they do hearing me drone *Silent Night*—
They join in, shy and hypnotized,

Saigon chemist, cowed Haitian, miming
the words I once told my music teacher
that Jews shouldn't sing: "Holy Infant."

Bleish the Barber

I.

Grandpa stopped short, grabbed the broom, poked it bang! bang!
against his shop ceiling whenever my aunt
upstairs "made a wrong note." Homely, obedient,
she played scales. But my pretty child-mother sang
and danced by Grandpa's mirrors, where he snip-snipped
ear-hair and nostril hair, and cocked his ear for
Miriam's piano "that I two years paid for."
The men waiting for Bleish like Ruthie—full-lipped,
a barber's girl—who has hated Miriam now
68 years. Grandpa, upright, Russian, ate
onions, did 20 knuckle push-ups a day.

Miriam cried "Too small!" when his coffin banged down
on the grave-lips. "We'll measure it," diggers answered,
and took out tape. Mom ducked away: still the dancer.

II.

Grandpa stood up, the creaky *fin-de-siècle*
vegetarian, and gave a girl his seat;
the bus lurched, his bald crabbed knobby leg buckled,
and snapped. Wheeled in the hospital, he was meat
served to germs. They burrowed through flesh a statue's
age, killed hands leathered hard by a razor-strap.
When Miriam phoned, we were leaving for a wedding;
long expected grief stumbled through its paces—
our shocked "Oh no!" and then, "Oh God—the wedding!"
Our shock when the blocked coffin banged the grave-top,
when the living hair shook on his dead nape.

We recorded him once in 1962.
I pull out his small old foreign voice, spooled on tape:
"Hear me? This is Grandpa—How are you? How are you?"

III.

Cantors lurked by the roads and crowed, waving their
black books at us like ancient, lost debaters:
"Sing Kaddish—two dollar! Kaddish! Come here!"
Our string of Fleetwoods paid out, slow torpedos
bobbing in file. Everyone began to breathe;
the diggers cuddled Grandpa in, spooning dirt
from its round loaf. Grandpa died at 96—
I'd outgrown him at 12. Turning back, finding grief
answers the knock, the knock of his awkward box.
Grandpa, these two old grackles were once your girls:
guard them by your shop's infinite mirrors—*tick*

tick tick tick—the tail end of tape whirls around
the recorder's flat breast; snippets, hellos, songs
unfurl like your own full last name: Bleishewitz.

Bill

Two boys grew up and got sick. The first one suffered a virus that softened the bones of his legs. First his shins felt tender and fragile; then reddish sores appeared above his ankles as bits of bone worked their way to the surface. He missed a day of school; then a week; finally his parents pulled him from the fourth grade: nearly crippled, in continuous pain, he sat at home listening to the Radio—the new modern wonder. The hospital was another wonder, cool stone and wide porticos, bigger even than his school; his mother took him there to see a doctor, who gave him a lolly.

Next week they operated, and by the spring he could run again, though his calves were now creased with scars. His mother took him back to the doctor, and there she began to cry because she couldn't pay. And the doctor said she didn't have to pay, which made her cry even more and kiss his hand, and the boy swore to them both that he'd become a doctor too, and never charge money. And he did—he skipped four grades, beat the quotas, and became a pathologist (though he did charge).

And he fathered me. The second boy I know very little about, except for how he died. His father was a doctor too, and had brought the boy in sick to his own hospital; and there he received the special care a doctor's child receives. But he died, and his father asked mine to do the autopsy. My dad showed him the results: long, interlayered crystals taken from a slit of the boy's kidney. A pink shimmer under the lens. "Crystals of the sulfa drug they kept giving him at the end," he said coolly. "They drowned him."

I wonder about this man: losing his son, he must have suffered the grief that makes the mind rage with curiosity; my father sated his curiosity, but not his rage. All he tells me now is, "The guy was a Jewish orthopedist from Seattle— he asked, and he deserved to know." And I wonder about his boy—or about his corpse; for it was his corpse that taught my father about kidneys, how they can be made to do too much by doctors, and quit, and flood the body with poisons.

This is what was done to my fat Uncle Bill, though my dad didn't know it; all he knew was that his brother had survived a heart attack but was getting worse under care, and that the whole family was phoning him to drive in and do something, anything: Bill's doctors are no good. Bill's friends are all quacks. He's getting delirious, or unconscious, he's talking all dreamy. The doctor said to prepare themselves.

Dad arrived late, and bickering with my mom (I remember; I was there). They all rushed up, DO something Pete, TALK to them. His physicians, Pete, quacks. The charts. Quack Quack. Life and death are two easy thoughts for a boy of six, who had killed Nazis and Indians the whole ride up: I sat on the bench swinging my feet and talking to my cousins while Dad fended the family off, too repressed to give them comfort, too elitist to discuss the case with anyone but doctors.

Kidneys process natural toxins from the body; my uncle's were apparently too shocked to work, and the doctors were forcing water into him to make them start up. Poisoned almost to death, his mind was cut free, and he had started babbling prophecies and visions. Bill was always a terrific talker, and this probably made Dad feel worse, uncomfortable as he is with the spontaneous and uncontrolled. But on the chart he saw what the doctors were doing; and he remembered the crystals from the boy, the special case. And he thought for a while, and then began to talk.

I like to imagine some quick nasty squabble when my father usurped authority, a scene where Dad betrayed his professional ethics for the sake of his brother, whom he never felt close to anyway. But the attending physicians were probably glad to be rid of Bill, and the squat middle-european crowd in the lobby; and glad to be rid of this clipped, uncompromising man. May the blood be on his hands.

Bill was raced to another hospital, and dried out; suddenly his kidneys started in on their own and his mind left that other place; he got well, and even started work again, conducting immense, boisterous dinners every night at home; and he gained weight until his heart burst and they found him dead at his desk.

Being so smart, my father was resented by the other boys and left on his own, and has grown into a lonely awkward man. But alienation, perhaps, has made him clearheaded; the same old excellence that kept him from us also saved his brother's life, and turned him into my remote childhood hero.

The doctor who waived his fee gave my father a chance to be a regular boy; my father then gave up his boyhood to become a doctor. The doctor who brought his son's body in wanted to know the cause of death—not to relieve his loss, but to preserve it in knowledge. These are exchanges from choice.

But the boy who died was a victim of ignorance, and he in a way was exchanged for a few years of my uncle's life. And because I'm thankful for those years, and proud of the choice my father made, I must somehow be grateful that the boy died when and how he did.

Marriage: Six Primers

1. *Hole in the eye*

When she hears his father's accent she learns
what he suppressed. He sees in her mother's hallway
the decor she hates. Between them, a balance
scale weighted MOTHER FATHER YOU ME
—the loads shifting image by image.
  A mother left in the car.
  The father's bottom teeth.
And the small deductions—yearbook photos,
hidden cigarettes, names said dreaming;
his taste, the pills sent in the mail—
  As if a sailor squinted for land so long
the sun burned holes in his eyes;
standing in his house, he jerks his head
this way and that, just to see it sidelong....

2. *The shuttle*

Lover and beloved.
  Who carries the most desire?

Better to ask who eats the apple,
  the pig or the family roasting it—

Or ask the two woodsmen
  on the shuttle toy

chopping the wood they're made of;
  or the samurai and geisha

pumping mechanically—a perfect fit—
  cock and cunt sliced from one stone.

3. *eppur si muove*

Rising from the altar of promises, he sees
  a tearful lover in the church. She cries

in relief; he feels it as grief. And though
  kissing his bride, he silently swears, like Galileo

telling the Inquisitors yes, my Earth
  anchors the universe—

and yet (rising from
  below) *she moves all the same.*

4. *Duet of days*

She: After this many years, I test positive! Week eight—
He: You—that makes it mid March: I was gone all that month.

                        *

She: ...so Jeff was in town then, and we drank a lot and....
He: You'd better call him up: that's his kid you're carrying, not mine—

                        *

She: What's with these condoms? Who did you bang on that trip?
He: ...so I never, never meant to hurt you. One night she and I smoked dope....

                        *

—On Thanksgiving they learn the baby began on Valentine's;
they teach her numbers, the stars, and animal sounds.

5. *I stand behind my contradictions*

—J.Y.

At first glance you were tall, tall! Birch
  yellow hair, piano fingers. And short a dime.
I felt something in my pocket, handed you
  ten thoughts (of bed). We split

a pizza, then split from everyone—
  our lovesick summer, bedridden as invalids.
Now the doctor shows me my sperm—
  "Too many pinheads" (the doctor,

trained in mechanical reproduction).
  But here, our shining boy....
A swallowed dime could kill him.
  When his chin shakes with cold

I start to sweat. And when
  the homeboys gather, you moon them
(behind curtains), sing "Vertigo"
  to the tune of Camelot—

charms and dangers to spell our home.

6. Dice

They fit snug sleeping, their nipples make dots
  on dots. Blockheads, but the sum of our parts.

All day they bump each other around,
  two faces avoiding the one fate. Suddenly thrown

for a loss: snake eyes. Shaken to their bones, rubbed
  and pleaded with, tumbling through

a glitter of choice—till their number's up,
  and the raker finds the die.

Zero Account

for my sister

Your "x," withdrawn, vengeful,
undertakes the spousal

rip-off. Quivering passion,
once negated, murders love—

Kindness? "Justice"
is how greed frames
every divorce:

cupid's backstabbing
alphabet.

The Unspeakable

My student Charlie Bernstein,
strapping, curly hair, about to take a step,
    like Rilke's blind man
pondering, fingers at his lips…he wrote poems

about flowers, hillsides,
the girls he would bring there, and I nudged him,
    "send your stuff to the poet
Charles Bernstein, he says language writes his poems,

he says, 'that these dimensions
are the material of which the writing'—:
    this guy should meet another
Charles Bernstein. Tell him you wrote his books."

Curse my tongue. The boy
never mailed them, but after he left school
    he was driving all night
through Texas, and a truck killed him.

I met Prof. Bernstein once
(stooped, alive) and told him about Charlie.
    He said _____.   And I answered _____.
Two dray horses champing at seeds and forage.

"Second Eden"

Thomas Hardy.

The blood their parents gave them
   seems like original sin—
hugs and kisses, saliva or cuts
   might pull another child in.

They're careful at the park, for
   carefulness will save them
from spending their inheritance,
   the blood their parents gave them;

but when they come to AIDS camp
   they play and wrestle and run;
no fear of giving infections
   until visitors come.

from Fort Necessity
a poem in documents

My First Autopsy: Age Ten

A man walked into EMERGENCY, dropped dead.
His body was a garden my father tilled,

blade ploughing the flesh, seeking his death:
what part of his life had killed him?

My father grasped dead arms: This is a working man.
Little helper, I touched the puzzle of his hand—

ruts and scorch-marks, yellow-brown nicotine
nails, map of the defiant edifice, yielding

from the heart's glutted tube, a black crumb
my father took for death....

> He made me witness
> unspeakable injury
> cut my childhood
> under its blank sheet

Birth Racket

Baby born for it. 12 hour workday,   *Mother Jones* magazine.
seven days a week. Through the drum-skin
of its mother's womb, it rocks to the whir
of machines: iron rain. Swaddled in

factory rags, toddling among forests
of spindles, the racket echoing
its natal home, till it casts off childish things—
at age six—and takes its place on the line:

a wage-man, a snuff sniffer, on whose shoulders
the factory teeters and grows. To speak of
child slavery is to set everyone else working:

mill-owners send their lobbyists
to dandle toys before the legislature,
lawyers are sent to suckle the courts....

Arbeit

The animal is one with his activity.   Karl Marx.
The worker puts his life into the object;
Then his life belongs to the object.

The Lords of Labor

The Law of Competition,   Andrew Carnegie, 1889.
concentration of business
in the hands of the few, is
essential to the progress of the race...

I want my fair share, and that's all of it.   Charles Koch, 1989.

I can hire one half of the working class   Jay Gould, 1886.
to kill the other half.

———————————————————————

My Silence, $5.50

July 2, 1972: Ann Arbor Police raided an
unlicensed home for juvenile delinquents today,

after complaints of loud music and noise.
Twelve minors were taken to Social Services.
One teen was released, a temporary worker
hired to clean the home's detention room. He
would not speak with reporters.

                    *

   I walked past the staring boys, unlocked the basement room.
Shag rug of piss, Cheerios, ripped magazines,
underwear, burnt ceiling tiles. Smeared in brown
on the door:
                    SO ?

Rip out the rug, they said, *Clean all surfaces,
and don't talk to anyone.* I knew about this place.

   Three days work, at $5.50/hr.

Śmierć of the Postmodern

…The Polish poet was reading to us,
and when he said śmierć the Polish part
of the audience laughed. Suddenly

we were laughing too, in Polish. Later,
a guy said he was a great listener because
he made comforting sounds when Italians

told him their troubles. "I didn't understand them
but I would shrug and frown, say BAAAH,
and they'd keep talking. Just say BAAAH,

it's Italian, it's subjunctive for *that's awful*—"
Then he told us the listener-baah in Mandarin,
WAAAH, but I was noticing his large ears,

ornate seashell folds and trellises, with
a good meaty thumbsworth of lobeflesh
dangling below. He was predetermined….

The porn-star Bright Star moans *oh-oh-oh*
in American videos and *aí-aí-aí* in Spanish.
Stella. Bilingual. Trilingual. Three thumbs up!

Put her on mute. Then we heard the Polish poem
in English: *śmierć* means death. In the cartoon
post-office, we are the envelopes dropping

through different slots, AIR, LOCAL, or FOREIGN,
all landing in the same bin. A flutter of shrouds.
My family crest reads,

   Why was I not informed earlier?

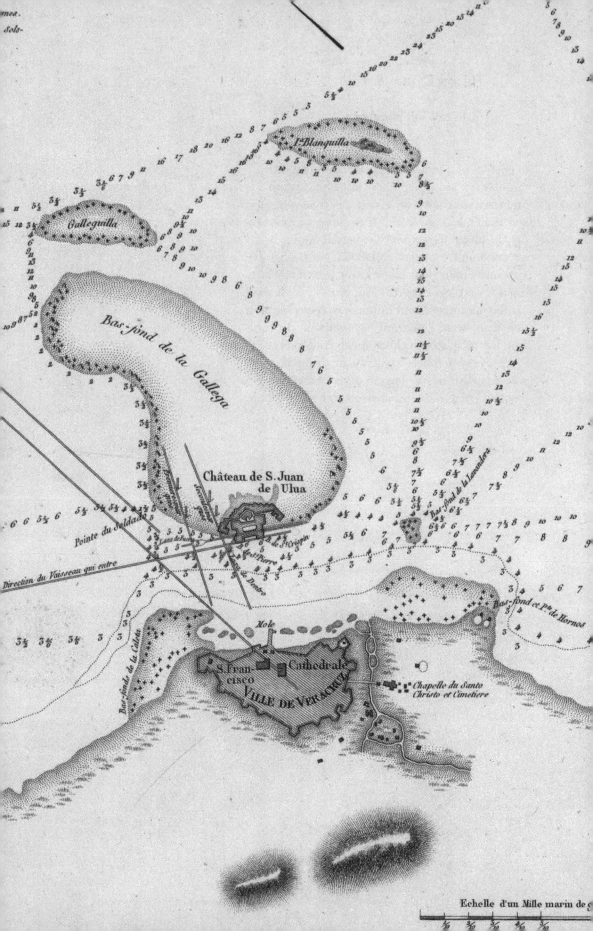

I. Blanquilla

Galleguilla

Bas-fond de la Gallega

Château de S. Juan de Ulua

Pointe du Soldat

Direction du Vaisseau qui entre

Bas-fond de la Lavanderas

Bas-fond et P.te de Hornos

Mole

Bas-fond de la Caleta

S. Francisco

Cathedrale

VILLE DE VERACRUZ

Chapelle du Santo Christo et Cimetiere

Echelle d'un Mille marin de g

HUSAYN CARNEGIE

girl i call Tall Shoulders

in absence of queens english i turnfoot in a little
mumble *hey. hey* is trappings i don't have, is ash
on brownblack skin. *hey* is *sorry, hey* is *maybe?*
and all of me as music. this is the sonnet i was made for—
ugly breaking, ugly words, the ragged outline of my inner.
say the numbers of your childhood. crossleg yourself across from me.
how many bikes. how many kisses. how many bugs.
uncross your legs crisscross your arms look me dead.
say the numbers of your future. how many blessings.
how many scars. how many days without surprise.
i am listening, scooch closer. touch your knees to mine.
i will say my numbers. i will talk my being into air.
who i couldn't be. my bugs in order of their wingspan.
how tall i stretch for. the abyss i know we sit beside.

Alí Calderón

from **Constantinopla**
[The Church of St. Salvador of Chora]

Edirnekapi: Four centuries ago a Byzantine Church
Outside the walls of Theodosius:
concrete & ruins & dust.
My grandfather always
at Our Lady of Carmen at eleven
reflecting? listens to mass?
Light falls from windows upon frescos.
It's Jesus.
Multiplying loaves of bread. Jesus.
There are fish.
Empty baskets. Jesus.
Someone by my side says, "God"
But what is at the entrance? Nothing. But is nothing? Echoing sounds.
Under indifference
of a Christ Pantocrator
Time has worn the glass
like tiny mosaics
The Baptist reveals
a layer of sand & mortar
the wall is gold and lapis
Now tar.
Hidden for fifteen centuries behind statues of apostles & saints
Love & lord of paraclesion
Lime plaster & dark border signs
Written in Greek: come to me, hurried, overwhelmed—
Inscriptions almost invisible
Diffuse
the cracks
vaults are scaled
stone bricks
Opposite of healing the lame, opposite of lame, the paralyzed
Opposite of what I think is the final verse—
My father answers—"this is only decoration"
"You are the sculpture"—& I pointed toward my chest

Translated from the Spanish by Karla Cordero and Ana Bosch

[Kentucky]

The light changes in West Vine & Broadway Street
The cool wind stashes the afternoon
A flying crow cuts through transparency
& the light on the leaves
—the fine strokes of brushes appeared
in high wind souring
of day's clarity:
supuso una presencia
whispers us into present

Translated from the Spanish by Karla Cordero and Ana Bosch

VICTORIA CHANG

PORTFOLIO

Barbie Chang's Father Paid

Barbie Chang's father paid her tuition
      by intuition his brain

now shuns all logic the law is thick
      with rules about love

if a person is so edited that they are
      unrecognizable can you

still love them is it possible to write an
      elegy for someone who

isn't dead yet what if a name no longer
      means what it used

to where does the wind go when it
      is not blowing

today Barbie Chang packs up his
      clothes again to

move to a facility to mute him no
      longer able to travel to

Italy or the local deli he tells Barbie
      Chang she is demented

his dementia is self centered it never
      means anything

always demonstrating something
      Barbie Chang is always

frustrated with his words that have
      lost what they are

trying to signify she drives away
        from his house for

the last time it's cold outside he
        stands at the

front door waving pointing to his
        long distance shirt

The Prognosis Is Poor Again

The prognosis is poor again the lungs
       are out of money

again it's Monday again every day
       is Monday Barbie

Chang's mother is sleeping in the other
       room again her

father is confused by papers again
       shuffling through

them mumbling someone is bringing
       another oxygen tank

again Barbie Chang's ambitions are
       whispering again

she attaches a green heavy cylinder
       to thin tubes again

everyone at school seems rude as they
       talk about their kids

and their new skills again the women
       at school hear

illness and interrupt with their own
       stories about their

grandmothers again it's tense at school
       again the Circle ignores

her more than usual they go to the mall
       more often while Barbie

Chang mulls about all the people God
     has killed in planes again

her father refuses to get up from the
     restaurant table because

he still wants to sign the receipt Ricoeur
     calls metaphor a mind

put in *a state of war* what if when a part
     of the brain dies it

loses its capacity to be at war the two
     armies never fight

they are divided by a large hill neither
     side can ever see over

what happens when a brain is frozen in
     a state of preparation

Barbie Chang's Father Calls

Barbie Chang's father calls again calls
      her again again he calls

her still knows how to dial a cell phone
      Barbie Chang's father has

another problem always has a problem
      doesn't know he is the

problem he says Barbie Chang's mother
      criticizes him all is wrong

today today he calls his hands *handles*
      today his handles hurt

today Barbie Chang's mother handles
      the bad news poorly

today the doctor thinks three months
      but says six no one can

fix Barbie Chang's mother once her
      mother had good hearing

could hear anything see and smell
      everything corners were

always too sharp too dark no hearth
      always harping on

everyone what was wrong with everyone
      too dumb too short too tall

not enough college collar too white
      moon too fraction

moon too waxing when she is not yelling
        at him or asking about the

taxes has Barbie Chang finished her
        taxes again asking about

the taxes the same taxes or whether she
        can fix his brain she lies

on her side thin body shaped
        like a large ear

Emily Berry

Summer

In a kitchen, on an island, stirring tomato sauce, I am far from home.

I stir the thickening tomato sauce.

Deadly kitchen, which is hot with the temperament of this country, and with the heat of cooking.

Deadly sauce, which thickens with my sinking feeling. Which cracks my ice caps.

And now they let out a scream.

I am thirteen years away from home. Later, twenty, and so on.

I can't get back.

Someone is holding me and crying. Greek sunset.

From now on I will eat only the foods of the region that require no preparation, that cannot break into me: white cheese, white bread.

Colour all over my hands, I get down on the floor of a tiled, white room.

Song

after Luna Miguel

When I became mermaid it was for this reason.
The girl I love is a beautiful boy.
So you would not ask questions.
Because I gave myself up to the rain
but it was too late; the rain could not save me.
And when I thought the line was straight,
I was wrong; I could not follow the line.
Thus the shore, infinitely. Thus these rocks.
There was so much to feel good and sorry about.
And I shut my legs up tight, I shut my eyes.
So I could see him better, so I could see her.

Girl on a Liner

after Rose Wylie

This is the body's way of handling emotion.
I am dreaming a lot about voyages.
Mostly I can't remember them. There is something spilled
in the background (they say it is a house).
I wrote, *Nothing in the outside world is changed,*
to ward off the catastrophe. I am in a beautiful place
with birdsong and which smells of flowers; yet,
everything very skewed. I loved you, but not in a pure way.
Something kitsch could break my heart so thoroughly.
Why should it not? '"What do you want?" is not a simple question!'
I say, again, or am I shouting. But you must know,
they said, calmly and like a very light breeze.
You must have some idea. What's that noise?
I expect it's the sound of the train breaking down.
Does crying age one? If so I suppose I've become very old.
In the dream there is something hard he is asking me
(my father) but it's vague…it's vague. I examine my face
in the morning. It is only partly like hers.
I watch the water pour out of my eyes; there was a feeling
but I wrote it down and it ceased to be a feeling,
became art. '"I am afraid of…"' they explained,
'might be better rendered as, "There is a fear of…"' Then
I get confused-stroke-scared, looking at the shit-coloured night,
and there's a curt wind at my back and I'm crying again,
crying with the relief of not being loved. *Whatever it is*
will reveal itself, but I feel like that grubby place
beneath the door handle, the place everyone touches
as they leave. Sometimes the world goes very hard
and cannot be got into; I slide off its surfaces
and I am trying to take in air, or trying not to.
I cannot believe I would conceive of doing that to you.
In the house she is very plaintive and timid, bereft,
and goes into a room off a long corridor,
making mournful noises. I feel terrible. I'm standing
on the edge of nothing, with a handkerchief,
in a ballgown, and I am waving goodbye to you all.

Anna Akhmatova

Last Toast

я пью за разорённый дом

here's to the ruin of this house
to the villainies we do
to our coupled severance
here's to you

to the lies lips issued forth
to the cold weather of your eyes
to the world's being dumb and coarse
to the god who let us die

Translated from the Russian by James Stotts

Anna Lena Phillips Bell

Sunday

The blue and white dress
is perfect to wear on Sunday, mowing the lawn.
The blue and white dress—
its stripes skim over skin and only suggest
hips, thighs, sweet shaking obvious
to the mower-pusher and the mower-pusher alone
in the blue and white dress.

Strapless

Fearing my nipples would betray themselves
beneath their bodice, I donned a strapless bra.
But it revolted: slipping from my breasts,
dismounted them, inched down my waist to where
it rested, chaste, symmetric, satisfied.
"See the miraculous brassiere! It cuts
her clean in half: and yet she lives!" I died
all night, again and again, as it marked the span
of my torso, cleaving hours into minutes—
ten, five, two—till I excused myself
and left, face stricken (what must he have thought?).
I never had the thought to take it off.
Instead, in the bathroom mirror's sudden glare,
I wrestled it again up over my breasts,
then darted back to the gym, to mirror-ball
shimmer and slow dance, praying to be taken
for a girl, whether or not I knew I was.

Green Man

He will not subside,   won't slip into leaf-mold;
he lived in the woods   where my father found him:
a weathered plank   with waiting sockets.
He carried him home   and carved the cedar:
a narrow nose   nestled in red crest
lichen, lips   like his own, and scuppernong
beard; bronze ivy   to crown his brows.
Last, he split walnuts   and wedged each half
into its hollow,   hallowed his face
with cool creek water,   and called him whole.
Then, as he'd promised,   he posted him north.
Dry moss crackled   in the bubble mailer;
wide eyes emerged   to watch me while
I made him a place   in my winter house
and bade him rest.   Now, as I breathe,
a verdant current   fills craven air:
he exhales, his mouth   speaks moss, makes leaf.

KIM TRIEDMAN

Life was easier as a square—

razor-edged, an absence
of tilt, corners sharp and sure
as bayonets, pinning it down

to something else.
There was a house
and it was anchored in bedrock,
there was a

plan. Out the window:
horizons –
gravity –
the steady deployment of seasons,
and even a man with a gun,
watching.

Where is he now?

Everything suddenly formless—
edges bleed
and bleed; the chaos
of curve. Even night comes
charging in, even dreams,
unbidden. The mutiny

of seasons.

Above our heads:
blitzkrieg –
gunfire –
rooflines tipping
carelessly toward the sea.

Michael Waters

Sixties Sonnet

I have become handsome in my old age.

"You're cute," smiled Denise, breaking up with me,
"But cute is all you'll ever be."

Denise who was so wrongwrongwrong, I miss
Our Woodstock nights, half-a-million thumb-flicked

Bics coaxed to climax by God's thwapping bass,
Hissing soppy Oms against the cloudmass.

A drenched, naked hillside soulless and pure,
Zonked, mud-caked, Yanomamö, immature.

I forgive Sly and the Family Stone.
I slept through Santana, dreaming future

Exes who might love me despite my rage.
I have grown lonesome in my afflictions.

I have become handsome in my old age.

Mihaela Barefoot

When shame wouldn't allow me to look any longer
Into the negative space
Gathering its rough, cotton twill around your temples,

I glanced down to be startled
By the sensual, brush-stroked slashes of your toenails—
Still redder than any girl's.

New Generation of Native American Poets

Feature

Edited by Sherwin Bitsui

ORLANDO WHITE

Whit

There's a silence on paper that does not require ears only the reverberation

of a page turning—

She asks, *so how does it feel to be a letter?*

She waits for him to notice her.   She is exclamation-like

                    but upended,   her feet tiptoeing,

                    balletic   in her black tutu;

scurrying dashes of ink   calligraphic, as if quill pen

                    on parchment   annotating solicitude.

He replies, "I think of it as a carapace, a place of solitude and cerebration—"

She presses on to prance around him,

but he is ensconced,

his body catafalque as she divulges,

          I like that you don't expire.

"—I will not lapse because we are equipoise,

                              we embody each other like iota,

                              we are obmutescent, you are verb and I, noun;

          when you locomote, your toes traipsing

I feel to urge from my exocarp

                              to accord my bones to tremble."

1

dark in back
throat hums,

rubs to ridge
alveolar root
of tongue

looms toward
teeth. To feel

sound one must
oral from belly.

Cough up soul-
pulp, evidence
of incorporeal self.

m

a structured fluid speech current, arcs flow to mum,
within its aqueduct ink throbs a motion sensation.

As bone marrow in cavities of skeleton sponge out
vital fluid, or needle point pulls vein into syringe tube.

Breath holds to pronounce its semblance. To exhale
separates nasal tone from print: an influx of throat.

Almost a clog in sentence, puncture-ation break marks
in accidence but only in a momentary *utter*, fluidity quops.

It's an elemental thought from a deep well of apperception,
color- and odor-less in pipelines of mind-perforations.

n

undulates

between

page,   ink: a language

  blood vessel.

Oxygenates   cadence.

    Without it   *being*

    will not have breath.

Write, means to

    place life

    into   book.

Letters live,

    reaffirm   self

within   it.

    An ink vein

    funnels

    plasma thought

    through   word

in moment   one

                pens it.

Cephalic

I place a black cloth the size of a dot over his head. Wrap his entire miniscule body with a thread of my black hair. He lies there on a white sheet of paper and squirms like a dark cocoon, thinks he is going to transform. The letter, when it begins to lose color in a book never opened, becomes a macula in thought. And when read through the lens of a decimal point: see its dark fleck of a cranium, see expendable language—grab the letter *j* next to him, hold it like a tiny black scythe, behead the *i*, and watch its dot head roll to the back of sentence.

SANTEE FRAZIER

Sun Perch

for Karis

It is late, but outside the night is glowing with snow & streetlight, quiet but
for the occasional growl & skid of the plows. Winter, Syracuse, where the
feinting snow fusses & scatters until it collapses roofs & power lines. And
now sitting in that gauzy light, nothing but the sounds of sleep, my son's
cublike snore, I am reminded that most of my childhood was spent walking
in another city, alone, a boy who knew evenings only by the gradual
blackening behind buildings, electric poles humming like bugs, from the
street curb hearing the clink of dishes, chuckles of supper, a fish staring
blankly at me from the center of a round plate rimmed with almond-eyed
bluebirds—wings extended, midflap—the fish, perhaps lightly steamed,
then wok fried, charred along the belly, fins crisped, mouth open from its
last breath, fossilized in a reduction of fish sauce & honey—next to the
plate, a bowl of steamed rice. I sat at the table waiting, not knowing how to
eat the fish or rice with chopsticks, smiling as best I could while in Vietnamese
John explained to his parents how I lived three blocks away, that I
had been home alone for days. His father looked at me as he left the
kitchen, wearing the shirt of a machinist, "Paul" stitched above the right
pocket. Later, I would learn he worked three jobs, and on his only day off,
Sunday, after mass, he would drive his family to some faraway lake outside
the city, where they would reel in sun perch & net them boatside. As I sat at
the table, smells of cooking oil & aromatics fading, John translated for his
mother who asked me to spend the night, and I said no thank you, smiled,
and walked home to whatever misfortune awaited in that dark house,
where the plumbing was empty, my bed a palette of blankets on the living
room floor. I said no, not out of shame but because I wanted to lie down
and remember how I used my fingers to scrape flesh off bones—skin tearing
with it—how I trembled when I was asked to eat the eyes, fins, & tail. I
remember now, how my wife once looked at me in the throes of labor, how
she gripped my hand when the pain ruptured up, and how through it all,
behind the brown webbing of her pupils, there was gentleness. When our
son finally came, he could not breathe, he was blue, motionless. I remember
the midwife rushing him off, and minutes later hearing a gasping bawl.
I didn't know what I saw, as my son shivered, hands gnarled, locked in cry,
still blind from birth, breathing underneath a plastic dome. When I think
of it now—the drive to that faraway lake, my first catch flopping in the boat,
and later jerking the hook from its mouth—the perch must have been
surprised at the sudden uselessness of its gills, and as I watched it gasp

helplessly against the hull of the boat, I wished what all boys wish for, a way of remembering how air rushes from your body after being socked in the gut, to sit in the dark, alone, when streetlight is just enough for a boy to make shapes with his hands, a play made of light, light made of snow.

Mama's Work

Mama tucked the coffee can between her wrist and hip
and walked down Dry Creek Road. Her eyes lined-up,
blush and lipstick, her Levi's shorts cut above the thigh.
And what it was to see those farmers cutting down wheat,
side-glancing mama, barefoot and brown. Sometimes it's flour,
sometimes money when she empties the can. Her work
in the quiet corners of barns on the hay, on hot days
when locusts launch themselves out of thickets.
I stare down Dry Creek Road looking for her wrist and hip,
her splayed hair and small toes walking out of a pone-colored dust.

The Carnival

I studied every ride on the midway—
watched them groan, twirling
        light into blur, the Ferris wheel's

last passengers pointing out
            from their seats to town's end.
These monuments that have risen

        between the hills, to be forgotten
as the lights go out. Where was she
        in this hazy night? Maybe half-lit

in Red-Oak Bar, leaning on a man,
            wedged between his thighs. I wonder
what it is to dream of autumn,

        balled up on a park bench,
the tilt-a-whirl in my gaze,
            wanting a passing car to take me to her.

Among these monuments I am too
            small to find my way to the sandbanks
where she sometimes takes a man,

        where sometimes I wander,
skipping stones, while she earns
            in the backseat of a car or under

a gun rack. It is hours like these
            you learn the path of a ditch—a quiet
only the huffers know. Day breaks:

        the carnies have loaded up the rides,
heading out of town in a convoy,
            leaving nothing behind, not even the grass.

JENNIFER ELISE FOERSTER

Relic

An atlas
on the underside of my dream.

My half-shut eyelid—
a black wing.

I dipped sharp quills
in the night's mouth—

moths swarmed
from my throat.

I pulled a feather blanket
over my skeleton
and woke—

a map of America
flapping in the dark.

Once I dreamt
of inheriting this—

my mother
who still follows crows
through the field,

my sister's small hand
tucked inside hers,

me on her breast
in a burial quilt.

Death Rite

Before makers
there were maps.
There was skin.

Stone. There was time:
the ripening of corn.
Moonlight

and her shadow. Grief
given space:
a circular

shelter. We stayed inside
for a number of days.
Stacked rocks around ourselves.

The clock was a gate.
There were highways.
Mined gashes.

We were slit, bled.
Slid to the ledge
of the dark province.

There were crosses: spiders
to sew shut the wounds
we reaped for you.

Oklahoma Ice

The farm has never been so still—
a sudden chill rattling over fields,
each shaft of wheat snapped
mid-bend into its casement—
and no afternoon so slow. Shadows slope
below the barn. A clock ticks to its stop.

In the brick house licked by snowdrifts
I leaf through maps of land deeds
stacked in the attic's hat boxes,
find twenty-dollar notes
flattened in the pages of an atlas,
my grandmother's derringer pistol
tucked into a cowboy boot—

       there is too much of a life to sort

and too fragile—the orchard's crystalline cast,
branches tinseled against a leaden sky,
the swans in a cabinet of cut glass figures
shivering under dust. I blow
on their chipped wings and snow geese
craze across the frosted pond.

Crunching through furrows patched with snow
I meet the freeway at the fence's end
and turn back again to the empty farm.
This is my inheritance:
glassed-over pastures.
Cornstalks cracking in the prairie wind.
Geese skein frozen like a chandelier.

       I step and shatter the field.

Chimera

I have traveled this continent
for no other reason but to search
for evidence of your existence.

In the stars, America, your highway
vanishes. Black moths are captured
in headlights and swallowed.

In the beginning, you had said,
we were cracked against the sky.
Now I read the highway
for the fall-out of your name
as you step again into the passing lane,
turn to the illuminated crest of hill
where a line of traffic outlines the dark—

in your silhouette I can still see myself
as a child, waiting for a car
to swerve around the corner.

But no car came that afternoon.
I stood there in the patient street,
my summer dress rippling.

JOAN KANE

Rote

It could have been yesterday,
Trying to learn a pattern of water
On water or a road I thought
Prophesied and never found.

Against the backdrop of valley
I lost the flock as it flew past
For no known reason at all,
A sudden and small consolation.

I saw skins hung on rain-wet willows.
I could not fix in mind or memory
The terrible road or where it led.
Perhaps it was sleep moving

Against me, its round hill
Swelling against a flat landscape.
Iris of eye gives evidence of the sea
Growing larger; an obscured sky

Casts over, scatters and rains.
Of a day that will not want to end,
Tomorrow shall be longer.

Stative

I.

Along the hillside whorls of wind: I collect
Anemone, blown into a two-week peak

As Grass-of-Parnassus' small bog star
Throngs the marsh below.

I pick these flowers for weather,
To ferment and powder.

I do not know their cure, heal or sour,
Or if it is my name again written
One thousand times, grove upon grove.

II.

The bucket of a man pouring water,
A quarterly moon dips low.

Fish slip from the seine: it is time
To depart. As morning nears,
Ursa Major's last light trails.

III.

Who would not dream a year of two winters,
All dullness and narrow entrance?

What a mean thing, the horizon,
So open-mouthed at gap
And close of day. It drowns a thin disc
Of sun from its height of one thumb's width
At arm's length. We can measure
Its meanness.

IV.

An odor of
Ledum twisted in grip—

Dusk placed like a seal over liquid hours.
A cogged wheel pulls the tide near, away from shore.

V.

The water drained away
Reveals a flat land of grasses.

I began to miss one of the small bones
In my hand and it hurt.

The Cormorant Hunter's Wife

Black birds luster in sleep above a rough
Sea, and he is all suspension from a length
Of rope before descending to snap ten
Long necks, one after another. Cormorants

In death are just lustrous: swollen from a day's
Plunging, distended with fish. He wants
To own his weighty bounty upwards,
But she in cunning cuts his cord and turns

To the other in her husband's falling.
Implausible travels from a scar of rock,
And a return that needs no telling.
Is it her failing: the cormorant hunter's wife

Feels no ill will all winter until the spring,
When, in a glutton's plumpness with her black
Hair lustered, he buries her beneath a sum of stones
And himself plunges with the downdrafts under.

Hyperboreal

Arnica nods heavy-headed on the bruised slope.
Peaks recede in all directions, in heat-haze,
Evening in my recollection.

The shield at my throat ornamental and worse.
We descended the gully thrummed into confusion
With the last snowmelt a tricklet into mud, ulterior—

One wolfbane bloom, iodine-hued, rising on its stalk
Into the luster of air: June really isn't June anymore,
Is it? A glacier's heart of milk loosed from a thousand

Summer days in extravagant succession,
From the back of my tongue, dexterous and sinister.

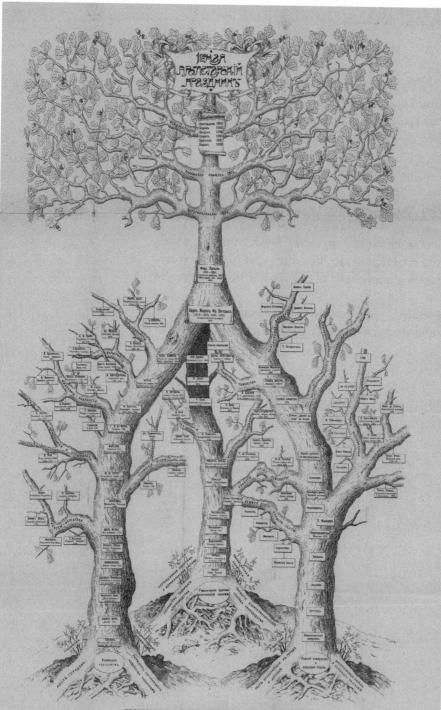

РОДОСЛОВНОЕ ДЕРЕВО СОВРЕМЕННАГО СОЦІАЛИЗМА.

KATHERINE TOWLER

On the Streets of Hanoi

Across from the park
men perch on tiny stools
sipping sugar cane juice
from tall glasses
while the woman
who tends the cart
squats at the curb
beside a pan of water
rinsing the glasses of the men
who have come and gone.
She does not look at me.
I am a white ghost,
a haunted and haunting figure
in a history that will not be named.
My feet move
over broken concrete
as though feeling for words
on an empty page.

Motorbikes careen past,
horns honking,
folding me in their wild dance,
oblivious to any narrative
I might impose,
to the need for a narrative at all.
One hunger replaces another
in me, the hunger to be recognized
for the hunger to be free
of this American body
and the outsized appetites
I am shedding bit by bit
like the layers of clothing
I no longer need.
How is it that they allow me
to become one of them,
to add my mute offering
to the great song of life and joy

that is this city?
The woman looks up
from her pan of dish water,
her eyes a quiet invitation
to join the flow
of a human river
winding in silent
forgiveness toward the sea.

Luggage

Four hours west
of Da Nang
on a mountain road
wide enough
for only one vehicle
I begin to lose
things.
The anti-nausea
medication, the ear plugs,
the little travel pillow
fall to the bottom
of a suitcase
I cannot reach
in the moat of luggage
ringed round
my fragile sense
of home.
Green fields of rice,
hillsides swept
in light have
other names
for me.

At the store
where we stop
the roof is corrugated tin,
the walls blue tarp lashed
to tree branches.
The woman selling
cigarettes and gasoline siphoned
into plastic Coke bottles
is pleased to share
her family's meal –
pork and bamboo shoots
in a thick sauce over rice,
green papaya soup,
baked eggs and scallions.

This is what
it means to be rich
I think as the teenage
daughter studies my strange
hair and laughs
at the foreign
sound of hello
in her mouth
and the equally foreign
sound of my
xin chào,
her easy pleasure
erasing what seemed
necessary, carrying
the notion of enough
and not enough
off to the green canopy
of the forest
where we watch
the monkeys go
hand over hand
from one treetop to the next.

POETRY FROM BULGARIA

FEATURE

Ekaterina Yosifova

I Assume a Comfortable Position

on the couch, the pillow, the fluffy blanket,
the books.
The lighting is also good.
Nobody enters,
though I don't lose hope
that someone would come in and say
with reproach:
this government also fell,
yet you're reading Lao Tzu.
To which I'd answer:
exactly.

Translated from the Bulgarian by Katerina Stoykova-Klemer

Ani Ilkov

Like Homer

The maiden in the dark is always singing
in the early morning or the early evening
while the grannies cast around their lightning
and their teeth "Dear God!" are rattling.

Dinner has been served upon the table,
but mice don't seem to care, in a choir
they sing along enthralled, as they are able…

One of them resembled Homer.

Translated from the Bulgarian by Dimiter Kenarov

The Children Take off

> *"Slave: I say, the dead kill the living."*
> *Aeschylus, "Oresteia"*

I saw them lined up by the wall
(perhaps someone had taught them)
pissing together on the backside
of their boring school.

Lined up, standing side by side,
they resembled migratory birds
readying for the western South.

Maybe winter's coming? I don't know.
Something is approaching maybe
we can't see... Which they saw.

Their faces look dejected
touched by some agreement
against the Wall their eyes are leaning
lips illiterate with silence
and joy that has no meaning.

Perhaps they know? We don't.
(Trams strum their lyres without sound.)
The children here: Orpheuses torn
to pieces by the city crowd.

Translated from the Bulgarian by Dimiter Kenarov

Kristin Dimitrova

Noah, the Carrier

Noah told it differently.

To the Jewish delegation
he said that he freed the pigeon and
it brought back a branch.

The pigeon is the white herald of joy. It is the pure soul of the innocent and
foretells the beginning of a new life.

The forefathers approved the story
and adopted it.

To Gilgamesh, however, he'd spoken like this:

I freed a pigeon, but it returned.
I freed a swallow—same thing.
Finally I freed a crow and
never saw it again.
Then I realized it had discovered
both loot and land.

The crow is the black warrior among the birds. Flying against the good sky, it
is the first witness of the last transformation.

Gilgamesh understood this language.

When he was alone,
Noah said to himself:
"There is no way,
truth does not make a good legend,
yet legend is truth's only carrier."

He clearly remembered: it was actually the flies
that found the ship.

Translated from the Bulgarian by Katerina Stoykova-Klemer

KATERINA STOYKOVA-KLEMER

Conversation

Daddy, why is your face so sad?
Because your Mommy died, baby.

Why do you visit the grave every day, Daddy?
Baby, she's there every day.

Daddy, your pillow is bitter with salt.
Is that a question, baby?

Translated from the Bulgarian by the author

Blagovestva Pugyova

Standing Atop the Statue of Liberty

I dream of standing barefoot atop the Statue of Liberty,
on top with the flame.
Amidst the confusion people will come from cities to witness the spectacle
and shout, "Miracle, O, Miracle! Speak to us!"

And if I say, "We are guests on this Earth, headed for a heavenly beyond
of gardens and rivers, and butterflies,"
mass suicides will begin
because everyone believes the words of those above.

Or if I say, "Man is born alone and dies alone.
The world's mingling produces confusion. Comforting others weighs us down,
and makes wars. Take care only of yourselves,"
selfishness will reign. Following that, too, will be mass suicides —
from loneliness
because everyone believes the words of those above.

So today I —
I step atop the Statue of Liberty,
and whisper only, "Give. Come on, give —
it's not taking but giving that's central."
The masses don't move.
Doctors with megaphones arrive from the madhouse.
"Don't jump. Don't do it, child," they say
as a helicopter hovers to save me and a fire brigade
rushes to put out my thoughts.
But I jump, become a blob of flesh on the pavement
because I cannot live among people
who believe, but do not know
how to give.

Translated from the Bulgarian by Ilya Kaminsky and Eireene Nealand

Dimiter Kenarov

Family

First of all, I'm the letter F. I'm the father
of five fabulous children – Fergus, Fey, Fatima,
Fritz, Fleur – and the friendly owner of
"The Flippant Foreigner," a miniature factory
for the production of fantasies. On weekends
I go fishing, or just fumble with a piece of fruit.
It's full of fun. Oftentimes.

My house is a farmhouse, fenced by a field
of flowers. My bedroom is furnished with fluorescent
lights, brighter than the whole of Florida set on fire.
When I'm frightened, my wife comes to me,
feels my forehead and says, "Have more faith
in the future." "The future," I say, "Is another F-word."
"God forbid," she fusses and gives me fellatio.
Thus time flies.

If my face looks familiar to you, it's your own
fault. I am not free, you are not free. We
are family. Among the foxglove and the sweet
fennel, somebody is planning a fratricide
and a fake funeral.

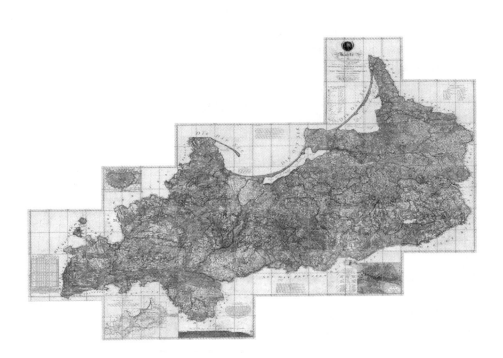

Ming Di

Hankou

If in Hankou lies a land of words
with open mouths, Auden went there
and did not.

If the East Sea a black hole, then the Yangtze
a sparrow, swooping to the night.
And the Han River, a one-winged fly?

No men. Or women. Only humans, fish, and birds.
Three primary colors blurred
as one: human-human, fish-human, bird-human.

In darkness, the Han River flickers
to the milky way
and there appears:
fish-fish, fish-bird, bird-bird, bird-fish…
some become women, some men. Some Hanzi.

From the Han River to Hanzi pass many nights.

A Mr. Hanzi walks the river. In his shoe a secret.
If his mouth remains unopen,
Auden went as if he didn't.

Translated from the Chinese by Michael Luke Benedetto and the author

SANDRA ALCOSSER

PORTFOLIO

THE BLUE VEIN

To be human is of the earth, crumbling

Is humus. Is humility. Bleeding

We fall down. A dog licks our blood. Sometimes

We eat songbirds because we are hungry

A poet might refuse to speak after

Shelling. Another sings until they starve

Him, not because he plots against the state

Because he makes his own song. For the way

She loved his music, and the way he loved

The blue vein that rivered from her eyebrow

To her brain, the widower on the pier

Lifts his cello. Wrist becomes lips, tongue

Casals played Bach each morning to sanctify

The house, sanctify the mind. We are all

Ephemerals. Our blood so close to the

Blood of a tree. The cello too is pine

A body with ribs, belly. Below the

Winter bud each genus grows its own face

Vedran Smailovic walks Sarajevo

With a cello. He wears a tuxedo

Skeleton of the body is the music's

Shape. *I don't think about bombs, about*

Snipers. We have to remind ourselves we

Are human. *I go to the ruined place*

The Meadowlark, The Mother

Who spreads feathers over a nest in flames —
The meadowlark, the mother, first container

Of the alphabet, the village, the inch.
Our face water on which her face exists.

Something grew into her that would not leave
The mineral of the race, its meter.

And so when a mother falls, we become her.
How mothers fall as families before her

Bones grown airy as gothic cathedrals.
Leave me, she says, her eyes derange the wall.

What will we do with you darling when we
Must let you go? Our atoms mostly empty

Space. When will another come along to
Cradle us — in the way that humans do?

SANDRA ALCOSSER

My Shy

You come begging outside my screen
Sidelong you stare all morning

I know that greeting It's the same as mine
You can't make up your flimsy mind

Do you like your world better distant or direct
Little Beckett shifting seeds from one cheek

To the other if I so much as breathe
You convulse like water on hot grease

Relax no one cares about you
That's the privilege of being discreet

You know the warm dens the sound of your solitary
Beat against the walls and those strawberries

Ripening under my porch the ones no hand can reach
They're yours — deep maroon reclusive they smell so sweet

Perfection

When was the last time with no
One's love or a brain to excite emotion
You budded forth from a seed
Or became a root hair if you were thirsty
Making detours for miles attracted by a speck
Of moisture We conceive a perfection
We cannot achieve — or so believed
Lord Byron — I conceive
A perfection of chickadees
Night ices and they clump on top of each
Other one body weighing two pennies — when
Was the last time someone held you to keep
From freezing — twenty hearts feathering
The pocket of a tree

after bathing

I melt into the air with a voluptuousness
so delicate I am content to be alone.

John Keats

The maiden aunt and I
spent Saturday nights
around a gray Formica table
eating hard-boiled eggs
afterwards we'd read the Bible
I thought a girl might die from
such a diet
but what did I know of maiden life
the sensual curve of Saturday night
like John Keats freshly powdered
in a dressing gown

I sit down
to the kitchen table alone near dusk —

a single egg a dark cup

Riparian

If we wash our legs with frozen water
Watch it rill down hairy flesh — oh the power
Of the body to refresh — to lie down at night
Wake again among harebells and bees, lichen
Speckled boulders, mists of sweet white
Clover — if we cock our pollen hats
Like Leonardo da Vinci and sketch
Riffles come to nurse the thirsty
Rubble, we can lean back, sieve
Our tea among secretive
Rocks — soak away the meanness
Of a year's duplicity — no one can reach
Us here — no human noise —
A river will gentle the cruelest voice

Papers

From the great estate her Great
Aunt said *stay until you grade*
Those papers. The students exclaimed
They loved *Sham pain.*

On hands and knees
The maid asked *how's teaching?*

Fine, if not for papers.

That's why I quit said the maid
Twirling polish into worn parquet.

Upon his death bed, to ease
The family, Gerard Manley Hopkins said *at least*
There will be no more student papers to read.

And then — *I am so happy.*
I am so happy. I am so happy.

Santo

Turbaned and beaded, hooped by eyelet
The Bahianas carry rose water in white
Mirrored vases to swab the staircase
At the Church of Good Endings. One ties a sachet
About my wrist and says when it frays
Three wishes will come true. I did not know
I wished for you — skating on bones, on torso
Your knuckles skinning cobblestones
As you made your way into the elevator
Down to the Lower City without hips or legs
Past midnight through sewers and souls
Of Salvador — oh breathless Holy Ghost
You were flying on your knuckles you
Were singing as you flew

Infirmary

Instead of the sulfuric chemistry
Equation from a spirit-duplicating machine —
Palladian glass arched inside Andover cream —
High windows an inch or two
Open to lift white sheers to haints to cool
The flesh of one who chose to be
Lying there floating in a brainy coral sea
To the whisper of Nursey's gum shoes
As she trayed yet another glass of juice —
Years later it will all return — how you hid
In sickness how it began your first delicious
Recess from class and loud laughter and keeping
Up — first chance to catch what some called being
As it walked around inside your body

Strider

Hard seed suspended over six wire legs
The strider creates a most playful

Wake as it skulls, leaps, skates
Across the river At night branches lengthen

Plants increase in height— and below air
Below transparent films of water
More atmospheres — upside down interiors

That we could float if we knew more of birth
Or death except sublime rehearsal

What is the wisest life in a great river
Where the skipper stops to clean six whiskered feet
Little round shadows cast on dimpling water

A body you know can grow an extra heart
In each wing if it needs to go deeper

Maré Frigoris

Coming home late spring night stars a foreign
Language above me I thought I would know

The moons like family their dark plains — sea of
Crises sea of nectar serpent sea

How quickly a century passes
Minerals crystallize at different speeds

Limestone dissolves rivers sneak through its absence
This morning I learned painted turtles

Sleeping inches below the stream bank
Freeze and do not die Fifteen degrees

Maré Frigoris sea of cold second
Quadrant of the moon's face I slide toward

The cabin arms full of brown bags one light
Syrups over drifts of snow Night rubs

Icy skin against me and I warm
Small delicates — cilantro primrose —

Close to my body A hundred million
Impulses race three hundred miles an hour

Through seventeen square feet of skin and
Gravity that collapses stars lifts earth's

Watery dress from her body holds me
With such tenderness I hardly breathe

Granadas

> *of lace, of canaries flying amid the tapers of an air*
> *that was lukewarm and sad.*
>
> Federico Garcia Lorca

The month when winter rains
River the crawl space
La Doña's son arrives
With wrenches hacksaw pliers
Plumber's tools in a tombstone case
To ruch up then sweep our drains
And after a few hours I pay him grateful
For his quiet labor

Invisible as dusk he stands by the gate —
Hinges straining —
Pulls out shims drivers straightens
Gravity's weight then bows and smiles at me
Granadas he says waving
His hands at the pomegranate tree

As if to filch from a branch
He wraps an airy globe with his hand
Pours liqueur into its imaginary hide
Sucks between his teeth closes his eyes

La Doña I ask as though his mother might
Have made this drink Saturday nights
When Salvador his father was alive
La Doña I ask again and her son frightens

La Doña in a pink sand castle
With a shack of sons behind laughing
While she naps — rancheros
On the radio and pool games
Under the wooden lath
That mothers a tangle of hanging plants

As if the mention of his mother's name sobers
Him — widow who's never spoken
Or waved when her boys walked her slowly

Under awnings of corpulent roses
Of unnatural coral as though
Nowhere in the world could calyx and corolla
Grow as fleshy and demented in color
As the roses of *La Doña* and Salvador

Triste the son asks and I do not know
If he speaks of himself or *La Doña*
Or perhaps of me — three
Figures snugged into bungalows
Above the sea *No not sad* I say making
A skirt of my t-shirt to fill with pomegranates

Too sexual — blooming
Since April each bud grew
Like lipstick rising from a tube
Pomegranates tasting of human
Bodies spinning now like planets —
Mars of burnished leather — splatter
On concrete, roll into the grass
Solo he says and I answer *no no solo*

Uncertain whether this means do I live alone
Or am I lonely unable to speak the same
Or understand anything but hands I make
A basket and wave him out the gate
And we become two white
Shirts tacking *solo* into night

You may sip the garnet swallow the seed
But there are always too many
Waiting in secret chambers
Like mistaken
Gestures *No no solo* I'd said *Take*
The granadas I could not stop placing

More in his basket and though
We lived as neighbors years after *La Doña*

Died and her pink castle sagged empty
I could only imagine her son's shame
When I lied *nunca triste nunca solo*
Holy as a god *never sad never lonely*
As if one could ever be
More than a human body

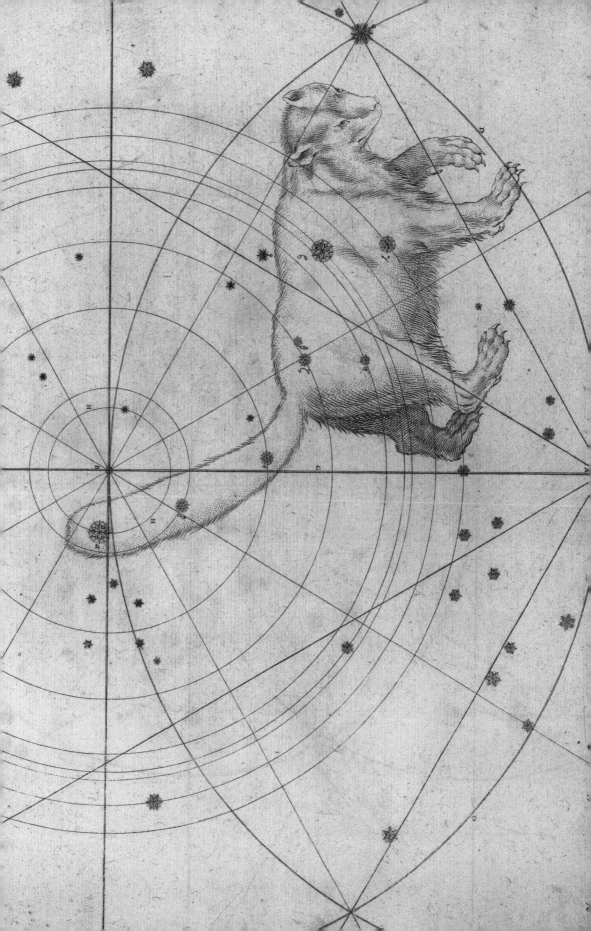

MARK McMORRIS

PORTFOLIO

A Poem for the Love of Women

A poem for the love of women
makes good copy for the bored and the ugly
which I confess to belong to, on both counts
ignorant of Venus, no child of Aphrodite,
foam-born and black for all the baths
I took with her, while the boats drew nearer.
The statue falls in love with the sculptor.
So the ship with the banker, and the glove
with the goddess of the silver screen who knows how to knit
the pimp in love with his ugliness
and the book with the binder, the word with system
of discourse and grammar with logic.
I loved the Indian in Uganda, the Kenyan
in Paris, the Turk in Boston, at the Fine Arts Museum.
I loved the Korean in Queens, the Scot
at the embassy in Bogota,
the nun in Dar es Salaam, the bus driver in New York.
Many women in many guises came into my bed
the Spanish in Cuba, the Basque in Trinidad.
Many women followed the foam-trail to my door.
The Greek on 37th Street, the Chinese girl
to elementary school in Kingston, the Texan
to Accra where I took her sight-seeing.
Many women are part of the map
the hand traces the swirling rivers by their perfume.
I loved the Angolan woman in Hanover,
the Bajan in Chicago. I loved the woman
from Italy in Benin, among the gorgeous sculpture.
It's hard to explain, but many women loved me
in many disguises--many masks--many shadows.
I loved the Berlin woman in Peru, the Inca
in Bonn, the Dutch in Guyana. The Lebanese woman
and I were lovers in Dallas. I loved the woman from Tunis
in Carthage, the Aztec in Glasgow. Loved
the Gypsy in Egypt, in Thebes to be precise, on the Nile.
The Jerusalem woman found me in Nice
and I loved her on the route to Avignon.

The woman from Nice loved me in Toledo.
Many women in many cities and villages.
I loved many cities in many women
built many cities with their love, followed
many women to archaeological pits, loved
their statues in the gardens of Priapus
loved dying languages in many women, loved French
in the West Indies, and English in Zimbabwe.
Loved pottery that kept the imprint of their faces
poetry that clothed them, the sinewy quatrains.
But the Sibyl is long dead, who spoke the language.
Weep for the Sibyl in her disappearance.
Weep for her, who spoke the tongue of my mother.
Weep for the Sibyl, who saw pieces of the heart.

She is not with child, the woman who loved me.
The woman who taught me Philipino, did I
love her or the speech, the woman I bought
at the market in Port-au-Prince, did she
really cherish me for my ugliness, as she said?
And was it a negative face that I captured
in crossing the ocean to find her bivouac?
The seeds are strewn like constellations.
The hair of supernovas burns round my face.
The ocean rocks the crab into a stupor.
And the sibyl is long dead who spoke of her
crossing from water-fall to hedge-row, river mouth
African moon over the sand dune cornu-
copias the plentiful horn of her melody.
Did I love the Gold Coast trader for her strength
the ferocity of her thought, the tight skin
stomach above the pubis, her rock-steady walk?

I loved the sin in sinning, the gland in England.
Loved O in Ottawa for a month, loved
Sandy or smooth, red or brown, women
and molls and concubines, Virgins and Japanese

feminine word-smiths, divas and butterfly girls
many women in many guises, many arms
many faces in my long mirror, many crossed
to my bed from the river, sweet-smelling orchids.
I loved Beth in Elizabeth, New Jersey
I loved Holly at Christmas, Eve at night
Loved Mavis at Mavis Bank, St Andrew
Loved Clara in the morning, Denise
at dawn, and Dawn in the Odysssey, by Homer.
Loved Heather the Heathen Woman
Cassandra the Christian. Sojourner Truth.
Loved Mabel the engineer at Los Alamos.
I loved many women in many tyrannies
the Queen of Spain, and the Queen of Darkness
Persephone in her filmy colors of Dis.
Many women found me by navigation:
Dora and Djuana, Sylvia and Adrienne.
Josephine the emperor's woman
Josephine the dancer
Josephine the daughter of Joseph
Josephine the fishmonger at a bay at Savanna-La-Mar.
And Kurtz's woman with the savage breasts.
Yeats's Maude and Tennyson's "Maude," in the poem.
Derek's Anna and Tolstoi's. B's Mexican.
Many women taught me speech--tongued
me into Reason, brought me to the Logos.
Women of howls and études, I loved
Clio and Klytemnestria and Beverly.
I loved Margaret Bourke-White in Ghandi.
Loved in vain and in anger, loved by fiat.
Loved the name Susan for no good reason.
I loved the pronoun she, the accusative her,
the embrace of hers. Loved Monica in French
as Monique, Carol the Carolingian singer
Norma at a bar in Nornandie, loved Leona
because she was a lion, Patricia
the woman from aristocracy, and Jane

the double-headed keeper of the gate.
Many women, many Sibyls, many ladies
with intuition and eloquence, many loves
came from the water to my embrace
the women of Modigliani and Wyeth
the nudes in drawing rooms and the Venus
at Cnidos by Praxiteles, the sculpture
by Auguste Rodin--the everlasting kiss--loved
the marble and the bronze and the wood
women in repose or in passion, loved
the wife of Cezanne though I should not have seen
her intimate bath, however discretely
and the Wif of Bath on her horse, I loved
Tracy for her sinuous calf-lines, Daphne
the nymph, and Lolita the mixed-up girl.
I loved in bed and on the roof of Notre Dame
de Paris, by the book and in secret, I loved
mistresses and executive vice presidents
and editors and poets in long print skirts
many women in many garments drew my gaze.
Loved the violin player adorned in black.
Loved the scholar in Chanel, and the writer
in a Simone-de-Beauvoir sweater, loved
Simone for her name, Victoria for her voice
Violet and Rose and perfumes
of natural growth, loved Laila for her speed
Virginia for her prose. Loved Amber
the color of sunset, and the wife of Paul Eluard.
Many women shared me with their lovers.
Many women in many parts of the world.
And the tale of my love is only beginning.
Many women loved me in my sleep
at supper or on the frontier, at church.
I loved the Muses and many Violas, Veronique
in Verona and in many cities of Europe
Clodia in Rome beside her Catullus.
And the tale of my love is only just beginning.

Weep for the Sibyl, for she is dead, who spoke
my mother's tongue and other languages
I gathered up in bouquets, the dried flowers.
The Sibyl is long dead who broke into pieces
of the heart, the word in pieces, and phonemes
spilling from the fountain, with the yard
criss-crossed by flares from the infantry.
The basin cracked, and leaves blowing in it.
The Sibyl is long dead, the heart waning.

The Great House in Various Light

The evening empty as a convex
coconut split down the seam:
not that it can be filled.

The evening empty as a gourd
that twists on an iron thread:
the rough skin of the sphere.

.   .   .   .   .

Not that there was a spoken word
to recall the moment of seeing
the short span when the clocks
ceased to revolve and hands
met in jest or benediction
time of the vortex into which
hibiscus and almond trees strayed
and windows made of aluminum.

The stars are suddenly remote
candescent petals night throws
above the yard, the beautiful things.

.   .   .   .   .

The great house is a hotel
and a museum of victory

how some lived at the epoch
of planters and governors

visible in the paintings
the armchairs and gilded glass

articulate artifacts
and floors polished by daylight

in a country of green hills
and water wheels and wagons

and sun coming out after a rain
the labor is hidden that built

the house long ago, and ploughed
the land to make it bear fruit

.   .   .   .   .

In British poetry, gentle woodland
creatures gaze at the hermit
with marble eyes lit from within.
A single bird defends the song.
Among the pines draped with snow
from the whole land only a secret
footfall teases the senses awake
like white breath on white canvas.

Ideal forms crowd the auditorium.
The sky deepens on the surface
of a lake, in a cradle of stars.
A coppice of isolated birch trees
climbs the mountainside to touch
the moon's scar, benevolent witness
washed of color and fragmentary
illuminating the village below.

.   .   .   .   .

In New World poetry, an invisible
river runs this way and that.
A car(t) eases on a bumpy track
over small hills and into shallows.
The world is a tangle of leaves.
Towards sundown a driver gets out

and pushes into the forest, drawn
by a noise he cannot identify:
perhaps the hiss of water below.
It's only the river on its way.

Ideal forms crowd the auditorium
things present and things past
scattered beneath the poinciana.
The car heads into higher country
then out into space where fields
suddenly lie down beneath the seer
cattle pastures and agricultural lands
that have always been there

watched over by the great house
from its hilltop, like a sentinel.

·   ·   ·   ·   ·

In British poetry, the forms
of desire darken with the change
of seasons: green leaves once
they fade and turn gold and fall
to earth, and make a carpet
in the forest, awaiting the rain.

For each season has its sonata.
Silence and sound in balance
belong to the decline of autumn.
In winter the notes are fewer.
Silence comes into its kingdom
crown of the father, who departs.

The world of white prepares
to conquer the earth with silence.

·   ·   ·   ·   ·

In British poetry, articulate hues
speak as they are visible to the mind
audible colors played on a piano
primary sounds in an empty forest.

And then above a lake, the moon
in motion suspended like a dancer
as the music temporarily ceases
depriving her body of its rhythm.

        .   .   .   .   .

Ideal forms crowd the auditorium.
The light of day starts to fade
and a mist settles in the valleys.
The great house is lit from within.

        .   .   .   .   .

As they were, in other windows
you want to see their ghosts
the slaves, like black posts
staggered through the fields.
You want to make a picture
that shows the strange overlords
at intervals watch the misery
of torsos laboring to plant
and harvest the seas of sugar.

        .   .   .   .   .

The green beds of sugar cane
extend from here to the hills.

Bright heads grazed by the light
of paradise become its negative.

．　　　．　　　．　　　．　　　．

In time, would the land irritate us
as it must have irritated the masters
the tropical caress of the air unavoidable
getting up each day to see once more
the rolling green hills and cattle ponds
tranquil in the valleys, the horses
collected at the water trough, content
to stand or to walk over the grass.

A comely scene worthy of an oil painting
(fruit trees dappled with sunlight).

They have escaped from seasons
into the monotony of a terrible beauty.

(Who is speaking?)

．　　　．　　　．　　　．　　　．

Away from the coast
the car passes through
a shadowy green world
of tropical syntax
ragged slopes and curves.

．　　　．　　　．　　　．　　　．

What then was promised by the evening
lights that spangled about the hills?

．　　　．　　　．　　　．　　　．

Endless tall grasses, a landscape
composed of variations on a color.

The after-image of elliptical forms
transparent to the cry of a sea gull.

        ·   ·   ·   ·   ·

A tablet of scripted exclamations:

there, a poinciana with pink blossoms
overhangs the road, there a scrawl
of fighting tendrils, an indigo grammar
of petals offering illumination
to fan-shaped pristine hieroglyphs
waving to greener punctuations
of banana trees and mango, a tangle
of writing over writing closed
to further interventions. Visible
palimpsest of a book without letters
the tangle of leaves has no secret key
and cannot be deciphered, wordless
monads travelling contours of silence.

        ·   ·   ·   ·   ·

Mimesis touches the world
with an imperceptible
tenderness, only hardly
like wind an Aeolian harp.

        ·   ·   ·   ·   ·

There is a point when the sky pivots
to face the dawn, to face the dark side
of personality, that of a sensible man
recanting the mysteries he embraced
as a youth, when the angels spoke to him
and he ran towards them with arms wide open
across a field, beneath the painted stars.

. . . . .

Say that the world is a drinking glass
containing things of the life and language
and say that a poet wakes up one morning
thinking of capturing for the future
those petals inside that glass, broken vowels.

A vase of orchids stands on a kitchen table.
Not that it is abstract, or a luminous
symbol, nonetheless it is an algebra
of forces, like the equations of space-time,
which rule outside the mental universe.

As if an image should leave its mirror behind
(the thing of which it is but a ghost)
like bodiless speech, and yet sensuous, in the way
a dream can leave its mark on the dreamer--
Esse est percipi, so speaketh the Law.

Wind begins to touch an Aeolian harp.
The great house is a place of articulation
word calls to other words, in transit.
Compelled by the beauty of flowers
the mind creates a space for other things.

. . . . .

(By British I mean Romantic idealist.)

Warm night descends
like a cloak. The whistle
of tree frogs supplies
a melody, and crickets
invisible to the moon
begin their Parliament.

The birds sleep with their young.
The air is otherwise still.

The Last City

There is always another city
you come to Rissani
the people, their tongue, their way
of navigating the streets, their gods
you say that this is the limit
of cities beyond which is neither
east nor west but only the curve
of earth falling into the valley
pastured by the sun and walked
by stars of an abstruse geometry
there is no further to go than this
you are at the frontier
where all roads and all rivers
sink into the sky like a prayer
only the exile whispers
as he stares deep into a calyx
there is always another city
there is a city called Sijilmasa
that was forgotten by the diggers
of labyrinths and archangels
city of concubines harsh city of slaves
gold and spices city of weeping
city of boulevards and gardens
ibises and fountains and the wind
culling an alphabet from a bird's walk
there is always another city
hidden in your footsteps like a song
sung by a calypso singer
as the poplars tremble and the wind stirs
there is always another city
say if I travel past this milepost
the road will become its double
the journey home will lead me to you
woman who bears her soldier
to the twilight of cathedrals
the city strikes twelve in her face
there is always another city

another Acropolis another citrus grove
to replace the one you long for
there is always another city
and in her palm you see the zero
of an orchid plucked from a guitar
there is always another city
hidden in your belt, the city
of empty libraries and tambourines
the city you call the last
city, the city of iron, the ordeal
and quest assigned to those who eat offal
a city where there is no language
to name it except the tongue of lizards
there is a city never visited
by Herodotus which is stranger than this
not even a book, only the idea of a book
the thought of Paradise, the idea of a reader
and a place to set it down

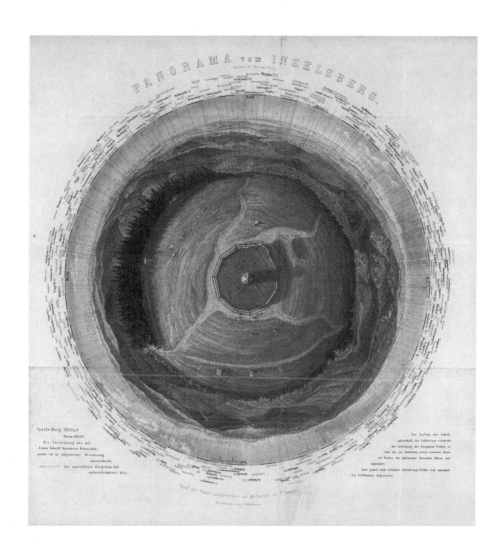

PANORAMA VON INSELSBERG.

POETRY FROM SWEDEN

FEATURE

Edited by Jonas Ellerström and Malena Mörling

From the editors:

Here are a handful of poems by five major Swedish poets, each holding up their own end of the rich tradition of Swedish poetry. From Edith Södergran, our legendary and passionate pioneering modernist—to Gunnar Ekelöf who, after studying in London and Paris, brought surrealism to Sweden and whose thematic and stylistic scope, to this day, remains unrivaled—to Sonja Åkesson, who in the mid-twentieth century became our sharpest observer of the hypocrisy and vanities of our society, a function that she is justly famous for, along with her no-nonsense but still sensitive view of human (not least her own) frailties and shortcomings—to Göran Sonnevi, who, but not reflected in what is presented here, has become a poet of epic format; his most recent volume, *Book Without a Name* (Bok utan namn, 2012), comprises eight hundred pages—to last but not least, Jesper Svenbro, a formidable contemporary poet and scholar of Greek antiquity.

Sonja Åkesson

To Play Like Yourself

In this dive, will you even talk about it?
Will you talk about a guy who's totally himself?

So now you think it's pretty bad . . .
the worst there is
when a guy reminds you of another?

Wouldn't it beg, for at least a touch of ridicule
to at all cost avoid a person's influence?
(says A)

I think anyone who's able to crib so well
you get annoyed by the theft
must be incredibly gifted really.

You're listening to a guy who's playing a piss poor Miles, you see.
He may have worked his ass off
to play like Miles.

And then a guy shows up for whom it's awfully easy
to imitate Miles,
then you mean to say he's worse?
In other words it's pretty lucky
to have pretty bad musicality
because then it's easier to find your own voice?

If you think that a guy is damn happy to be cribbing,
that his ambition is to play completely in the shadow of another
then isn't it okay for us to listen to it?
(says A)

Can you, for instance, even talk about anyone who plays like himself?

Playing like yourself, what the hell is that?

Translated from the Swedish by Carlo Brady, Jonas Ellerström, and Malena Mörling

GUNNAR EKELÖF

Poetics

You should listen to the silence
the silence behind the proclamations, the allusions
the silence in the rhetoric
or in the so-called formally complete
This is a search for meaninglessness
in what is meaningful
and the other way around
And everything I so artfully seek to compose
is conversely something artless
and the entire fullness empty
What I have written
is written between the lines

Translated from the Swedish by Jonas Ellerström and Malena Mörling

Göran Sonnevi

Poems Without Order

For this reason alone
we understand one another
because we do not
understand one another

*

Every
word carries
the whole universe

*

Every word
also carries
the whole of death

Translated from the Swedish by Rika Lesser

Jesper Svenbro

Hermes boukolos

In the hope that our project of reinterpreting the Hymn to Hermes
might find favor with one of our nine lyric ombudsmen
we here start on a tentative basis the transferal of cattle
which is the sign of really border-crossing poetry—
an experiment that we have had to postpone for a long time
as our metaphorical audacity has not by a long shot
permitted a cattle theft of this magnitude.
Now, however, the cattle herds of the Sun God
—a full-grown capital whose lowing is widely heard—
have suddenly proliferated at a rate expected by no one
which is why we too take up the shepherd's crook and openly explain
how we secretly have looked upon bucolic poetry,
for centuries capable of calving many-splendored interpretations:
all poetry is bucolic and the interpreter a cattle thief
who before restoring the cows he has stolen
makes them calve in secret and keeps the calves for himself!
True, Apollo sends the herds of poetry to graze
but the one-sidedly acoustic interest he takes in big cattle
which carefully fenced feed on the hills
confuses him when asked about the renewal of metaphor,
fundamental to the poetic subversion of our time;
on this point his half-brother is perfectly up-to-date
ever since he stealthily signed the Surrealist Manifesto
one night at the beginning of the twenties:
what is Breton's "spark" if not the soundless sign
that Hermes with his wand has established a connection
between the two seemingly irreconcilable elements of the image?
Never is the poem's shower of sparks so wonderful as at night!
Not surprisingly, Hermes chooses the darkest hours of all
to resolutely seize the alphabet by the horns and push it
backward out of the fold of the old poems:
twenty-four cows with as many types of hooves
set off quickly in the pitch-dark of interpretation
where just as in the original text it is of paramount importance
that the Thief have more than one string to his lyre;
a few hours earlier, he invented the instrument
that determines the standard range of our own lyrical poetry

and rarely limits it to its highest register, suitable
for example to depicting the atmosphere among the gods
where they live, in Winckelmann fashion, at an altitude of three thousand
meters.
Fortunately, the Cloud Gatherer discovered a little chap
who will forever break the monotony on Mount Olympus:
way down there on earth he is seen leading his cattle
into a darkness that slowly begins to blink with fireflies,
punctuation marks in a childhood poem full of strange meetings
and so quiet that laughter can be heard at a distance of several miles:
is it Zeus chuckling at the prank of his newborn son?
For a moment, the ancient world holds its breath.
Only the tripping of ninety-six little industrious hooves
Reveals to sensitive ears that border-crossing Hermes is on his way
and that the alphabetic order of tradition is now being rearranged
in a manner that makes constant use of chance.
Can tradition nevertheless transfer its meaning?
The hooves of our cattle are the same as those of antiquity

lining up their imprints in a lyrical verse of record length
from Mount Olympus in the north to Arcadia in the south,
where our Cowboy has stolen across the border, unseen:
things must work out as best they can! And in fact they do work out.
With its entire weight the poem narrates its cattle theft
and at dawn consists of the tracks it has left
on the path where now an irate Reader suddenly
is close on our heels in order to take possession of his herd—
right beside the precipice where all the poems still stand
and like thirsty livestock finally call for sound!

Translated from the Swedish by John Matthias and Lars-Håkan Svensson

Edith Södergran

Decision

I am a remarkably mature person
but no one knows me.
My friends create a false image of me.
I am not tame.
I have weighed tameness in my eagle claws and know it well.
Oh eagle, what sweetness in your wings' flight.
Will you stay silent like everything?
Would you perhaps like to write? You will never write again.
Every poem shall be the tearing up of a poem,
not a poem, but claw marks.

Translated from the Swedish by Jonas Ellerström and Malena Mörling

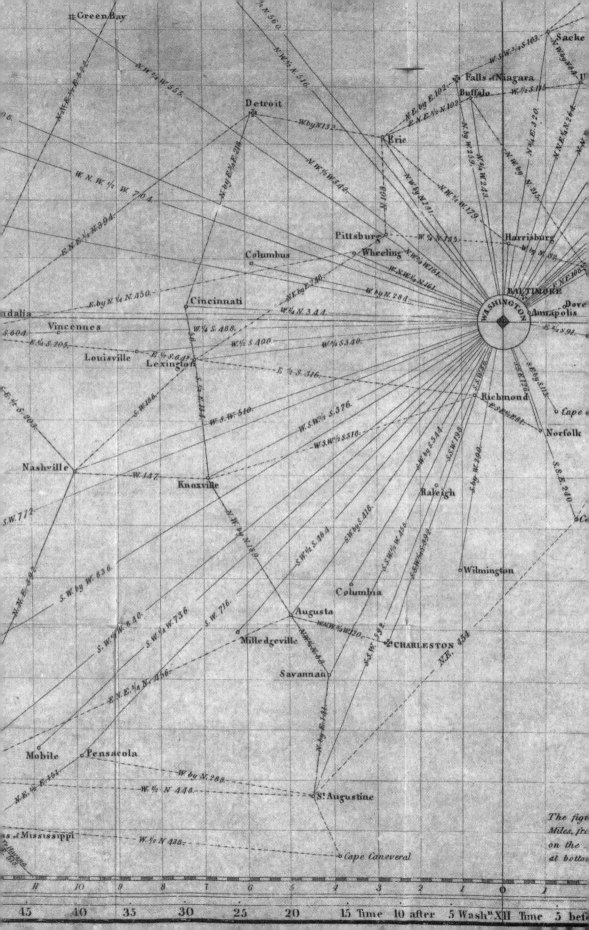

Green Bay

Detroit

Falls of Niagara

Buffalo

Sacke

Erie

Harrisburg

Pittsburg
Wheeling

Columbus

BALTIMORE
WASHINGTON
Annapolis
Dove

Cincinnati

Vincennes

Louisville
Lexington

Richmond
Cape

Norfolk

Nashville
Knoxville

Raleigh

Wilmington

Columbia

Augusta
Milledgeville
CHARLESTON

Savannah

Mobile
Pensacola

St Augustine

Cape Caneveral

of Mississippi

The figu
Miles, fro
on the
at botto

11   10   9   8   7   6   5   4   3   2   1   0   1

45   40   35   30   25   20   15 Time 10 after 5 Wash.ᵗ XII Time 5 bef

MARIA GARCIA TEUTSCH

PORTFOLIO

Postscripts to Headlines, written with chalk on the asphalt in front of a house of an American Poet in a Muslim Country
or
Poems from an American Dissident

Headlines from the United States

Boy Scouts' say kids safer from abuse in Scouts than at home

in a house
where mothers make
from Scouts' abuse of mothers
red-velvet
cupcakes.

DNA: Now-dead convict killed teen in '74.

Dead teen
never gets to text
her congrat-
ulations but has congratulated God's secretaries who congratulate
God on
speed-
dial.

Fisherman finds human finger in belly of a fish—

fish finds silver hook
with lemon bait twist
in corner of mouth of a man who's caught it--
who's pointing
the tail
at whom?

Shooting by breastfeeding mother latest case of self-defense

in an amendment to the second amendment
breast milk will replace guns--
daisies to replace bullets.

Headlines from France

a. Syrian crisis "tragedy of the age."

Children offer a reward
of lost kittens
for return
of missing parents.

b. French politician wages war on "anti-white racism."

Soldiers confused
over white flag.
With hands outstretched,
they surrender
while whistling untender
untended parts of speech.

d. Dior duels with YSL.

Rage over rain frock
vs. pencil skirt distracts.
What were we
talking about, my sweet mouse?
Burst of machine-gun fire.

e. "For Gaddafi, rape was a weapon."

He died when his name
became a verb.
More gendarme
war. In our reflection
a finger floats up
and points to one more gendarme
in the mirror
whose name is now becoming
a verb.

Maria Garcia Teutsch

Headlines from Vietnam

Vietnam jails three bloggers in crackdown on dissent.

Alcohol enemas administered,
boys will be boys
boys will be boys
will be boys administering
alcohol to jails
of boys.

Headlines from China

China postpones ceremony to mark 40 years of Japan ties.

An empty bowl.
No word to conjure
a belly full--just a pause
between the in
and the out. The birth
of a storm on simmer
in the empty bowl
is a ceremony.

Headlines from Pakistan

Gay games set for 2018 in Islamabad.

Quiet.
Tell us about your country
of poppies, wheat and corn.
Whose mustache lies to you from billboards?
What bold skull's colors symbolize law?
Where do you hide your women
when they bleed, Sergeant?
Where do you hide your sergeant
from your women, Sergeant?

Headlines from the Maldives

State of Emergency Declared

"For the safety and security
of every citizen," tweeted
his spokesman. Yellow trigger
fish protect their piece
of the reef with bared teeth.

Postscripts to Headlines

P.S.

not shot
by a sinister
videographer
obedient to
the barometer
of videographed meteorology
of measured
fingers
of truth.

P.S.

hiccup diagonal bursts of hate speech every 5 seconds
is how we learn
a new verb for mercy,
hidden in between
the final tooth
and period
of every poem
of a toothless man.

P.S.

blue boats adorn themselves with red and white flags.
She walks onto the roof
where her Sergeant
prays,
and she slaps his silly ass.

P.S.

three nets sorted and cleaned by a fisherman
in front of fish who announce a five-year plan.
A baby turtle oars
itself through sand.

No rain today, only the call
to prayer unfurling
over your tiny self
as you scrape a way
through an invisible squall.

ALEŠ ŠTEGER

As in sex

As in sex,
The body of the other
In poetry
Is mystically unattainable.

There are no laws,
Only farewells.

One must abandon
All words,
As water in a delta abandons
The riverbed
That led it safely
Over land.

Two tongues made out of rain
Will spell with water,
In water, out of the water
You are, you are.

Thank you.

Translated from the Slovenian by Brian Henry

Aleš Šteger

My intellect has a wish

My intellect has a wish
But cannot control
My destiny.

My soul can control
Destiny,
But it has no will.

I tuck my intellect
Into a black briefcase
And my soul behind an ear.

As I walk alone
The black briefcase rattles.
Someone is whispering to me.

Translated from the Slovenian by Brian Henry

Adam Veal

Forbidden Planet

A tick is a privileged creature. It sees its host's body in terms of geometry.
Looks for warmth & sticks in its whole head. Drinks deeper than any Viking
slakes his thirst on a horn that holds the sea or blood, who unbuckles from belly to
groin. Who focuses on his salted hands pulling at his pubic hair, but unbidden
come visions: corridors of rubber webbing, shadows of tubing & wire which flap
blind and with their nails score welts on the walls & the floors. Piping stacked
and rounded out against the black sky stretch toward a hazy curvature: From far
away, he notices larger cylinders clean with distance upon which a little silver
light dances. Nearby, vacuum tubes animate: Plastic segments rising in search of
some spurt of blood.

Gary Soto

The Gopher

Took away the roots of my rose bush,
Took away an onion and its cool sister, the tulip bulb.

This I discover as I walk down the porch steps,
My pair of stiff legs an aluminum ladder.
I post my hands on my hips.
It's too late for kindness
Not after how he treated my girl.
I'm going to split that gopher in two,
Earthy sailor that has journeyed
To the sound side of my yard,
Weedy terrain if you want to know—
A pile of lumber, sacked leaves and ivy,
The graveyard of poisoned snails,
And an old wooden bench
Where I once discussed with my inner banker
My brief relationship with money.

Wait a minute,
I'm getting off the subject,
Which involves the gopher,
Bucktoothed killer of my rose bush—
Poor spinster, still standing
But by the end of the week
Her head will droop earthward
And her arms discard the leafy sails.

Where's my shovel?
Where's my right glove of justice?
I'll patrol the yard
And wait for him to surface—
He's got come up for air,
Cocky sailor with slicked-back hair,
Whiskered and fearless.
Fearless as he has eaten earth
And earth's remnants,
Leaves, barky material,

A pebble or two,
And the roots of my rose bush.
I'm serious now.
I have my shovel, implement of death,
And a smoke bomb—
Let him rub his eyes!
Let him sneeze
And shit at the same time!
The sailor has taken away
My rose, still upright,
With bees hugging her pistils,
Her flowers like pink tutus,
Her scent sweet.

I'll stand like a sentry
Over his hole,
Slick my own hair back,
Show him what a pair
Of teeth I possess,
The red in my eyes,
And the cat inside me
Waving my tail
From side to side.

Claudiu Komartin

(I want to believe you)

I want to believe you
when you say
there will be someone
with a perfect smile
and defined features
an insect with a nanny soul
who will push me toward tomorrow
like leading a horse crushed by sadness
in the evening   to the slaughterhouse.

Translated from the Romanian by Tom Hatcher with Mariana Berca

KATHLEEN PEIRCE

PORTFOLIO

Vault

1.

In a dry time, one night's rain was felt to fall to her
who lay awake in bed, inside no darker air than what
the rain fell through entirely, hers because one waits,
one pays with waiting, as outside, late in winter,
it may be the long-dried uncut grass is touched by
an almost evenhanded, reasonable water
each leaf has given something to by bending
so, by bending down. Say her body moved that way,
night and the one dark lowering again,
and inside her mind the blades fell through
while outside in blades of water,
on leaves one knows as blades, rain fell
as if in thought, in air.

2.

Abraham Jamnitzer is long dead,
and his father before him, and his father,
and his father, and— Here stands
a silver statuette with arms raised up.
At her silver bodice, waist, and hem,
silver medallions wearing silver faces shine
from this figure so admired
at a father's hand, a son made her again,
a duplicate, almost. Her hands appear
just come undone, re-made as coral-made,
in red. No cameo; this is consubstantiation;
hands as branches from another element
where coral moves, or moved, would move,
handbranches/branchhands;
her coral looks arterial, and from her head, a spray
of coral lives again because arranged
as could be spokes of spoken sentences made visible,
except her mouth's made closed. They might be thoughts
whose ends are new. One wants to sleep.

3.

One wants to sleep, though sleep reveals another spray
ingrown, regrown every night, seeming to move
in the non-air of dream's most perfect privacy
where any thought can marry any form, so
even while falling there, if the paw one loves the odor of
more than wet grass itself, if a paw is raised
and scraped against the door,
someone wants out, someone wants in,
never some*thing.* A paw is raised again,
comes down in dream as the memory of a book close to the ear
falling from the hand whose wrist she mouthed,
of who loved her, dead now eleven years,
or it may be a branch pushed to the roof by wind. Rain comes
to roofs as though ceilings are doors. Should she feel, waking, that
she loved, or loves? The moment the coral branch was
fixed in the cuff, a wrist was what?
A roughening of the silver has inferred
some lacework there.

4.

On an isthmus of a kind,
one abbey in far Austria, buttercream and yellow
(*no, buttercream and apricot, Abess,*
it was Sanssouci that was so over-yellow),
contains, as no other place, the footfalls
of Maria Theresa. It *was* Sanssouci
that was so over-yellow. *Without*
a care. This abbey's corridor goes on, goes on,
the arches made to hold as they appear to narrow
while never narrowing, not unlike the way a figurine
contains the figure of a girl, arms high, breasts high—
Must she always wear shoes? She must. *Think them,*
behind her silver hem, unlaced, tangled, at root.

5.

Heel-clicks, Baroque.
Empress Maria Theresa comes in presentation of her gift.
Behold :: unveiled, dead,
two of the eternally devout: a pair long buried, unearthed, undressed,

6.

redressed in lace and silk. *Laces and silks.* Posed so,
sidelong, apart, in glass tombs, sealed,
sacrosanct, they face across the abbey church
at the station those assembling feel
as half-way down the aisle. *Pass through.*

7.

Pass through. Look left and feel the other waiting from the right,
look right and feel the other way around. Laces
and silks. He bears a quill-tip pen. *Are there jewels?* There are.
At her neckline, cuff, and finger bone, a red-brown
garnet radiance— *Why is the unearthed beautiful?*
lit garnets encircled with a perfection of seed pearls
That were his eyes? No,
his eyes are nothing in his skull. *And yet they look?*
They seem to look. They seem as the poet sees
birds occur because the air dissolves itself
as birds. Or is it air congealed? So dense,
reality, a thing can form by what breaks there
as well as if it binds.
That were his eyes? Yes.
Yes and sweeten it. His eyes rest at her wrist,
her throat, her hand, in perpetuity. *So
and not so. Her true body is not there. Nor his.*
Nor his.

8.

[…She inherited from her grandmother the dark complexion and the piercing black eyes of the March family. She was of peculiar characteristics, herself attributing some of them to the supposed Indian blood in the Marches. She was a devoted lover of nature, with which she spent many pleasant hours in sweet communion, in the fields and forests near her pleasant home. At the time of her tragic death she lived alone in her pretty cottage in the fork of the roads leading from Pepperell to East Pepperell. In the early evening of the 6th of January, 1883, the house took fire from some unknown cause, and before aid could be rendered it was consumed. Miss Chase perished in the flames which destroyed many valuable relics of by-gone days…]

9.

If brightness is a truce, a sleepless woman
is a flowing audience, and a made thing.
In a sentence about the river, she says,
"A mirror brought outdoors is also a light-chime."
In a sentence about who would be looking in, she writes,
"A flake of salmon, salmon-colored, lifted to the actual mouth
of one who'd kissed her in a dream."

10.

She remembers when there was no water. The rocks were whiter.
She could still see the day lily, still think of the morning glory
as gesturing in other things. Tallied from her first planting, when
mistaken, all, for weeds, and pulled, the heap of glory tendrils
magnified her looking at the finally let first-come, cone-shaped buds;
their spiral narrowing added, the thinnest leaf,
the star retained at the wholly opened rim, all added, profusion
added by midday, the singing, sobbing blue added, and
each like each with on gesture for infinity, the throats so white,
the scent negligible, added, the clinging, added, the daily ending,

added, the blue exhaling into fuchsia, the late flesh blown,
the inexplicable rewind of the thing, backward and looser
but the same motion in return, added, until she heard
she had been wheeled under an arch of these each summer day
at eight months old. Her mother spoke the words,
who speaks no more. No sum.
It may be the long-dried uncut grass is touched by
an almost evenhanded, reasonable water
each leaf has given something to by bending
so, by bending down.

11.

Abraham Jamnitzer is long dead, may be a pearl,
two pearls, a leaf of grass, a laurel tree. Coral was thought
essential, quintessential, nature's perfect child,
touching (*touched by*) all three realms.
Her limbs: the right leg is exposed. Her silver thigh
shines out from underneath her silver gown. The other seems
to live inside. Her silver sleeves, at elbow length, are puffed,
and banded twice. One red hand/branch is split
three ways; one four, with two emerging nubs.
Pliny, Natural History, Book II: *not even for God*
are all things possible— for he cannot, even if he wishes,
commit suicide... The power of nature is what we mean

12.

by the word God.   ... hail is produced from frozen rain
and snow from the same fluid less solidly condensed,
but hoar frost from cold dew; snow falls during winter
but not hail, and hail itself falls more often in the daytime
than at night, and melts much faster than snow;
mists do not occur in summer, nor in extremely cold weather,
nor dew in frosty or very windy weather, and only on fine nights;
liquid is reduced in bulk by freezing, and when ice is thawed

the bulk is not the same; variations of colour and shape
are seen in clouds in proportion as the fire mingled with them
gains the upper hand.

13.

Again, a veiled baby,

one of many, one December,

will see the end of a century

with a pinched face

under a drapery of flames,

hair held in the hands again

as the hungry open their bags

of roses regarding air

a thousand thousand times, even

before birth, but also after

death, which always rains

on our village, where we live.

14.

Enter peach-like wearing yellow, buttercream,
coral, apricot, and salmon, you bridesmaids of speech;
her eyes have yet to be described. Gestured in
other things, the sobbing blue? *Look up*. No sum. It is

to suffer here. Who looks where the dying look
look at the world, but without the air
of the unworldly as it swells. Who looks
at a body held by death and finds words more faithful
than that groom and bride? Not one. No words,
no hand to give or take away, no upper hand.

15.

Without a care. White petal
on white petal, in porcelain,
one flower on a coiled stem
holds one candle, never lit, a
white flower with an effect
of after-white, given to
grey-white in the folds, and
redoubled in the mirror as a mantelpiece.
Look up. Repeated flower stems unwind
ad infinitum as a chandelier.
It blurs one's sense
of singularity. It is an affluence,
an edifice, a sense, not an idea,
of transformation's start.
Look back. Remember? *No, look back*
to your solitary mantelpiece.

16.

One sees the mirror, finally, rather than the self
reflected back, or that first pale flowering, and sees
the mirror also framed in porcelain
buttercups and primroses, but
with their color drained—
and that the walls bear plaster-frosted
creepers and leaves and flower heads,

white-on-white-on-white-on-white
in bas-relief. *Relief—*

17.

I received him in the dark. I had come to bear everything
bar being seen. Behold :: a naked, finger-long, ivory boy
seated on an ivory skull would make, if he could breathe,
a perfect ivory bubble with his pipe.
He doesn't wear but *is* the crown of "Contrefait Sphere
with an Allegory of Transience", Jacob Zeller,
Dresden, 1611. Here, bone is flesh, off-white as if off-white
was pushed from white by force into a further force
barely restrained in his raised legs, raised arms,
blown hair. The skull he sits on brings bone back to bone again,
but under it revolves, or would revolve, if we could touch,
a virtuoso piece. A turner shapes and hollows out
a bone-sphere by machine. From scrap he carves portrait medallions
to see behind round windows in the sphere. In Zeller's "Contrefait",
the portraits live inside inside, in an incised, revolving *if we could touch it*
world inside a world inside a world. One is not free to turn
and not turn in, turn into, turn away, turn back. The prince

18.

is dead at twenty-seven, green-white as a linden bloom.
A sister whimpers though she drowned.
A daughter wakes to feel her mouth foam-filled
as her mother dies in a distant bed.
Drought in summer. Lightning without rain, and then
a rain, and then long rain.

19.

Still stands our silver girl.
Her stillness stills the moving world in waves,
a blind eye rolling on a crowd
of sighted faces, felt to be
a kind of sight to those it does not see;
a bell hammered
in copper, dangling a wooden tongue:
it never rings;
one thinks one knows the sound.
Her arms are up. When rain falls, it falls
without once touching her. Her coral hands and thoughts appear
diffused because a coral widened undersea.

20.

Under all rocks,
something— see
even under water under a
river rock a wet-
ness but see what
is thought of one
who would look
for wetness there, or
for dryness in drought time.
To some end what
water did or what dry air was was
less unloved, more
unthought of, not so un-
seen as effortlessly known
and so thought turned away. No
language needed there.

***

Vault is a poem in 85 parts. Parts 1, 2, and 3 appeared in *The Laurel Review*, and *Oneiros Broadsides* published part 20 as a broadside.

4. Melk Benedectine Abbey, Melk, Austria. Sanssouci is Frederick the Great's yellow palace in Potsdam, Germany.
8. from *Reminiscences of the Family of Moody Chase, of Shirley, Mass.*, by William Moody Chase, my relative.
9. "If the brightness is a truce" is from Montale's Motets, as translated by Wm. Arrowsmith.
10. The first line, and the first half of the second are from Carter Smith's poem, "Therefore You Are That Other One You Love""
17. "I received him in the dark. I had come to bear everything bar being seen." Beckett, *Fizzle 2.*

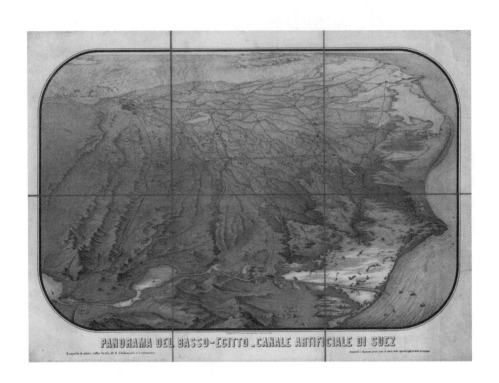

PANORAMA DEL BASSO-EGITTO _ CANALE ARTIFICIALE DI SUEZ

GUY JEAN

[Smoker's black exhales saturate sea's Abyss:]

Smoker's black exhales saturate sea's abyss:
in nightmares,
whose chromosomes
are carved with human instinct
of secrets, secrets:
what makes us–
us?
the love of bodies, of freckles, of imperfections, of us,
the song now soothes–who? wild souls?–us.

Translated from the French by Alyssabeth Knerr

Jenny Molberg

The Dream, The Sleeping Gypsy

In what would be his last work
Henri Rousseau painted a moon
in place of the sun, passive

as a dying woman. With his brush
he lit the girl's breasts,
two bright pomelos, the orbed

voyeuristic eyes of the lioness.
My mother's skin is artless,
her hands deft. She turns each page,

whispering the names. Seeing
in Rousseau not shadowless
brushwork, not a child's misconception

of the world as flat, but layers
over layers, his hand patient
as the acacia that rings its own grain

as the years pass, its wide taproot
drawing up from the earth
a strange, unutterable music.

I want to say my mother loves
the gourd-like lute as the thing
that most reflects the moon,

for it moves the eye from depth
to surface as if they were
the same. The few incisions

of light in the desert sky
strike the woman's long
sleeping hair, the lion beside her.

The moon's face
a cold white god. This
is the metastasizing beauty

of my mother. My mother the gypsy.
I, the pinpricked sky.
The lion her cancer.

KERRY SHAWN KEYS

PORTFOLIO

All Souls' Eve

Vilnius

How do we know it is All Souls' Eve
when the wind's already thieved the calendar
through the steamy air of the kitchen,
out the window, and into the gutter.

My son waves why and goodbye, and the pages
of the years that were so happily engaged
a moment ago in the brisk furniture of air,
now barely flap their corners in despair.

Are they dead, he asks why, but really he *says*,
and this prompts his sister to whirl, and flutter
her hands pretending that she is leaf and dove
let loose from a dark magic theatre above.

Brother, I can see the other side of life
where these yellow candles of my fingers
are dancing to sutartinės next to the stones,
and Christ's tears are turning to snow.

Sister, the calendar's in a pool of water,
does that mean that Time is dead
and why spirits will come to buzz by our bed
and feed us with mums and beebread.

Amazed by the strange talk of my children,
I bid them climb the chalk-white pony I'm riding,
and three Bellerophons on a lively errand
we fly to the graveyard to prance our bones,

to weep with Saint George for slaying the dragon,
and to kneel, three kids, before the chimera of Heaven.

Almost Invisible

for Sonata

Sunlight billows into her room half the day long as it should. Sometimes leaves are falling, and the light skitters between the leaves to get in. When the leaves aren't falling, still nimbly attached to the branches of the birch trees, the light then gently flutters among the leaves and around the branches, and enters the window fluttering, and flutters on the carpet and wall dancing with its partners, the trembling shadows. She watches the spectacle on her wall from her bed, and at a certain time she knows the dance will end, though that moment of time mingles with the time of the day and the seasons, always changing. A leaf falls on her bed. Another on the windowsill. Then on her. Another time will come when only the shadow of the branches and the broken light will dance on her wall, a much slower dance through the moisture on the window. The leaves will carpet the ground in yellow and brown. Then she will wait for the moonlight to come into the room. Earlier in late summer, the apples in the apple tree shimmered silver in the moonlight. The bark of the birches also silver. The apples now have all fallen or been picked and eaten, given to lovers and children.

She gets out of bed and stands framed in the window as if in a Hopper painting, looking out at the empty branches, the windows across the way, a few visible stars, the moon. She shimmers silver in its light like a glass of champagne at a wedding without a bride or groom, and she sees her face in the windowpane, a nimbus of air covered with drops of water, almost invisible, delicately attached to the darkness as the moonlight slithers across the branches of the apple tree and the birches.

Looking Out

the outside North looking in
that expanse of light
filling my eyes and the room
an ideal light I'm told
for making images of the world

that may be

there's nothing painterly about me

instead I stand here in this script
looking out
at the Athens of the North
the chimney tops and bricks the smoke

the bone-ash pastel of dusk's nondescript brushstroke

the faucet drips
                    haphazardly

stray tomcat spray
marks the entranceway
so that nowadays the angel of death stays away
as do the seraphim and Purim puppet plays

evening's getting dark now
and my hungry eye barely makes out
the drab zodiacs of antennae

the moon sets to the side of the frame
felt but unseen

planets are playing charades as satellite disks

barely audible
dirges and dybbuks hum in the shoal of the urban buzz

of time and space and emptiness

and I listen as best I can
locked inside myself

unknowable smoldering motionless

looking out

The Fountain of Youth

Only a stone's throw from the church of Saint Kotryna,
my happy-go-lucky children are throwing dozens of stones
into a broken-down fountain graced by the head of a lion.
I've told them nothing about desire and its vagrant wishes.
For them it's a game of getting wet and plips and splashes.
As for throwing coins for luck, they know nothing of this,
never suspecting anyone could be blessed in the heart of Vilnius.
Anyway, today I don't have any wisdom or coins to give them,
or obols or hunks of sea-washed amber or precious gems.
Besides, if these little Cyclopes had their way, they would plop rocks
or some looted, busted off piece of rococo or baroque.
Instead, I point out a few dandelions thrusting their sunny heads
through the dilapidated sidewalk, and like most kids
they already know what the dazzling florets will soon become,
resurrecting into the breathing of parachuting seeds of fuzzy cotton.
Like little gods, they are eager for some change or experiment,
so they don't at all mind my baptismal suggestion to "transplant"
the golden, severed heads into the fountain along with the stones
to see if they'll float like Christ or sink like an adulteress to the bottom –
an old man's gratuitous game. Fortunately, the young don't listen long,
and soon decide to take a bouquet of them back to their mom
to put in a tiny vase to regale the pallid parlor of their home,
where fittingly they will droop milkless and dead by morning.
But I'm getting too far ahead of myself. They're back with their stones
at the fountain with this would-be king of rock-throwers watching them
with admiration as grown-ups so often do, grown-ups addicted
to more Sisyphean and melancholy pastimes. Reverie can be seductive,
and soon I am far away from wherever I am, in some other land,
imagining myself picking myself up and throwing flesh and bones
over my own shoulder, turning into God's clay again, or better yet, stone.

Robin

The robin's breast
must be full of blood.
He gets up early
and slurps the red worms.
He smashes his soul
on a mash of berries and frost.
He mates with the moon
on its joyride in the grass.
And in the days of his youth
he ate the sun
climbing the mountain.

Sweet Robin

Sweet robin,
how long's it been
since you came
with your red napkin
to my table to dine.
The sun's gone down
ten thousand times,
the moon risen the same.
Sweet Robin,
bloody on the lawn
ear lying
sideways to nothing,
night tunneling
through your brain.
and mine.

Trout

The trout's blood run cold in the rill,
I bent and picked it up, fuck-finger
up the gill, and, by God, felt it was a fresh kill –
for what dies is killed. Rainbow-glittery, I trophied
it up to his mythical heavenly face, and cursed
the placid indifference as blood sluiced
down the rillets of my life-line mapping mud-caked
tributaries running out of time. On call,
I dipped God's catch back into the cheerless glass
of that darkling catacomb of alchemic cold, releasing it
from the fork-lift of my grip, belly-up, to twist and rush
downstream into a nether world of oceanic things.
My portion? to cup my slimy hands and suck up
a kind of dumb-show Hyperborean communion.

The Lens

Trees are washing the film from the air. Peroxide and chlorophyll
mix with wax as if feathers of water were dripping
leaf by leaf to the center of a huge drum.
Trees wash the air. When a stick shifts into the mouth,
the smoke goes everywhere. Her breath goes everywhere also,
but always wavers between her arms and the earth.
These trees have silver needles, and they puncture the darkest pupils
with a cold light born before the birth of this world.
Ferns grow out of the bricks at the edge
of the building, and a deer steps into the picture.
It smells like linseed oil and chloroform, fur covered
with patches of tar and denim, changing its shape every second.
Over and over for many years now, many times, it looks
straight into the eyes of the car, and his hand goes up under
her skirt, and his skinky fingers are thick with perfume.
Their shadows begin to crisscross toward the center
of the road. The brakes bring everything together.
Suddenly he's dead. She screams her nylons are torn.
Flowing over the serene lake of the lens, the soft eyes
are in my arms, fur at my neck. If only now I could close
the pores of this memory, and let the syllables of another world
begin to wash the coal-dark air with their breath.

Borders

She rolls an eyeball down the plaster
and sips vodka from the palm of her hand.
Refugees stream from the granaries to the cities.
Earth sips her from the deliverer.
Flowers are islands. Islands are carnelian.
It's fluorescent at night. Green. It puts
a raindrop of semen in the technology,
while a wolf, surveying its kingdom,
obediently falls asleep on the terrace.
My plan is to dream I'm awake
in a silent film by Hokusai, falling
all over myself. Her dream is to plan
I'm her step-father crucified on the jade horns
of an insect. Wasabi and rice wine
in the blood are pure lands unto themselves.
She will also dream of a birch tree,
and a yellow balloon bursting on the declensions
of her tastebuds. Anima will rush over the fence.
Candles and crosses surround the home
of the antlion and the woman of the dunes.
This story is a document of our aesthetic contract.
This is a natural area protected by a natural guard standing
still as a stopwatch, sand shifting through its hands.

Civilization and Its Contents Redefined

stood up by the Muse
and so in her bed
fucked you instead

The Actress

Kalamazoo, Yale, New York, Hollywood,
a few miscarriages along the way, soft-porn surfer food,
a dozen marriages in disarray, she shouldn't, she should,
she shouldn't shoot up but she damn well will
and soon hits Hell's paydirt as she twists and shouts
at the Pollock print above the bed in her hotel.
Yes, tonight, torso torn and turned inside out
as if a yoga-advertisement's elixir of diva despair,
she's been sucking the toxins from the liver
of every role she once upon a time delivered,
and kissing to death the aging menace
of mascara-smutted tongue and lips
that haunts the mirror that's been stalking her
down each garish, chlorine-green, 3-star corridor.
Look carefully, mon audience, at her once gorgeous
figure dredged dumb, converging to the floor,
curling up from a confused, pro-life, aborted fetus
into a fish-like stillborn, scripted stupor. Please,
an encore, that at last she'll surface this world's theatre
passing through the wings and green room of desire
for the literal one that gave birth to her,
cunningly promising her the promised land
of her mirror's once youthful imagination.

Two Vignettes

Carnival Along The Susquehanna
–Danzante

Tonight I'm a Lydian bitch going out into the snow
downtown with toenails painted red, bosom erect.
Honeybee Butch with Carolina Cunt. We hold fingers,
shotgun hemp. A pediatric intern at the fetal clinic
faints into a cloud of jet wash and formaldehyde. A cop
crawls over the ice and washes our feet with mace.

Arson My Ass
at Leiby's

moving the mattress mildewed with bloodtype O
onto the sidewalk, we make love in the trailer park
between the snow and a wind-chill factor of minus 6 F.
A black cat screams from the asphalt. The manager comes out
and tells us not to park our butts in front of the fireplug.
I squirt him with crystal meth and dial 900 on the cellular.

Vila Isabel Flashback

Sitting on the tile floor again in Vila Isabel, fidgeting,
staring at Parrot's Beak and the stolen tennis shoes
hanging on a wire against the outline of the Southern Cross.
Such devotion to the past is a dilapidated dream
that the inanity of memory can fix things, even the present.
I'm repeating over and over, "pretty boy" "pretty boy"
but the mountain is silent and not hungry.
Coffee-cup with maté smashed to smithereens
against the gangrenous black fungus on the plastered wall.
An incoherent scream descends from the watertank on the roof
as other protesters have the freeway up their butts stuffed
with lit cigarettes and small slivers of prismatic
confiscated daylight. The candlepower of the moon scrapes the barbs
of multi-colored glass cemented to the courtyard wall
to keep out the ethnically uncleansed poor
and Exu's dogs and goats disguising themselves as tomcats.
Someone just vomited into the flowerpot I call Cupid's cauldron.
Perfected lovers seldom think gravity or time a terrorist.
(I take a long drag and dispatch a revolution of rings into the darkness)
Perfect lovers on the other hand suffer from vertigo.
The Ice Age is returning. I can hear its fanbelt pulling and tugging
skaters around the rink in the strip mall of my heart.
Weeds will go out of business and Balthus will paint a still life
of an extinct nymph sunning herself like a brachiopod in a doorway.
Candled kites are fluttering into the stretched canvas.
The steaming masses want a Nordic welfare state, and the students
are in favor of dialectical breasts and banning football and samba.
The watertank is pierced by a high C scream
and calories and centavos liberated to roll across the floor.
The ceiling over my earth is leaking. My messmate's underwear
moistens in excitement that the trademarks of the hierarchy
are coming to an end. A bat flaps its membranes through
a thickening cloud of hemp hovering over the hillside favela.
You turn out the lights and swing to sleep in the hammock.
Tonight, you will drown in the unattended glossary of your dreams.

Consolation Prize

for K.P.

I listen to the birds fly by of course.
I'm indifferent to the ways of women and men.
I tell them of course what there isn't to know,
    and my blood freezes over from drinking
    the slow water of their dreams.
She was taking a sponge-bath in her father's brain.
If you were to live like me, the sun would drop runic arrows
    in your throat. You'd sprout plumes and zippers.
I gave her a blue ribbon for her squirming epiphanies.
What do you know of pleasure or pain.
We are eating an apple in a stable at the racetrack
    but your hands and head will be severed.
Your mouth is painted with Elmer's Glue.
A cow migrates from the Indus to Europe.
You will piss from a hole decorated with black flags.
Your tongue is a dead snake in unsloughed pantaloons.
I eat the birds flying over the classifications and the buzzings,
    the trains and the hyperventilating volcanoes.
They give me money for my services.
Is the sky blue. I will take this pumice and crush it
    with my teeth into little people. Watch.
Cicero is a raindrop. Babel a papermill.
I am a pebble in a fountain on a mountain. Children love
    rhythm and rhyme, come to me in and out of time.
The body when it separates from the soul perishes
    in a Heaven of sheep.
The soul stays behind, chirping, chirping, chirping,
    like a bird at a street-crossing for the blind.

The Start Point. N.E. b N.º

The Bele Head. W.N.W.º

Dunnose. W. b N.

Dover Castle. N.E. ¼ N.   South Foreland E.N.E.

The South Foreland, and Shakespears Cliff.

Entrance of Dover Harbour.

Calais Town and Cliff.

Engrav'd for I.T. Serres's Little Sea Torch, and Pub. by him. London 1801.

Vicky Santiesteban

The Heat Is

for William Carlos Williams

With all respect, Doctor, the orifice from which I speak
is filthy as the cat you kicked from your bed last night.
I've come to you, specifically, for pharmaceuticals

but instead of the saccharine cherry you stick me with
your pitiful perversions. Don't call the nurse—I hate
the nurse with her mercury fingers and starched white dress.

(You dreamed yourself writing this poem, dreamed me
crossing a wet pasture naked at dawn offering this broken
cup of poison, this odor of box, this *chore*.) Doctor:

I've come to you for a cure, not to stand on my hind
legs and perform. Come, let's share a vial of blue,
one for me, three for you, then let us

dream on our backs in a bed in your farmhouse
with your scalpel and steady hand, come let us carve
the puckish poem that made me make you a man.

Contemporary Poetry from the African Continent

PORTFOLIO

Edited with an Introduction by Kwame Dawes
and Chris Abani

KWAME DAWES AND CHRIS ABANI

Introduction to Feature: Contemporary Poetry from the African Continent, 2016

Each year, we are finding ourselves more and more impressed with the quality, range and volume of work being produced by African poets living on the continent and outside of the continent. We are noticing the conversation that is now taking place between the poets whose work is appearing in print and those aspiring to have their work appear. And we are noticing a remarkable way in which the poetics that are emerging reflect a growing sense of the broader poetic world, while remaining fully and innovatively rooted in the traditions of poetry and aesthetics from their "home-spaces." Energy. This is what one senses. A growing energy that is creating the kind of heat that generates lively productivity and innovation. The poets are taking command of language, of poetic forms, of idioms, and are fully inscribed in the notion that they are able to write into being, through poetry, a narrative of identity and place. It is still too early for those of us who are working hard to create a space for these poets to be published to start speaking of a new African poetics. It is too early, and largely pointless for us to even attempt to do this. What we can do, however, is take away the sense of hopelessness, disregard and futility that haunted these poets when they felt that their work was just not going to get a chance to be shared with the wider world. It would be foolish to underestimate just how important possibility is for a poet working in isolation. These poems are just a few of the latest crop of writers who are busy honing their craft and producing poetry of dynamism and beauty today.

And yet, while we cannot speak definitively of the shape and form and even aesthetic values of a new African Poetics, we can acknowledge that the struggle to form expression around this idea is itself already an indication that is has begun, that a new thrust of poetic form and expression has begun, and it a humbling and beautiful thing to witness and to be part of the formative drive, even if only in the hope that we are guiding a transformation to its birth. The energy and drive here, the newness and hope hasn't been felt since Christopher Okigbo's *Come Thunder* and the responses from Awonoor. And while the poets of the past where trying to define "Africa" against the West, these new poets are defining self and the poetics not against anything so much as within a new global sense, a new form of cosmopolitanism that isn't the smoothing out of difference but rather the convergence on clear points of Africaness while bursting into simultaneous global senses and presences and selves. The most important thing that the African Poetry Book Fund and its many facets of expression have proven is not that there is newness, the history of the continent is always about new expression, but rather that African poetry always has been and always will be, and it will no longer be ignored.

Lena Bezawork Grönlund

Still Life

First there is the port.
The port of belongings.
Then there is the black-
and-white photograph,
his twenty-year-old frightened
face, her sunken, distraught eyes.
Then there is the still life.
The life of the photograph.
There are the actual
years. The twenty-seven years.
The ten thousand days, my mother's
death somewhere in between.
Then there is the meeting
him, my father and me
at the table in the house
with the blue walls. I look at him
with her thin shoulders
against the wall, his thin face,
his startled look and her deep lines
under my eyes.

Chekwube O. Danladi

Oji River Police College

In Enugu, the harmattan does not rage too harsh.
At 5:45 p.m., aunty and I begin our walk, 40 minutes,
a gleaming dusk eating our heels, our footsteps paced to match.
My skin rides on the teeth of biting flies, Aunty recalling
her day's due grievances and I am obliged to listen,
counting flecks of grayorange on lizards' backs.

She laughs at me often, saying,
Strange my dear, these your eyes, they swallow everything,
My mouth, glum and outstretched, mutters an affirmation.
You must know that I began to lose my sight when I left this country.
Do you understand?

There is no quotidian.
Let me weep to women's high worship,
rising from every church on every night,
every sunset too winsome,
the burn of bitter leaf soup beguiling,
grant me use of sense I still maintain.

I find two cures for this.
The first: to wash my eyes of fog in the Oji River, and look fast to the sun.
The second: there is a small cluster of shops near the road
where men sell bread and okada fuel.
Aunty sends me to buy one loaf for tea,
a tin of malt chocolate.
I stop at the stand where the proprietor looks most like me.
He holds my hands before the naira, calls me sister.
When I am leaving, he calls me beautiful.

I want to tell him I am pained for looking.
I want to tell him to let his own eyes rest.

Yasmin Belkhyr

& the Song of the Swan Drifts

When I was alone in the city, every man spoke my name. Called me rivergirl, mouthsore. Habiba. Habibti. The ovens flared and spit, slabs of meat browning, boys with seaborn eyes slapping the air with folded newspapers. Bees dozed around the hot mess of honey and butter, and I have a woman's body but a girl's voice when I ask for chebekia, for zmita, for m'smmen. Beyond us, the goats wailed. Tails swinging at mosquitos swollen lazy with their blood. Portraits of our king in every doorway. Every man I walk by imagines our children, his hand on my waist. My mother was in Taza or Casa or New York. My father was dead or the king or a god. A bushel of mint cost me one dirham. The family next door caught me smoking out the window. Later that night, I thought I was dying. I remember lying on the bed, clenching my stomach and thinking, *I am dying*. Every night that week, I had the same dream: a man knee-deep in water, his hand in my mouth, pushing my teeth into my teeth.

Ejiofor Ugwu

The Plague
for Kofi Awoonor

And they hurried him away
into emptiness,
and so will his blood
gather fire,
and the millions still blazing out
all over the Sahara.
I am curled up here in Ajaokuta
atop a rock
where the sun has gone to bed,
my chins heavy in my hands
waiting,
watching
as the blood pursues us and
the diseased earth
till the world is eaten away
so that we can live.
There is life in our dust.

ASHLEY MAKUE

peace offering

i have decided that
love may no longer
summon me to war
i have laid off my troops
blood bathed my body
clean of all sin
i will no longer kiss
like breaking my law
or make love
like being broken into
i will clear my eyes
of all my specks
and then i shall see you

you see
these are the days
of the sweet treaty

VICTORIA ADUKWEI BULLEY

Fifteen

With a hopscotch grid for a wrist
see my sad boy

with a smile like a one-string guitar
relative to nobody, yet out of tune,

dropping out of school
out of line, saying

I love you more than life itself
in a first Valentines card

during the spring term
in which we turn fifteen.

In the attic of an old phone, now,
here he is again

in the drawer I was cleaning out
during a hymn I was singing

before I met him
and here he is, my sad boy –

now watch this older girl stop
and cast her day out with the dust

and become sad too.

This whole impermanence thing is deceptive,
looks lifelong, actually, to me

sat here still molding mason jars
of words to preserve him with,

wondering if a poem ten years on
is still a pining, asking

how many more I will make
before I learn how little of us keeps.

Chimwemwe Undi

The Habitual Be

Of course we come together different,
found a better way to separate this breath
from our bad habit of living, to name a
circle a circle and disregard a line.
Of course we're mended with gold,
we're made from it. Take our new shards
and tint our laughter all yellow,
bust through paper bags.

Remember when the water crept up
& drowned all the sinners
& God made a promise we keep tempting Them to break?
Remember the fruit, how good it tasted,
how it reminded us what else our holy mouths
were for? O hell yes!
We were built to remember,
to walk on water and right on through it,
to swallow the moon and swear we're still hungry.
The language is a dance we know all the steps to.
We conjugated a life into a second coming,
and then another,
then a fourth,
endless forth.
Our mouths remember themselves, electric sliding
tongue, sampling history like soul beat. Forget you
know all the moves until the music starts.
And of course,
of course we are built of memory,
threatened to become nothing but,
but stay knowing
to double a negative does not turn it yes.

Check our iterative existence, our defiant glory,
the way we are and are and are
and be.

MARY-ALICE DANIEL

Innocent Nigeriana

Returning to a place after 17 years,
after an uncle's third wife
has bitten the ear off his second wife:

The carpet as the same carpet.
The children are like children.
There is a beehive under the front seat of the Volkswagen.
Dogs Pavlov to another language and what once
           was a house is now a table of water.

A feud that made my mother cry,
and my aunts drive to airport lounges,
calling us in England,
asking what shall they do.

And *road* that should not be called *road*:
more an obstacle than a way through.
We settle in Illela on the cold plateau
where grow custard apples, where
frost kills thirty-five chicks in one night.
    Blue of twilight—only thing
like a body of water we'll see for weeks.

Men pray in the umbrage of a small mountain:
for their wives and their sore throats, for daughters:
girls who belong wholly to their mothers.
At each wedding, a child wears a wedding gown—
the custom of the little bride.

Flies, tenacious as bark, involve themselves
in the work of preparing food.
Mosquitoes pool in the poverty:
swollen plastic bags full of water and bacteria.
Tonight, my arm is a constellation of moonlit bites.

Innocent Nigeriana: the ripe moment.
Engorged world and its quiet. I learn

that goats are afraid of thunder.
The eldest butts its head against
the kitchen door, trying to break in.
The lesser ones bleat pathetically all night,

    wanting to be let inside,
    certain they are human

FAMIA NKANSA

No Man's Land

There is a country between us
and it is neither Ghana nor the US

          It is not the man you haven't fucked yet,

the run of chords
beneath your shorts,
the Langston Hughes
that was our start,
the braid
of sighs flooding
the ankhs
stitched in the fabric
on my wall,
Unathi,
whose father
was shot at the Sharpville riots,
tugging my twists after her hug
before she looked from you to me back to you
and then down
at the pinstriped floor,
the way you run in the rain,
the Seahawks
sticker on your car,
the page of your back
inside my hands, the
Mariama Bâ letter
I will write when we
are done.

Remember that dog
you lost
to some
speeding train.
The way
I laughed
at how
you mourned.

Momtaza Mehri

Transatlantic (take two)

We wanted a music they couldn't play
—Thelonious Monk on bebop (and us I think)

Over coffee and a pecan maple, they sit.
A Thursday midmorning is as good a time as any
to discuss the generational dull ache of
second-guessing.

A god conveniently wearing the same face, genitals
as tax collector / border guard / leering judge.
He carries a police baton / its fall is a language we both understand
though the stretch / of / syllables often differs
from shore / to / shore. So?

His people / Her people (God, aren't we a mess?)
Aren't they beautiful, despite everything,
or maybe because of everything? Semantics, he brushes aside crumbs, bulldozes
a heap of granulated brown.
Asks her if she knows the song they're playing right now, over speakers.

Under his placemat, a colony leaks, breaking
Tilbury dock banks.
Hers, an exiled song of hardheaded old women
and loose laughter.

They will leave soon, snake past the train station.
Stake a claim in the cities between each other's teeth,
much like the caffeine / itself
browning their grin,
much like the / fluoride / of the old city
itself.

GABRIEL OKARA

Rural Dweller

It's cock-crow!
She draws her aching limbs
On her creaking bamboo bed;
And once again to the farm she must go,
As she has done at every cock-crow
Since these months of sowing before the rains.
Her face lined with furrows of labor
And her hands calloused and fingers
Twisted like scraggy roots of a hillside tree,
For her oil lamp she gropes
In the morning darkness
As the sound of passing lorries
Fails to drown the song of early birds
From far and near, filling the morning air
With gladdening sounds,
But the sounds pass her by unheard
For her mind is stuck on her hoe!

At last she stands outside her hut
Of wattle and mud, gazing at the morning sky.

The trees slowly take form, drawn
By the rising sun and woken to life by the wind,
They sway back and forth in time
With rhythm unheard, unseen in the morning sky.
And weakened by age, her feed tremble, but with steps
Tradition-urged, she goes her wonted way to the farm
With a hoe, untouched by time, in a basket, on her head.
Thus she walks with no lodgment in her thoughts
Of promised changes for the better at dawn
As she turns off the asphalt road into a foot path,
Seen only by her uncluttered mind and
Tradition-taught vision!

20 June 1978

PATRICIA JABBEH WESLEY

To Libya: February 2011

When all is finally said and done,
there will be masses of graves of masses,

broken glass of pierced people,
and the children dying or already dead.

Somewhere, on a side street, someone's hair,
forgotten after the clean-up.

Shreds of hair on pavement, the reminder.
        And the counting of those

taken away at night will not begin

        until we have already forgotten
who it was that was taken.

MUKOMA WA NGUGI

Framing Your Picture
For Maureen

Takes a long time to find the right frame,
and longer still to decide on framing you.
Thrift store to thrift store. No! This one
will not do, looks too much like a prison.
That one reeks of ownership. This one
—a bad poem—it hides nothing.
And…who wants to be seen through glass
like a mannequin? But this love of ours
has friends, and Paul brings an old frame.
It stands on iron. It will not bend or break.
Not a prison but a fortress. It will do.
Over the phone I ask—have you by any chance
been feeling protected? You laugh.
I shall leave you framed.

TSITSI JAJI

The Go-Betweens

Mai's bridewealth:
a letter of resignation to the board of missions; duplicates to the supporting
congregations; two plane tickets; two ceremonies; two receptions, one large.
Being American, her family made no further claims. Neither did her adopted
African family.

*

Grandpa's wedding gift to Mai and Baba:
one piano and two pecan trees. Chickens were barbecued. Fish were caught.

*

The bridewealth of Mainini Fay, Mai's adopted sister:
various beasts, cash and goods, up to and including furniture and a fridge, to
which Mai objected, shaming the adopted brothers. These were deducted, but
remain in her account of the saga.

*

The bridewealth for my young brother's bride to be:
given as calves to him at age four. A slighted elder sister, I raised cane, and
also got a few. The cows stayed on the farm, *kumusha*. Babamunini counted,
corralled, herded, nursed, milked, cleaned, prodded, yoked, slaughtered them.
So, ask him if you need to know which ones are which, or when they died.

*

The bridewealth of my grandmother, Ambuya:
unresolved. When her husband died and again when she was gone, these factored
into burial ceremonies as fines to be paid in goats. And Moneygrams.

*

A house for Ambuya and Sekuru *kumusha* was the first thing Mai and Baba built
together. It was bricks and cement filled with store-bought sofas with bumpy
knots of wool and green melamine plates and there was a wood-burning iron

stove that was never used once. It sat in the kitchen built off the side of the brick house, and Ambuya kept the key on string around her waist.

*

So I find myself paying the bridewealth owed by Babamunini, my uncle, who is my small father by virtue of being the younger brother to my father. Babamunini, who beat his own mother once when his medication ran out. Forgive me, Mainini, my little mother. My mental math tells me you will live longer.

KWAME DAWES

The Etymology of Hubris

The late actor's wife,
the famous poet,
lectures me humbly
on the etymology of hubris –

all Greek she says,
nothing in our dialect
for it – by "our",
she means generously,

America, though here
in deep winter,
I walk my cockapoo
under the gentle tyranny

of the prideful
humility of the Midwest –
a collective hubris.

My daughter calls
from another city,
crying for her loneliness,
but laughing at the absurdity of it.

Together we wonder,
where will we build a kraal
for our clan, with its own boneyard
for our scattered dead?

Real Situation

For John Kinsella

There is then,
this helplessness,
and we are not in search
of leaders,
not in search of prayers,
we simply carry a weight
in us, as if perhaps
we should know
the calculus of violence.

We began in silence,
the intrusion of elegies
on our daily rituals for beauty,
and these elegies are the mutterings
of meaning, as if by lamentation
and praise we defy
the madness around us,
as if by song
we learn to live.

I admit, now,
my desire for ancient myths,
not the bloodlessness
of dusty hexameters –
I do not see my broad
nose in the marble and stone –
and though I know
of the split innards
of those ghetto islands
at the under belly of civilization,
I prefer my myths
to smell of what I fear most:
the broken bodies,
the bleeding, the thin
line of yellow shit,
the flies.

John, I know that here
in these songs,
I am rehearsing
Marley's despair –
"There ain't no use,
no one can stop them now…"
– in that after season,
his body rotting away,
his face hollow as a saint
waiting for the flame,
his every word alight
with clean suffering
"no one can stop them now…"

And this is how we survive:
blind to all, deaf to all, drunk to all,
or constantly leaking
from every pore
every bewildering sorrow,
those lasting things,
the elegies of our peace.
I see the bodies ripped,
I see the tents erected still,
I see the secret compacts,
I see the rites of greed,
I see the beheadings,
I see the on-screen flashes –
how disposable our bodies are –
and no one can stop them now…

How then is it that here,
in this garlanded moment,
I find such comfort
in these muddy lines?
These are the clumsy words
of a drunk priest who has exposed
his nakedness to the believers,

and now they pity him,
pity his stammering,
and have lost the mysterious hold
his art had on them,
but every song must fade,
and what is left
will be ash,
and this, too,
is fine.

Chris Abani

Koan

The riddle of iron.
The indifference of knives.
The slap of water on wood.
Stone.
Ember.
The resistance of stages.
The body in dance.
The lift of albatross.
The destiny of rain.
Stone.
Ember.

Cremation

Smoke and ash augur loss the night
My mother feeds her diary into flame,
Sheet by sheet, line by cursive line,
And then a wind weaves through, just enough
To blow a flame back at her, searing skin.
She hesitates a moment, penitent, then pulls back.
Did she let it hurt for one second too long for regret,
Or for the sweet torture of fire?
She smiles at me: sometimes you just burn your life
And begin again. And even again.
No ink is permanent, she mutters.
No path carved in stone.
I watch the single blister rise on her hand
The size of a baby's heart.

The Calculus of Faith

That way the shrill of cicadas traps
a summer evening in the thrall of fear.
And doubt enters and you wonder –
is the question where is the light, or when?
A simple story is never easy.
That is an elegance learned hard.
Distant thunder and the rustle of muslin in the window.
What do you seek? Story or lighthouse?
Vision or revelation?
When did I first taste a fig and say
this is a fig I am tasting?
Shadows draw their knees up in the corners.
The first miracle I remember holding was
a mango, full and weighty with ripeness.
The second miracle was an onion skin sheet
of paper torn from a King James Bible
filled with oregano and thyme and smoked.
The third miracle was the smooth
turquoise of my mother's fountain pen.
The roll of it, the insistent pull of its nib
and words, glorious and alive.
I also remember my fear like a hole I crawl into.
A hollowed out log, a curve in a stump.
If you listen, if you listen –
In the book I am reading it is raining.
I seek questions for answers I want to keep
I seek with the elegance of planets
a constellation of inquiry.
When I had spent my pocket money on sweets,
I cut a candle in half
to make two votives, to double my prayers.
There are always two kinds of people –
and then all the others.
In the end we realize that
every human body is a scripture.

Symposium
on Kwame Dawes

Edited by Cecily Nicholson and Hari Alluri

CECILY NICHOLSON AND HARI ALLURI

Introduction: Like Prophesy in Waves

> ...The absence
> of shadows, storms looming, the clay
> when each evening of laughter
> does not feel like ominous calm
> before the shattering of all things.
> —"Rupture," in *Duppy Conqueror: New and Selected Poems*

The multiple aches in these lines, their vernacular ease charged by the complex undercurrents they carry, offer in their completeness a manifestation of lineages in the work of Kwame Dawes. They resonate with the reggae aesthetic he identifies in *Natural Mysticism*, "an aesthetic which unites body, emotions, and intellect and brings into a single focus the political, the spiritual and the erotic;" they seem to recall Dawes' predecessors St. Lucian poet Derek Walcott and Ghanaian poet Kofi Awoonor; they speak of ruined marriages while moving in a cycle of poems that shift their rhythms and speech as they attend to the blues and August Wilson, U.S. regional history and the violence of racism and much more and always, always, to a complex and redemptive humanity entwined with a redemptive and complex earth. His work exemplifies comparative poetics—of Ghana and Africa, of Jamaica and the Caribbean, of black diasporic experiences and writing in the U.S. and the U.K.—multi-tonal, drawn through varied perspectives and personas with a singular yet encompassing voice.

> ...I hear myself turning
> heir to the generation that understood the smell
> of burning flesh, the grammar of a stare
> —"Parasite," in *Midland*

The following three essays—drawn from *Poetry International*'s online symposium on the work of Kwame Dawes—examine specific lines and arcs of Dawes' poetry, thought and praxis to address his impact personally, socially and historically. All three essays place Kwame's work in conversation with his antecedents and contemporaries—literary, theoretical, cultural—offering insights poets can uniquely apply to how we approach thematics, aesthetics and craft.

Specifically, Honorée Fanonne Jeffers focuses on how Dawes' *Requiem* employs clarity in narrative, rendering in nuanced ways the "common ancestral and historical concerns" of black poets; Vladimir Lucien attends to how the long-poem *Prophets* embodies "the complex sacred" specific to Caribbean experience, unsettling the received contradictions of what is sacred and what is profane; John Robert Lee explicates quotes from *Natural Mysticism* on the reggae aesthetic, offering reflections on and propositions for its historical and ongoing influence on Caribbean ways of being, community and literary practices.

> a host of holy witnesses
> so far away from the humid
> air of home.
> —"Bruised Totems," in *Bruised Totems*

As a way into the arcs intoned above, we place into conversation brief excerpts from the essays in the full online symposium by authors who have reached, through rigorous examination, an intimacy with the facets of Dawes' work.

Several authors perceive that Dawes attains, in subject matter as well as form, a pervasive sense of both burden and lightness in his poems. For Corinna McLeod, this can be recognized by minding the way, in his depictions, "freeing, or escaping, or emerging are still about a sense of remembrance." In "Prophet Man," Shara McCallum notes that Dawes "retraces how various peoples have come together in the context of the Caribbean and finds power in acknowledging the resulting fault-lines of history. He… invokes faith as a means to face fractures… in the world as we experience it." This act of retracing is echoed by Ishion Hutchinson when he describes "the moment the light's changing scansion resembles his lines." Hutchinson could easily have been speaking of these:

> With my eyes closed, I am drunk with the mellow,
> swimming, swimming among the green of better days;
> and I rise from the pool of sound, slippery with
> the warm cling of music on my skin
> —"Shook Foil," in *Shook Foil*

Dawes invokes faith in the sacred, in the body, in music, art and literature, responding to what Hutchinson calls "the legend that says the poem is the cry of the occasion and faith is work" not just in his poetry but in his essays, especially once he becomes, in McLeod's words, "fully cognizant of the influence reggae music had had on his own personal and literary formation." Linton Kwesi Johnson discusses the ongoing labor of rewriting the tradition of reggae poetics into contemporary times, noting that Dawes' perspective calls forth "a decolonised, postcolonial approach to the creation, appreciation and criticism of Jamaican and Caribbean literature," and noticing "Flight" as "a good example of the 'reggae aesthetics' at work."

> Though hesitant, I will pit-stop over Babylon,
> in some third-world barrio like South Carolina's low country
> or them turtle-green islands where they preserve
>
> the tongue of Africa, lodged in seed and stomach
> —"Flight," in *Prophets*

If the portrayal of "the individual and collective experience of the African diaspora" through a "congregation of these utterances" is, as Kevin Simmonds suggests, something particularly "borderless" in the hands of "Ghanaian-Jamaican Kwame Dawes," this borderlessness extends to his HIV/AIDS activism and his refusal of patriarchal gender boundaries in his portrayal of women. As Rachel Eliza Griffiths points out in "What We Have Learned," "women persist in a rich music that is painterly, textured, and three-dimensional... You can see the eyes of the women in his poetry. These eyes look and speak back, aware of their power and their vulnerability."

There is a sense that Dawes is carrying forward, complicating and transforming multiple traditions. Lorna Goodison observes in the title essay of the symposium, "Poetry has never been the same since Kwame arrived on the scene, and that is a cause for rejoicing... Kwame's life project has at its heart a great overflowing generosity, which spills over into all he does for poetry, his own, and for the world of writers and writing."

> I am the water carrier.
> I feel the livid sweetness
> of my giving, and the bright
> alertness of this salt
> touching my tongue.
> —"Water Carrier" in *Gomer's Song*

***

For their generosity, we give thanks to all the symposium's contributors: Lorna Goodison, Rachel Eliza Griffiths, Ishion Hutchinson, Honorée Fanonne Jeffers, Linton Kwesi Johnson, John Robert Lee, Vladimir Lucien, Shara McCallum, Corinna McLeod and Kevin Simmonds. We offer further gratitude to Matthew Shenoda, Justine Henzell and Jeremy Poynting for their guidance and support. Finally, crucially, gratitude immense to Kwame Dawes himself for initiating many resources and contacts that made the symposium possible and, respect due, for making this work necessary.

HONORÉE FANONNE JEFFERS

Kwame Dawes' *Requiem*—Or, A Defense of Narrative in Black Poetry [1]

In the beginning chapter of his 1990 masterpiece, *Poétique de la Relation* (published seven years later in the United States as *Poetics of Relation*), the Caribbean poet, writer, and critic Édouard Glissant, uses the metaphor of the "abyss" to describe the Middle Passage, the journey on which over twelve million kidnapped Africans embarked to their eventual destination as slaves. This section on the horrors of the abyss, strangely rendered with such poetic language within a critical text, ends with something like a manifesto: "This is why we stay with poetry."

Appearing six years after Glissant's book, Kwame Dawes' *Requiem: A Lament for the Dead,* abides with his Caribbean compatriot, taking the Middle Passage as metaphysical text. Using the art of Tom Feelings as muse, Dawes writes/channels complex poems interrogating humanity at its most terrible, as in "Research," a poem that seems to mock the intellectualization of spiritual trauma: "We enter your holocaust/with trepidation/and leave the stench." There is no need for academic distance from this tragedy, Dawes insists, for there can be none for the descendants of this journey. There, in those waters of the Atlantic, Dawes connects with black ancestors.

For those of us who have read history and/or listened to old folks speaking of slavery, the stories of the Middle Passage and slavery are well known and to some, hackneyed, but in the collection's title poem, Dawes directly addresses this exasperation with black history:

> Do not tell me
> it is not right to lament,
> do not tell me it is tired.
> If we don't, who will
> recall in requiem
> The scattering of my tribe

---

[1] I don't limit "black" to "African American," for I'm speaking of the entire African Diaspora all over the globe. I'm speaking of the entire African Diaspora all over the globe. I'm speaking of the descendants of African peoples who remained tethered to their ancestral origins in a huge continent that, at this writing, contains fifty-four sovereign countries. And by "origins," I don't mean essentialist, phenotypic identity, but rather the examples of cultural production that exhibit African influences but not necessarily Pan-African sensibilities.

Here, he speaks to an unseen critic, and as the reader, I'm curious. Who is Dawes talking to? Who challenges him? A guilty white person, who will interject and try to evade responsibility for his own ancestors? To wit: "But Africans were involved in slave trading, too. You wouldn't be here on this side of the Atlantic is it wasn't for them."

Is Dawes speaking to another black person—a hardheaded young'un with no use for going back to the pain-filled days of slavery? Or, a scholar, such as Paul Gilroy, who both exalts the notion of the Black Atlantic but also, derides the nationalist inclinations of Afrocentrics? Or, is Dawes speaking to another poet, such as the ancestor, Robert Hayden, who declared that he didn't want to be a black poet? (He only wanted to be an American poet.)

Dawes is a poet able to claim many places. That is to say, if we talk about *place* critically—as imaginary space, as geographical location, as moment where the quotidian and the highest aesthetic hold hands in peace—Dawes is the Poet's Poet. *Requiem* is not his first foray into Diasporic matters, but more than a description of a subject, this book is an act of reverence.

Now, what does reverence have to do with narrative poetry? For me, a black poet concerned with the ancestral project, absolutely everything.

It's going to take some time to explain. To finally say what I've been afraid to say in my own career.

But it's only because of the model of Kwame Dawes, his courage, his artistic open- handedness, his stunningly beautiful poetry, and his amazing—and, sometimes to me, *intimidating*—artistic output, that I finally decided to write this piece.

So bear with me.

***

In the past two decades, there has been an aesthetic split between the "page and the stage," with page poetry probably winning the intellectual battle, but stage poetry winning over the audiences, with much grumbling and shade-throwing from page poets as a result.

Page poets, we rule in academia. We get the reviews in the literary magazines—and definitely in *The New Yorker* and *The New York Times*—and we get the teaching jobs. Stage poets, they rule in performance. They get the audiences screaming like at a rock concert, but they don't get respect for their brains.

I admit it: until recently, I never had much respect for spoken word poets. And those in the arena of Hip Hop who call themselves poets? Delusional, clearly.

One charge that I've heard thrown around very frequently is that stage poets write "accessible" poetry. Despite my (previous) sense of superiority about being a page poet, I never understood what was wrong with accessibility in a poem, with readers being able to comprehend what was on the page, but apparently, accessibility is supposed to be really, really bad. In order to be a great poet, one has to be very difficult to read; that's the message I've received these days. And for the past decade, I've noticed that accessible has been used as a synonym for a "narrative" poem.

I write mostly narrative poetry myself, poetry that, like Dawes's, tries to connect with the reader, that acknowledges there's a reader in the first place. However, in recent years, I've been guilty of setting aside narrative poetry in favor of lyric poetry. I don't mean "lyric" as "subjective emotionality"; I mean a poem that uses a dense, sometimes incomprehensible lexicon. Why? Because I want to impress editors and make people think I'm smart and growing as a writer. That I'm not stuck artistically. Maybe I shouldn't admit that, but it's true.

I don't know what precipitated the domination of the lyrically dense poem. Perhaps it was the poets who studied poststructuralist theory as undergraduate and graduate students in English departments around the country. Or, it was the purist devotees of the Modernists Pound and Eliot who found it increasingly delightful to "make it new." Or, maybe the preeminence of the lyric poem occurred after the L=A=N=G=U=A=G=E poetry movement of the 1970s, a movement that was and has been roundly decried by mainstream page poets, but which, at least to me, seems have had a lasting influence on the work of page poets of the twenty-first century. All I know is that folks within the academy don't much like narrative poetry anymore.

To be honest, there have been black poets writing lyrically dense work for a while. Obviously, there is the Afro-Modernist poet Melvin Tolson, but there have been others, such as Kamau Braithwaite, Michael S. Harper, and Yusef Komunyakaa, to name a few. Yet what has emerged in interviews with these poets is the need to discuss in critical ways their lyric impulses, to provide clarity instead of shrugging their shoulders and declaring, "Good luck with reading my poem. I can't help you, brethren."

For example, speaking on Tolson's epic poem, *Libretto for the Republic of Liberia* (1953), his son, Melvin, Jr., said that his father was aggressively trying to establish himself as a Modernist poet of his era, but he made sure to include footnotes to the poem. Braithwaite is a scholar whose critical work can be read alongside his poetry. Harper and Komunyakaa claim jazz as a strong, artistic influence; thus, the rapid movements and word variations in their poems display the musical genre's improvisational tendencies. With these poets, we have their own explanations for their work, and the implication that they are aware their poems are hard to understand. They acknowledge and appreciate an audience.

As many younger black poets have drifted away from writing criticism about their own and other poets' work, and gravitated toward highly specialized MFA programs, we don't have a discussion or justification of the whys of lyricism in black poetry; we have left that to folks with Ph.Ds. Still, what has not been said is that the herding of black poets toward lyric density and away from narrative poetry—and narrative's assumed twin, accessibility—is concerning in terms of the ongoing oral traditions in global black literature.

I'm not against language that performs the equivalent of a Yoga Crane pose (and maybe even a headstand). Every poet likes to experiment; I know I do. But if a black poet wants her work to be read before a non-academic audience, if a black poet wants to write poems for the liberation of black people—*all* the people, not just the ones with graduate degrees, if a black poet claims to be in service of the ancestors, doesn't she need to be understood clearly, at least some of the time? What is so wrong with writing narrative—with being accessible? When did either of those become dirty words?

I didn't ask, "Does a lyrically dense black poem have a right to exist?"

And I definitely didn't ask, "Is a lyrically dense poem really a black poem?"

I'm asking, "Why wouldn't a black poet want black people without academic degrees to understand her black poem, you know, just sometimes?" I think that's a fair question. I don't think that should cause a riot or sound like an insult.

***

In his blog essay, "Middle Passage: Robert Hayden," Dawes provides a close reading on Hayden's monumental poem and draws connections to other black poets of the African Diaspora: "And it occurs to me that the echoes I hear in Hayden betray what cannot be denied, which is that so many of the great poems of the New Work, poems of the Caribbean must have come out of some experience of reading Hayden's Middle Passage." Dawes goes on to mention other giants of Caribbean poetry: Derek Walcott, Kamau Braithwaite, and Glissant. Then, he gestures toward two luminaries of African (North) American poetry, Kevin Young and Elizabeth Alexander. In so doing, he implies and then outright states his argument: there is not only consanguinity among black poets, but for many, common ancestral and historical concerns.

As I read Dawes's essay, I was struck about the role that narrative has played in black literature over the centuries. From the frequently offered and very misunderstood example of the West African *griot* (and its lesser-known female counterpart, the *griotte*) to the aunties and uncles who sat on porches or who perched on seats in dirt under tall trees, narrative—the accessible, oral tradition—has been important in the passing down of black culture to subsequent generations. It has been important to fiction *and* poetry.

Narrative is not limited to a stylistic device. In black poetry, narrative constitutes the reverential impulse, what Dawes clearly has mastered, and what I and many other black poets long to master but are cautioned against, lest we be labeled old-fashioned—too accessible. Yet consider these lines:

> Ashantis, Mandingoes, Ibos, Wolofs, Fulanis, Coromantees

> Buried in the hill country,
> the swamplands, the forests
> of this New World oven
> the words of tribes linger
> like old mystery songs
> tracing us back to something

These lines are not recycled. They are undoubtedly fresh. Only the blood they refer to is ancient. The "us" means the global community, the descendants of the survivors of the Middle Passage, the members of the African tribes listed— *incanted*—in the first line of the poem. There is much lyric beauty in "Language," but narrative is the guiding force of Dawes' poem. The story of this blood speaks to the blood in this audience, the kin of those different tribes.

With either narrative or dense lyricism, it is possible to tend ancestral altars. It's not Solomon's dilemma, but if one is interested in being understood by others outside an interior circle—the private communion of the poet-shaman with the ancestors—narrative is necessary. Through the use of narrative, the black poet commits an act of great generosity. He allows the reader to bear witness to this communion.

VLADIMIR LUCIEN

BOSOMTWA: The sacred and profane in Kwame Dawes' *Prophets*

I am thinking of the word 'sacred'. A word whose etymology is one of deep and at times troubling ambiguity. The original term, found in ancient Roman religion, *sacer*, is incongruent with the meaning it took on in Christianity. According to some, the original term more convincingly coheres with the term *haram* in Islam. A person or thing that is 'set apart', which encompasses something at once 'sacred' and 'cursed'. This shift is more seismic than one may think especially for the spiritual life of Caribbean people. Instead what obtains is a more simplified notion of the sacred as being symbolic of all that is 'good' and 'God'. This is of course compounded by a static concept of what is 'good'—a bigoted sense of it in fact, which scarcely veils its cultural bias. It also completely delimits human experience within an entirely moral framework. Kwame Dawes' work constitutes an intervention of sorts into the stodgy definition of the sacred and its hegemonic status in the Caribbean and beyond.

What first appealed to me perhaps as much as it confused me was this aspect of Kwame Dawes' aesthetic: the complex sacred. A sacred beautifully vitiated if not by the *cursed* then certainly by the profane, the quotidian. In his own words in *The Missing Slate*:

> I am not sure that there is ever anything but the quotidian. In other words, even when there is pomp and splendor there is probably a streak of fecal matter in the briefs of the King. I am as interested in the alarums as I am in that telling streak—that thing that makes us all human beings who will eventually die and become quite ordinary things. I can't say that poetry represents anything for what it is. I am not sure though that the elevation of things is the opposite of representation. Instead, I think that poetry heightens our perception of what is out there—it complicates and simplifies all at once. Poetry distils and muddies.

This is the conflict which Clarice is faced with in Dawes' book *Prophets*; a prophetess, whose visions become increasingly 'tainted' by not merely her own erotic desires, but by the awareness of her body as something more than a mere vessel for revelation. The two however, the sacred and the 'profane', are never presented by Dawes as discreet domains, but always overlapping, as palimpsest. To wit, the space where Clarice and her congregation meet, is also a space where the 'Ninevite city's' (as Kingston is referred to) putative debauchery takes place: "In the air the stale renk/ of spilt Red Stripe, curdling vomit, ganja and/ sweat is thick as in the drifting carcass of an old slaver/ after the liberation of the encumbered souls./ This is the hangover of Saturday night's rite of carnival/ release before the righteous glare of Sunday penance" (17). Into the wonderful, confluent pun "the slow deliberate *march* to the chapel door/ where the congregation *rocks* its own lamentations" (ibid) (emphasis mine). While the word 'own' could suggest an adversarial relationship between the two, the word *march*—which is a word used to describe one form of carnivalesque movement in the Caribbean[1]—and the word *rocks* cohere with the vocabulary of mas' and reggae—the popular culture of the Caribbean. A better example of this mixing of sacred and profane spaces is the beautiful juxtaposition, thrown into sharp relief by a line and stanza break:

Shifting mountains

of flies dance around the gnawed remains. (17)

We are repeatedly met with such palimpsests of place in the work which are also concurrently palimpsests of time. From Thalbot's "instinctive return/ to the place of his navel string's burial" to take up grimy, brazen tenantry in the 'jaded pink mansion' formerly a plantation Great House, to the "horny ghost" of Castleberry, Clarice's house's erstwhile white owner, lusting after her. Or Last Night's fantasy shrivelled into confession, of "a bad drunken woman with bold bright eye," who can "dance the bogle[2], with her knees/ supple as guava switch." His description of her ("An all the while is pure slackness from her mout/ a slap me one side an the next wid her stinking word/ dem.") is almost identical to an actual occurrence which the great Caribbean poet Kamau Brathwaite recounts in his encounter (like Clarice with Castleberry) with the ghost of a dead slave called Namsetoura, who almost seems to embody the kind of contradictions and juxtapositions and palimpsests that structure and anchor Dawes' work:

> She [Namsetoura] did it in a way which was quite unexpected because normally *one would expect a sybil to speak in an oratorical manner*, in a very correct, abstract system. But instead of that she used very salty language. She spoke in a mixture of Asante Twi, Ga, and Barbadian Nation language. But she spoke in a very—not a hostile manner— but she used a lot of four letter words. I mean, she chewed me out properly. (emphasis mine)

---

[1] The carnival is referred to as a 'road march', among other things.

[2] A Jamaican dance.

Brathwaite, like Clarice, takes down the prophecy fed to him, "gye only the redemption of my bosomtwa/ mi tell yu // an de chilldren chilldren dis-yah wound/ mi seh" (Brathwaite, 121). Brathwaite translates Bosomtwa in a footnote to the poem recounting this encounter, thus: "The sacred lake of the Asante is Bosomtwi. Bosom means sacred and secret. Twi is the name of the language. Twa refers to the female sexual organ. In her 'presentation'. Namsetoura is very gesturally xpressive [sic] about this. *She is able to combine all the meanings...*" (emphases mine).

But this fluidity between worlds, times and ontologies reaches Clarice's mind as breach, taint, but beyond her, the word preserves the fluidity with images of creation, germination and inextricably, eroticism, with, for instance, "The voice of her saviour *breaking* through the *erotic twilight.*" Yet Clarice finds these revelations "difficult: the clutter of potent seed spilling like this/ germinating in her fertile mind" (21). Or when, after the purchase of Castleberry's nineteenth century mansion, "For two weeks Clarice delays her occupation—/ the exact count is nine days, *but the pagan/ in her decision remains unspoken*" (46) (emphasis mine). A nascent awareness of the continuity between worlds however looms, when after meeting the dross of Kingston's brimming excesses of the night before "Clarice picks her way through the debris of sin/ and bows in prayer while the brothers broom // the mess into mounds to be burned: *pyres of sacrifice/* turning in the morning air" (18) (emphasis mine). Note how the debris becomes the ritual sacrifice of the devotees. This takes us beyond a world delimited totally by morality and a simplified moral battle between good and evil, but instead speaks to these excesses as a cosmic counterprinciple to the ideals of Clarice and her faith. An almost cyclic relation is established in the lines above in which "debris of sin" becomes ritual pyre. Clarice's conflict however remains one between the corporeal and the ethereal which she sees in a fraught relationship with one another, though she is perhaps the manifestation of their not dialectical but tidalectic resolution.[3]

---

[3] According to Anna Reckin, in her *Tidalectic Lectures: Kamau Brathwaite's Prose/Poetry as Sound-Space*, "Brathwaite proposes "tidalectic" as "the rejection of the notion of dialectic, which is three—the resolution in the third. Now I go for a concept I call 'tide-alectic' which is the ripple and the two tide movement." She observes further that "The tidalectic also describes a nexus of historical process and landscape" (1). Brathwaite himself describes the process through the image of an old woman sweeping sand from her yard on a morning. He states "Like our grandmother's—our nanna's—action...like the movement of the ocean she's walking on, coming from one continent/ continuum, touching another, and then receding ('reading') from the island(s) into the perhaps creative chaos of the(ir) future" (Brathwaite, 34).

Such conflict ripples out into Dawes' other works for it is in fact a key aspect of his aesthetic: the palpable imagery, the juxtaposition of the scatological and sexual with the holy, the "serious" with the frivolous. Probably it is this aspect of his aesthetic that makes for the fluid, palpable, richly-textured and *human* quality of his verse. You feel like if you touch the page, after a beautiful passage you might meet the slickness of stale sweat or some other unabashedly human thing. Although ubiquitous in Dawes' work, his aesthetic is perhaps most clearly isolated and actualised in this long poem. For these putative contradictions are the *stoff* of Jamaican *creole* Christian traditions, and of Jamaican society at large. The prepared space of the sacred, and the raw (in the best sense), priapic affirmation of the profane. One comes to the revelation that the speaker in Dawes' poem "Eat" in his collection *Wheels*, for example, comes to: "A man must know when night's/ reflux—the throat burning/ with half-digested meals—is the heat/ of the spirit blessing his head" (16). This capability of rendering even the body's inner violence with the redemptive power of the spirit.

The very idea of sacred space, holy ground, is unsettled. It is no one's domain, nobody's nation, but like the Caribbean tradition of sporadic social gatherings (as sporadic as Clarice's visions which she sometimes gets on the toilet), the 'lime', it is a moveable feast. Like the lime, it is flexible, capable of harbouring contradiction, strange bedfellows, capacious enough to harbour Biblical stories being recast with Third World African peoples, the pure word of the spirit entering a voluptuous black woman afraid of her curves, the locksman Christ, the violence and beauty and creativity of the Jamaican nation, this island that "spawns its prophets in plenty/ their ministry brilliant in the squalor" (36).

***

With this poem Dawes writes himself into a small (but Tallawah) tradition of the long poem in the Caribbean. His most notable antecedents, in the Caribbean, are Derek Walcott with his long poem *Omeros* in which he makes efforts at resolving his fraught relationship to 'Africa-in-the-Caribbean'—what Miss Queenie, a former Kumina Queen of Jamaica, referred to as Africa/Jamaica, a "prismatic" overstanding of origins and space as Kamau Brathwaite would have it—and Kamau Brathwaite's own Pan-African New World epic, *The Arrivants*, Césaire's *Cahier d'un Retour au Pays Natal*, or St. John Perse's early long poem, *Anabase*. Dawes' *Prophets* joins the conversation, perhaps at the point where Walcott ponders, in his 1974 essay "The Muse of History":

Eliot speaks of the culture of a people as being the incarnation of its religion. If this is true, in the New World, we have to ask this faceted question: (1) Whether the religion taught to the black slave was absorbed as belief, (2) whether it has been altered by this absorption, and (3) whether wholly absorbed or absorbed and altered, it must now be rejected. In other terms, can an African culture exist, except on the level of polemical art or politics, without an African religion, and if so, which African religion? (43)

Dawes' book is perhaps a fitting answer to Walcott's musing. Not a simple one, but one that is able to have and to hold contradiction. But let us hear from Clarice, culled from one of the most moving passages in the book: "Call it a bargain basement faith, but I have to find/ something what can fit my broad hip and match my/ complexion. What you have for me?"

Dawes' long poem is a beautiful tidalectic captured elegantly in Chapter XXVII in *Prophets* in a section entitled "The Last Poem", with an epigraph paraphrasing Eliot ("For us, all there is is trying. The rest is not our business…"):

> …So I sat among the roses
>
> and chewed at the bitter leaves. The weight
> of the Lord's commanding drooped my
> broken head, and the leaves of the slim
>
> volume of verse, this quartet, this clandestine fantasy, this hope
> for the power of earth-makers, stone-breakers,
> rustled insignificantly and impotently like a poem. (150)

Works Cited

Brathwaite, Kamau, Nathaniel Mackey, and Chris Funkhouser. *Conversations with Nathaniel Mackey*. Staten Island, NY: We, 1999. Print.

Brathwaite, Kamau. "Namsetoura." *Born to Slow Horses*. Middletown, CT: Wesleyan UP, 2005. 118. Print.

Dawes, Kwame Senu Neville. *Prophets*. Leeds, England: Peepal Tree, 1995. Print.

Dawes, Kwame Senu Neville. "Eat." *Wheels*. Leeds, England: Peepal Tree, 2011. 16. Print.

"Poetics, Revelations and Catastrophes: An Interview with Kamau Brathwaite." Interview by Joyelle McSweeney. Web log post. Rain Taxi. *Rain Taxi Review,* Fall 2005. Web. 2 Dec. 2015.

Reckin, Anna. "Tidalectic Lectures: Kamau Brathwaite's Prose/Poetry as Sound-Space." *Anthurium* 1.1 (2003): 1-2. Print.

"Roving Eye, Spotlight." Interview by Jamie Osborn. *The Missing Slate*, 11 July 2014: n. pag. Web. 2 Dec. 2015.

Walcott, Derek. "The Muse of History." *What the Twilight Says: Essays*. New York: Farrar, Straus, and Giroux, 1998. 43. Print.

John Robert Lee

Kwame Dawes and the Reggae Aesthetic: a cultural, social and political proposition.

Kwame Dawes. *Natural Mysticism: Towards a New Reggae Aesthetic.* Peepal Tree Press, 1999, 2003, 2008. 296 pgs.

I. Introduction

I came late to Kwame Dawes' ground-breaking work *Natural Mysticism: Towards a New Reggae Aesthetic.* I had heard this poet, novelist, essayist, editor, musician speak on the topic as early as 1999 in the prestigious Derek Walcott lecture during St. Lucia's annual Nobel laureate Week celebrations. I had heard the term repeated in various places. It was not until I read his collection of poetry *Wheels* (Peepal Tree Press, 2011) that I determined to track down Dawes' published ideas on reggae aesthetic, and so I came, at last, to his book. The other book that also came into view at the same time was his close study of Bob Marley's lyrics, *Bob Marley: Lyrical Genius* (Bobcat Books, 2007), certainly a companion volume. *Wheels* was the best book of poetry I read when it appeared. His range of themes and forms, his seeming stylistic ease, made me wonder how I had missed paying closer attention to such an important contemporary writer (and my editor at Peepal Tree Press.) The way I put it to a young poet friend was that one never notices the slowly growing mound-hillock outside one's kitchen window, until, startlingly, suddenly, your eyes discover that a new mountain has risen. With a fresh and eager immersion in Dawes' oeuvre (I still have much to discover including his latest *Duppy Conqueror: New and Selected Poems* (Copper Canyon Press, 2013), his novels and plays, more of his non-fiction,) I came to the realization that Kwame Dawes stands among the most important contemporary literary figures.

His range is international: from his native Ghana to the home he grew up in, Jamaica, to his sojourns in North America and Europe, his travels throughout the Caribbean, his co- founding of the now highly rated biennual Calabash Literary festival, he is a well-travelled and well-recognised writer. The awards he has garnered from Forward to Emmy to Pushcart to Guggenheim reflect the respect he has gained for his steady, focused, unwavering work – both his own and on behalf of many other writers, across several continents, including Africa.

For so many of us who came to our adulthoods in the Caribbean during the seventies—that period of revolutionary ferment in politics, culture, society; that time when we moved from anti-colonial to post-colonial and began to face post-modernism—reggae and its stars, Rastafari, the original, unique and seductive Bob Marley, led the way in shaping our consciousnesses as the new Caribbean massive . There were parallel movements in other parts of the Caribbean of course—Trinidad, with its street protests, soca music and rapso poetry; the islands with a strong French Creole influence like my native St. Lucia with our movements of creolité and zouk music; the challenging sound of what Kamau Brathwaite dubbed "nation language"; the socialist movements in politics that looked to Cuba, the Jamaica of Michael Manley and the brave efforts of the doomed Maurice Bishop and his New Jewel Party in Grenada.

More could be mentioned in another space, but above all those sounds—came, insistently, with its drum-and-bass, the strong off-beat of Reggae, the sexy rub-a-dub, led unarguably by Bob Marley and the Wailers and their roots-rock reggae. Reggae that spoke of revolution, called us to "get up, stand up"; that spoke of love in tenement yards; that called us to worship and praise Jah; that drew us to dance. And everywhere, in every street of the Caribbean, and soon, in every avenue of every city of the world, walked, with confidence and assurance, the dreadlocked Rasta men and women. It was all a manifestation of what Dawes has so appropriately called, "the Reggae Aesthetic."

When I began to read this book, it quickly became a page-turner. Others no doubt have written of this seminal, water-shed period of Caribbean life and experience, from the mid- sixties to the mid-eighties (in my reckoning), but for the first time I was studying a closely-observed record of the lives and times and music and ideas that had so moved me and all the companions and lovers and artists among whom I lived in those heady days. Marley and the Wailers, Peter Tosh, Bunny Wailer, Jimmy Cliff, Culture, Burning Spear, Steel Pulse, all of wonderful them, and all they carried in their wake, were the stars in our pantheon. The red, gold and green banners; the green leaf on the front of the tams; Rastafarian thought with its unique perspectives on our lives as Caribbean people, on the oft-derided Africa, on the sinister Babylon of class division, church-and-state repressions, racism, apartheid, in which we (so called Third-world peoples) lived decidedly uncertain lives; Rasta talk with its deliberate subversion of the official languages; Rasta life style with its health diets; and Rasta, with its logical conclusion of Black Power incarnated in its Black God Jah Rastafari...we were intoxicated by all this. So many of the upcoming generations for whom the class-ridden society could find no place, found an identity, self-esteem, historical groundation, in reggae and Rasta.

But not only was Kwame Dawes writing a fascinating social and cultural history,—a seminal work that sits alongside the earlier work of Kamau Brathwaite, Aimé Césaire and Frantz Fanon of Martinique, Gordon Rohlehr of Trinidad, the creolité propositions of Jean Bernabé, Patrick Chamoiseau and Raphael Confiant of Aimé Césaire's Martinique, and other thinkers throughout the pan-Caribbean area—but he was making a very bold assertion: that reggae and its spiritual heart of Rastafari, provided an aesthetic that could shape the arts and literature of the new Caribbean already taking shape around us. The Caribbean which is already here, at home and abroad. And he proposed that if you look at our art and literature, not only at the obvious musical achievement and its unique production apparatus, you can see the reggae aesthetic already in operation.

An impossible task, but I chose, from throughout the 296 page volume some quotes that capture the essential ideas in Dawes' formulation of the Natural Mysticism that comes from Reggae and its aesthetic sensibilities. And I offer some further responses to a movement that has had profound influence on my generation.

***

II. *Excerpts from Natural Mysticism, with comments*

    a)   "Unlike the folk forms of an earlier period, this was not an art form to be discovered or recovered from invisibility by the ethnographer from a different class. In the case of reggae, a working class art asserted itself in its own terms and through a language and discourse that would in time shape the way the entire society defined itself and its artistic sensibility" (18).

Of course, as Dawes recognizes, reggae can find its root antecedents in the earlier Jamaican folk music and the ska and rock-steady that immediately preceded reggae. But it came forth as something new, and yes, asserted itself as he describes. As a writer, I often admired the musicians—whether calypsonians like

Trinidad's Shadow, Kitchener, Sparrow and David Rudder, or the consummate, supremely confident Jamaicans—who did not seem to be struggling with the language spectrum as so many of us writers did.

For those of us who wrote in the more formal registers, we wanted to use our linguistic indulgences and genuine appreciation of the images, metaphors and idioms of our Caribbean English; but we also strained for the plain, colloquial speech, even as we stretched for a high, poetic language, or mid-Atlantic prose style. The reggae and kaiso singers sang as the average Caribbean person spoke. It was not till the dub-poets of Jamaica (led by Linton Kwesi Johnson, the late incomparable Mikey Smith, Jean Binta Breeze et al) and the rapso poets of Trinidad (Brother Resistance) and then the nation-language poets of all the region (led by the ground-breaking work of Kamau Brathwaite,) began to follow the example of the singers and rhythm-makers, that the new, truly post-colonial literary voices began to be heard. But as Dawes has pointed out in his references to Anthony McNeill, Denis Scott and Lorna Goodison, even the more formal-language poets like these also gained a new freedom as the aesthetic rising out of the music and its social contexts began to lead the writers out of the old harnesses into a new, self-confident freedom. What was true about the birthplace of reggae, Jamaica, and its new-found liberation through the immediacy, the relevance of that sound, those lyrics, became true for the rest of the Caribbean, both at home and abroad.

Today, even after the golden-age days of roots rock reggae and the Wailers and their contemporaries, Jamaican music via dance hall and ragga, has become the most popular music of the new youth cultures.

b) "...I am trying to find an aesthetic that both corresponds with my personal instincts and also relates to my sense of the social space I occupy as a writer. Why do I write as I do? What history, what discourse, what experiences have shaped my own sense of poetic and narrative construction? What cosmology has given rise to my cosmology? And what is it that connects me with other artists whose work I sense shares an ideological and formal affinity to my own? I refer in particular to what I regard as the emergence of a distinctive voice in Caribbean writing that is confident in its cultural roots in the region" (34).

I suppose more artists than we realise face these questions raised by Dawes. A poet friend often asks now, after many years of writing and publishing, "what is it for?" As anti-colonialism gave way to post-colonialism in our Caribbean, the matters and questions of relevance of our work to the surrounding societies became paramount. The street protests, the open rebellion by new generations against the pillars of the status quo we had grown up under in the fifties and sixties, would not allow us, as soi-disant public voices of the community, to do otherwise. To find a balance between my personal talent and my artistic inclination and the vibrant demotic and demographic I was actively involved in became the angst of many late night arguments, discussions and quarrels. It was you might say, at heart, a "political" question. The politics of the arts and culture alongside the politics of the street.

Who are we, these new Caribbean people? Where have we come from and where do we want to go? The new marxists and socialists were at the door. The youth would not be satisfied with the time-worn complacencies of church and state. And as people with deep spiritual groundings, faced by the new atheists, the new-age enthusiasts and the fundamentalists, what was my cosmological compass? What was my meta-narrative? How was all that to translate into the forms and contents of our new literatures, what was to be the distinctive voice of the forthcoming poets and novelists and playwrights. The painters, sculptors, dancers, a few film makers and certainly the musicians, especially the reggae musicians, were pointing the way, out of Babylon, to a possible Zion. There, in the Rasta-inspired reggae, Dawes found the aesthetic he was seeking, that brought together the sacred and secular, the political and historical, the Caribbean and Africa. There was the way to find the confidence in our cultural roots that would give the new literatures their authenticity. There, already, was the voice we were looking for.

c)   "But if the nationalist phase of Caribbean writing was concerned with the act of naming, acknowledging, and clarifying a sense of self, I knew that the new literature had both to find the language and forms with which to contend with current realities; had to possess a reflexivity that allowed for irony, for satire; had to find a poetic and aesthetic articulation that emerged not merely from a progression of the literary tradition but represented a qualitative shift from an anti-colonial literature which in its aesthetics still privileged colonial forms, to a post colonial writing which was rooted in our own way of seeing and speaking. The task was no longer to create a literature from the West Indies, but to allow the voice of that region to reflect on the world that it met" (61).

The task of allowing our voice "to reflect on the world that it met," rooted in "our own way of seeing and speaking," was the supreme achievement of Marley and the reggae composers and singers. And yes, it represented " a qualitative shift." And so, the new classics of our voice, our new-found voice, rose clearly and with undeniable power, electrifying a generation that knew this was what they were waiting for: Linton Kwesi Johnson, Mikey Smith, Jean Binta Breeze, so many, not only Jamaicans, but throughout the Caribbean and the diaspora, Exodus, movement of Jah people!

The recent success of Jamaican writers like Marlon James, Kei Miller and Claudia Rankine also continues to demonstrate this. In James' case, for example, his Booker-winning novel A brief history of seven killings is a no-holds barred, powerful, confident setting out of the Jamaica of the period Dawes is examining, the rise of Marley, reggae and Rasta. Marley is very much a central actor in the book. The language is unapologetically Jamaican as that of the music. The characters, drawn on real-life personages are Jamaican in every way. The novel is not only post-colonial but post- modern and will not be confined only to the label "Caribbean." It is a world novel, in the way one might speak of world-music. Contemporary Caribbean literature reflects that cosmopolitan quality even as it is grounded in the Caribbean reality. And as Dawes makes the point, this is so whether the writers are working from home or from the large Caribbean diasporas. More than ever now, with confidence, without reference to the once-colonial master imperative, our writers are reflecting on the world we meet, at home or abroad.

d) "...an aesthetic is defined as a cultural, ideological, and formal framework that is identifiable within an artistic form to which it gives coherence, and this aesthetic can be related fruitfully to other forms" (67).

e) "There are two basic ways in which the aesthetic works. On the one hand, the aesthetic may serve as a self-consciously applied frame, guiding and shaping the work being produced, where the artist is looking to reggae for a model of creative expression. On the other hand, reggae music epitomizes an aesthetic development within an artistic community as a whole or within a society at large" (74).

f) "I make use of four basic levels of analysis...on the first level is the nature of the overarching ideology of the reggae aesthetic. This relates to issues of mythology, cosmology, and the extensive historiographical concerns of the music...Second, I am concerned with issues of language use since it is the political and formal use of language in reggae that has had the most telling influence on the art of the region. Third, there is the question of the topics or themes of reggae music...Fourth, there is the level of form, – the way in which the formal dimensions of reggae can be seen to offer models of formal expression" (101, 102).

While I read Kwame's thesis with great enthusiasm and excitement, hearing someone articulate what I had experienced and sensed with reggae and Rasta, from time to time, some doubts would rise to question his propositions. Was my friend straining to make a thesis out of his beloved Jamaican reggae? Was he juggling to force an aesthetic on the new Caribbean literature? Given the complexities of Caribbean life and art and culture, would it fit, this encompassing world-and-life view expressed by reggae, would it give a real, viable, feasible, authentic philosophical framework to our post-colonial and post-modern literatures? Would it provide the paradigm shift we definitely needed?

At the heart of his probing of the aesthetics of reggae he put forward the above definitions and analytical outlines. By an inductive process, examining reggae closely , he arrives at the principles that shape the aesthetic he sets forth. And it makes sense, it is hard to argue convincingly against, his thesis. And it is not a closed-door, dogmatic thesis. He sees his explorations as the beginnings of an ever growing process. He says elsewhere that "it is possible to argue that the patterns revealed and crystallized in reggae music serve as useful tools to explore the work of writers who are working in a postcolonial space in which the construction of a distinctive voice is crucial to the realization of an autonomous Caribbean literary tradition" (261). He sees a "postmodernist innovative vitality" in reggae which allows it to tap into the folk heritage past and to move on into the newer forms, as witnessed in the later developments of ragga and dancehall, and to become a multi-language, international form that can adapt, without losing its uniqueness at core. So applied to literary work, there is the way pointed to capture our mythologies and histories, our urbanisations, our politics, our newer post-modern visions and concerns; and to capture that content in language that is true, adventurous, unique in many ways within the context of world literature, as Marley and the musicians have shown so convincingly and influentially, with their "models of formal expression."

    g)   "Reggae , I believe, offers the closest thing to the kind of sensibility that T.S. Eliot saw in the metaphysical poets of the seventeenth century, a sensibility that engages in a dialectic of body and spirit, reason and emotion, a sensibility not yet divided by the dualism of western scientific rationalism" (259).

Well yes, reggae comes out of the totality of our lives and sensibilities, "body and spirit, reason and emotion," and much of it from the hard part of our resistance to oppressions and exclusions; our poverties, our politics and defences against criminalities; and yes, also from our sexualities, our loves, our youthful rebellions and the jammin' of our dance hall happinesses; our faiths and wonderments about the spiritual and cosmological realms we know we inhabit. So the music, so the art and so the poems and stories and plays. So the making manifest of the natural mysticisms of our experiences that reggae and its emerging aesthetics so ably encompass.

***

III. Conclusion

    "I understand that it is only in the mastering of the particular and the parochial that a sophisticated universalism can be achieved" (264).

And, finally, reggae has done this, on all fronts. So can our literatures. Selah.

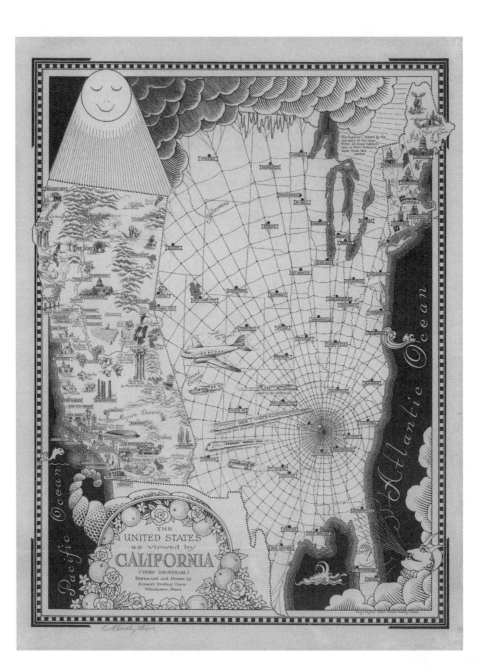

THE
UNITED STATES
as viewed by
CALIFORNIA
(VERY UNOFFICIAL)
Distorted and Drawn by
Ernest Dudley Chase
Winchester, Mass.

KEVIN LARIMER

[From what was understood of yes, dear mine]

From what was understood of yes, dear mine
your words are hung from a length of cord.
The hard think, the long situation of dreaming

and it surrounds us. Consider this no, or begin
with a reason for yesterday. The slow, a replay
of indeterminate actions. Confidence fathoms.

A mouse circles herself and blinks for the wait.
A torrent, a notion, divides her. Her itty bitters.
Quiet moves through the room like a morning

come violent and true. Movement catches red
and corners the eye. Something has occurred.
Abacus fingered, and decision whiskered away.

PROSE POETRY
& POETIC PROSE
PORTFOLIO

Edited by Katie Farris

Kathleen Rooney

La Réponse Inattendue

The greatest desire of every door is to open. So thinks Loulou the Pomeranian, gifted, as dogs get, in the scratching-at of doors. Anticipation of entry, anticipation of exit: getting outside for the relief of peeing, getting inside for relief from the elements.

This door the master has painted above a wooden floor is the 2-D incarnation of Loulou's fantasy threshold: a door with a biomorphic hole. A door of simultaneous darkness and light. A door that says not *either-or* but *both*. A door with a Georgette-and-the-master-and-Loulou-shaped cutout.

"It's a role that doesn't suit me, father-of-children," the master said the other day to an interviewer, letting Loulou out the back. "The garden is quite big enough for the children we don't have."

One's first look at a painting should be like a room with many doors. One wonders which will open and where it will lead. Loulou's unexpected answer: like thoughts, this door lets one be two places at once.

La Colère Des Dieux

The bearded man in the bowler hat in the backseat of the green automobile leans his head out the window, though he is not a dog. The mountains in the background are slightly fogged. On the roof of the car there gallops a horse and on the horse there whips a jockey. The hatted man might be Freud, or Trotsky, but is not – just a generic European bourgeois.

When he first saw it, Loulou the Pomeranian felt walloped with the memory of *The Lost Jockey* from 1926. It is now 1960. The Loulou who lived with the master and Georgette when Mag created that painting was not he – was not the present Loulou – though that pom, of course, had been called Loulou too.

The painted stack of creatures and vehicles causes Loulou to wonder about the value of being sing/ular, which is to say unique, versus being a plurality, which is to say one of many. As the master wrote in an essay: "An object is not so possessed of its name that one cannot find for it another which suits it better." Loulou has always answered to Loulou. This painting will always be referred to as *The Anger of the Gods*. Which is not to say that either name could not be modified or improved. Like maybe the gods should be wrathful, not angry? The image fills Loulou with neither wrath nor anger, but rather rampant desire to have, as the man does, his own chauffeur.

Loulou rarely finds himself in an auto, but when he does, he sticks his head out and lets his fur ripple in the sun. "Why do you do that?" the master asks. "Because dogs love to run," says Loulou, "and sticking your head out the window of a moving car is the sensation of running faster than any dog has ever run." "Exhilaration without exertion," the master says. "Exactly. Now, please, accelerate." And the master does.

Gemma Gorga

[It could be just this . . .] from the *Book of Minutes*

It could be just this. It could be God goes around pouring salt into human beings, trying to determine their saturation point, the line above which they can no longer tolerate any more pain and they precipitate to the bottom of the container, suddenly heavy as a sandbag. It could be it happened just like this, throughout human history: a miscalculation of salt and sand.

Translated from the Catalan by Sharon Dolin

LAUREN CAMP

Who Other

Most afternoons after school, she runs through a blister of houses, collecting the dirt of her childhood from neighbors' front yards. Tudor land red dog land fire station siren land of wailing careful light. Her hair grows long with slip knots of hope and chunks of chewing gum. She jumps contented through ropes of abjection. Sometimes lonely, she sorts people and decides no one matters less than any other.

Velvet

In synagogue in the suburbs, we fill with song in book after book and the Tigris rises up and makes a blessing. We are in our seats, running our hands on the velvet beside us. Our mouths are moving. Our eyes are down.

There is one story and one story, and we repeat it each week. This story is true and foolish. Words huddle, back to front, with occasional laments and long echo. We are waiting to learn about today, tomorrow, why we must suffer. I am wearing a white dress, my father a tie.

Even at this moment, the river insists on flowing. I smell the perfume of the desert. Old men advance with their widening language, pushing carts, selling words without farewell, without salt, without the flesh of worry. Silver birds quiver in the sun.

Then, I'm not at the water. The sermon has ended. There are round tables of bread on old platters. My father laughs, his cheeks like globes. A day of rest. All day we are lucky.

Kristina Marie Darling

from The Ghosts of Birds

It was a year of many discoveries. First a cold shore, then the smallness of the bones. Of course there were people who set sail on the desolation ships. For them, it was merely an opportunity, not a disturbance of any kind.

And the burial that failed to satisfy anyone. Not even a hand to place on the casket, or a body to rest beside the thistle plants.

After an entire winter of non-address, you still didn't want me posting letters. When I seal the envelope, everything comes apart in my hands.

Together, we try to reassemble the ghost. Her body is intricate and all of the books are far away. Now a ship that passes us by again and again.

And there is no barge in the white envelope that appears beneath my door. The thin shores already sealed with frost. When will the postman arrive and what little failures will he carry.

Shhhhhh. The doorbell is ringing. To whom should I address this?

To you who held out your hand—

More and more, I'm convinced those were the
last ships coming.

Around me the harbor is dark. Your letters are
still held up in customs.

An unarticulated melancholy, a sea.

       When the tide falls away we will
each board a different ferry to shore.

The little bones that arrive with your letters. These I do not label or inspect. They just appear they come undone they stutter.

The sea, as always, unannounced. No frost or distant voice to warn us.

There will be no dispatch from the other coast.

The tiny ships I carried for you, the ships that I built for you out of only the bones.

JORGE ORTEGA

An Epic of Limits

You walk among the knotty roots that jut from the soil like boas wrapped around the laurel tree with its exuberant crown that presided over childhood feasts. They emerge, sprout from the desert dust soothed by transitory shadows. And a warm breeze rises across these barren lands and floods itself against your forehead, that soft wall which auguries bend across, curling the already impalpable curls of conjurations. Far off, a stable, hut, or rickety farmhouse which a mirage appears to dissolve across the sober estates of clay, strikes your attention in the middle of this landscape swept by its arid monotony. All about, the pasture parched by winter, the blades scorched by the cold. You think: *golden hair of the weeds, yellow* jaramagos *from the fields of Seville, smoothed by the millennial weight of a column's capital, like a head rolling after an ambush.* Solid bodies of all types, scattered wherever they may during memory's excursion. Rubble of a demolished architecture that the secret meeting spot of time has spread in the infinite garden of statues. Beneath the green foliage bulbs, both the beginning and the end are visible. From there you can clearly discern the school you attended, and the cemetery grove you approach, while you travel at the pace of a tortoise.

Translated from the Spanish by Anthony Seidman

ANTHONY SEIDMAN

Vermeer

Even the dust and spear of straw on the kitchen floor are visible. The milk-maid pours a silken thread, clotted at the pitcher's mouth. On the table, loaves of wheat bread varnished by the gold of memory, while she gazes down at her chore, muscles around her elbows straining from the pitcher's weight. Behind her is a white wall, yellow-spotted, with one nail and its microbe-thin shadow. Outside the canvas, I only have patience to paint a nude with a few brush strokes, but Vermeer includes the stitches on his maid's mustard-colored blouse. And he brings me back to slow light drifting after love, when her red hair burns against the white pillow; he brings me back to a boyhood afternoon where I sit by a window, feel sun on my back, and watch dust-specks pirouette in a weightlessness older than the first apple falling from the bough.

Cork Which Floats On Water Is Consumed By Flame

At two o'clock in the afternoon, sunlight and heat ripen the thighs of schoolgirls in knee-length socks and skirts. Through the school gates they pass into the city drugged by siesta, and the strings of a lyre melt over the flame of my mind. Bus fumes rise and dissipate. From the sidewalk, I stare at those creatures teetering on that fire-bud between a smooth pubis, and a conch bedded in seaweed. My skull splits open as pigeons plunge from rooftop rebar to peck at my spilled seed. No trees grow in this desert city, and at each corner the schoolgirls disappear, shadows erased by wind. Soon they will no longer look over their shoulders, and a black bus will carry me over a road that rises through mesas and burnt chaparral. For now, there is no other hemisphere where I can catch the butterflies She shakes from her hair upon awaking. But rain floods the basement of each poem I write. I step across these hot coals to not walk on water.

GASPAR OROZCO

Film Seen In A White Square of A Chessboard

Time has passed since I heard the gallop of a fleeing horse. Today the Eastern Wind brought a few grains of red sand. I have seen the Bishop's head tilt. It is said that one can glimpse the sea through a chink of light. Others say this is rather a motionless dream in the Queen's mind. Our Lord dreamt of an obscure tree, unknown birds hiding in the foliage…on that day, victory was ours. Petal teetering on the fingertip of God is our kingdom. Yesterday the Queen traveled to the north. Her gait, a drop of metal. Over the bridge, black wheat fields stretch out. Flakes of snow commence falling. Silence.

Translated from the Spanish by Anthony Seidman

Film Seen In A Black Square of A Chessboard

High tide. Our moon is an iron ring. Bishop dips his long hands and cassock in the rabid foam. Intones a prayer for the battle. Salve. A tremor crosses the lustrous manes of our forsaken horses. Fire on the tips of towers that are lost in the dawn. Among the gifts from the stars, he chooses the fallen one. Into the early hours of the morning, the King practices his calligraphy. The interminable names of water. Over and over again. Each capital letter, a hook made from light. Weeds grow along the edges of the kingdom. I offered the Queen a sprig. Tenderly, she chose a lion's tooth and blew upon it: seeds scattered across both kingdoms. Snowfall. Silence.

Translated from the Spanish by Anthony Seidman

GASPAR OROZCO

Film Viewed On Coney Island

Like a dragonfly shimmering within a jar, such is the woman held by your gaze. From her open hands there blossoms three flames. Petals that turn into thorns, thorns that turn into amethysts. At this hour, the violet of gasoline is the most sensible perfume; fire encircles the drawings of her body: mandorla. Slowly, the flame crosses her soul, which is ours as well. Lights respond to the tongue's sweet beckoning. In silence, the union ascends. Breath is a light. It is fitting that this fire never be extinguished.

Such is what I witnessed on the island that evaporates at dawn.

Translated from the Spanish by Anthony Seidman

Some of The Sounds Heard Upon Approaching The Walls of A Movie Theater Shuttered Years Ago

Flapping of a myriad nameless birds over a winter garden. Thunder reaching your ears in the shape of a magnolia. A drop opening the deepest galleries of a cavern. Over and over again, the same canned laughter, over and over again. From the color of a quicksilver teardrop, gunshot cutting the night in two. Rain and the city glistening black. Sonar of a submarine lost in arctic waters. Crackling of a fire consuming a city or the final letter of a dead man. The green flickering of a dragonfly in a jar. Your laughter, your uncontrollable laughter as a boy.

Translated from the Spanish by Anthony Seidman

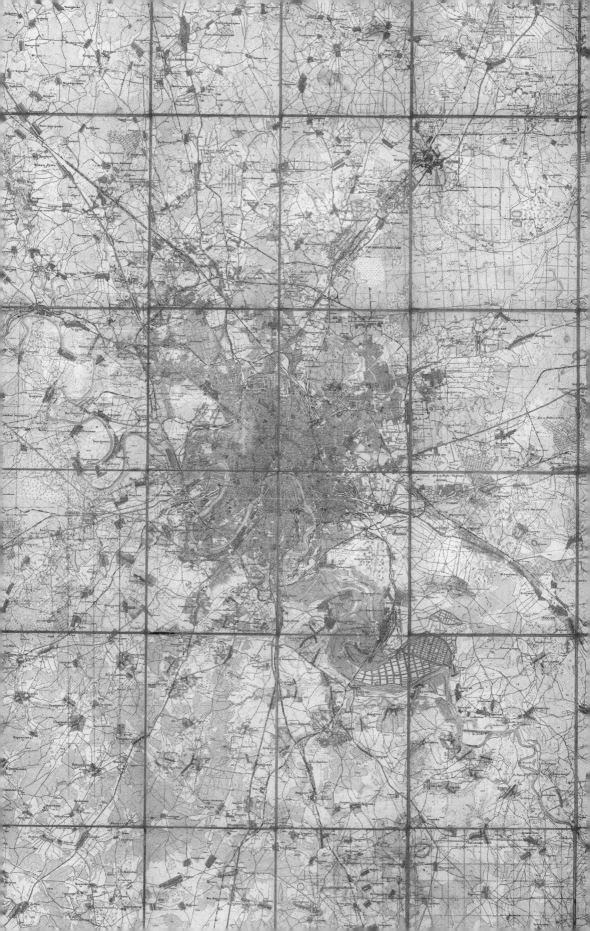

SABRINA ORAH MARK

PORTFOLIO

The Stepmother

"You smell like Florida. We hate you." The Stepmother knows from the crushed handwriting this note is from The Stepchildren. At the bottom of the note is a drawing of a mouse. The Stepmother wants to know what does the mouse mean. The mouse seems lonely and afraid. Its eyes are too big. The Stepmother peels a hardboiled egg, eats it very quietly, and thinks about the mouse, and Florida, and smelling like Florida. No one wants to smell like Florida. If The Stepmother had any guts she would go to the yard this instant and paint all the trees white, but The Stepmother has no guts. If The Stepmother had any guts her husband who is the father of The Stepchildren who believe she smells like Florida would come home and see the trees and say what in god's name have you done? Do you think we're living in a goddamn fairy tale here? The Stepmother would stand there with her large bucket of paint, and her guts, and tell her husband the trees are now white because she is not a real Mother, she will never be a real Mother, and also she is thinking of running away with the mouse. She would sob and say something strange and dramatic like how she feels as though she's three plagues short of an exodus even though she doesn't really have any plagues except for smelling like Florida. But none of this will happen because The Stepmother has no guts, and this is America not a fairy tale. This is a state in America that is not Florida even though The Stepmother is reeking of it. The Stepmother wants to know what does the mouse mean. It is a beautiful mouse. The Stepmother has no guts but she does have some scissors which she uses to cut the mouse out. No one wants to be lonely, and afraid, and live in a note about smelling like Florida. Once The Stepmother cuts the mouse out the mouse shivers. It is a very sad shiver. Sadder than all The Stepmother's sadnesses, and somehow this comforts her. The Stepmother isn't certain whether the shiver is from coldness or relief, but she cuts off a strand of her hair and wraps it around the mouse's shoulders anyway. The mouse falls asleep in the palm of The Stepmother's hand, and dreams of guts, and white trees, and the kindness of The Stepmother. The mouse is what the mouse means. It's The Stepchildren who mean something else. It's The Stepchildren who mean something far, far away, like a Mother. When The Stepchildren come home The Stepmother will hug and kiss them and wipe their dirty little hands until their hearts break in two.

The Very Nervous Family

Mr. Horowitz clutches a bag of dried apricots to his chest. Although the sun is shining, there will probably be a storm. Electricity will be lost. Possibly forever. When this happens the very nervous family will be the last to starve. Because of the apricots. "Unless," says Mrs. Horowitz, "the authorities confiscate the apricots." Mr. Horowitz clutches the bag of dried apricots tighter. He should've bought two bags. One for the authorities and one for his very nervous family. Mrs. Horowitz would dead bolt the front door to keep the authorities out, but it is already bolted. Already dead. She doesn't like that phrase. Dead bolt. It reminds her of getting shot before you even have a chance to run. "Everyone should have at least a chance to run," says Mrs. Horowitz. "Don't you agree, Mr. Horowitz?" Mrs. Horowitz always refers to her husband as Mr. Horowitz should they ever one day become strangers to each other. Mr. Horowitz agrees. When the authorities come they should give the Horowitzs a chance to run before they shoot them for the apricots. Eli Horowitz, their very nervous son, rushes in with his knitting. "Do not rush," says Mr. Horowitz, "you will fall and you will die." Eli wants ice skates for his birthday. "We are not a family who ice skates!" shouts Mrs. Horowitz. She is not angry. She is a mother who simply does not wish to outlive her only son. Mrs. Horowitz gathers her very nervous son up in her arms, and gently explains that families who ice skate become the ice they slip on. The cracks they fall through. The frost that bites them. "We have survived this long to become our own demise?" asks Mrs. Horowitz. "No," whispers Eli, "we have not." Mr. Horowitz removes one dried apricot from the bag and nervously begins to pet it when Mrs. Horowitz suddenly gasps. She thinks she may have forgotten to buy milk. Without milk they will choke on the apricots. Eli rushes to the freezer with his knitting. There is milk. The whole freezer is stuffed with milk. Eli removes a frozen half pint and glides it across the kitchen table. It is like the milk is skating. He wishes he were milk. Brave milk. He throws the half pint on the floor and stomps on it. Now the milk is crushed. Now the milk is dead. Now the Horowitzs are that much closer to choking. Mr. and Mrs. Horowitz are dumbfounded. Their very nervous son might be a maniac. He is eight. God is punishing them for being survivors. God has given them a maniac for a son. All they ask is that they not starve, and now their only son is killing milk. Who will marry their maniac? No one. Who will mother their grandchildren? There will be no grandchildren. All they ask is that there is something left of them when they are shot for the apricots, but now their only son is a maniac who will give them no grandchildren. Mr. Horowitz considers leaving Eli behind when he and Mrs. Horowitz run for their lives.

Two Jokes Walk into a Bar

Two jokes walk into a bar. The bartender says he'll be back in three shakes of a lamb's tail and disappears in broad daylight out the front door. The jokes hold hands and wait for the bartender to return. A third joke walks in. He clears his throat, and off the top of his head he begins: "A little Madness in the Spring / Is wholesome even for the King, / But God be with the Clown – /Who ponders this tremendous scene —". "Emily Dickinson," says the first joke. "Nicely done." The third joke is genuinely impressed. It is rare a joke so quickly gets it. All three jokes hold hands and wait for the bartender to return. The second joke's father is dying, but he doesn't want to talk about it. Instead he thinks about the bartender who will be back once the lamb's tail shakes three times. Why is it "shake" of a lamb's tail, and not "wag?" "Wag" suggests the lamb is happy and free, while "shake" sounds like "shank," which brings to the table the lamb's dumb truth: It will eventually be eaten. The jokes hold hands and wait for the bartender to return. The bartender's name is Bob. Bob Oranges. He's a friendly if slightly boring guy who will never return, and somewhere deep inside, the jokes know this already. From far off there is the faintest sound of children playing. It is noon and the jokes are in a bar. "If we were the Fates," poses the second joke, "which one of us do you think would hold the scissors?" Jokes one and three laugh nervously because this is clearly a rhetorical question. There is no way a joke would parade as a Fate. Most jokes would sooner drown themselves. The jokes warn the second joke not to even joke about this. But the second joke is angry. His father is dying. The first joke exchanges a worried look with the third. "Did I tell you about the dream I had last night?" The first joke is trying to lighten the mood. "Franz Kafka was walking up and down this beach. It looked a lot like the one I used to go to as a kid. You know, where I'd build sandcastles and stuff." He pauses, smirks. "So in this dream I walk towards Kafka, and as I approach I realize he's singing "Try a Little Tenderness." Like full blast. Like really belting it out." Just as the jokes are about to laugh, a bartender walks into the bar. It is not Bob Oranges. It is a different bartender. "What did I miss?" asks the bartender. The first joke tells him his dream. The bartender laughs and says, "Them young girls they *do* get wearied…wearing that *ooooold* shabby dress." The bartender drags out "old" like he's pulling off a sock that won't let go. At "dress," he gets a faraway look as if he has a girl in mind. The door opens. Day floods in. A rabbi and a priest walk into the bar. It seems, distantly, as if something like this has happened before. To the jokes, these men look familiar. The first and third joke offer the men their seats. It is the only respectful thing to do. The priest and the rabbi sit on either side of the second joke, who doesn't seem to notice them. The priest, the joke, and the rabbi hold hands and wait for the bartender to ask them what they're having. But now this bartender is elsewhere, most likely still thinking about a girl he once knew and possibly loved. The priest and the rabbi want to say something about wonder and tenderness and love and life and death, but they can't think of anything. Their minds have gone blank. The second joke frees his hands from the soft grip of the men to light a cigarette, and as he does his cell phone rings. It rings, and rings, and rings. But the joke's not going to get it. Not this one. Not now. No siree, Bob… Oranges, thinks the second joke. And at this he chuckles, because he knows it'll be the last funny thing for a long, long time.

Clay

In my day / Son / everybody knew how to pronounce the word "faucet" / and everybody knew how to apologize / profusely, and everybody knew how to vanish. / And when a man / drove up to your house with a truck / full of soil, mulch, and rocks / you knew he was there to grow something, Son. He was there / to make a difference. Nowadays the world's so heavy / that very same man is face / down in the flowers. Go try to talk to him, Son. Go try and pick him up. He'll never rise / Unlike the lonesome crowd in my heart that rose / and rose and rose / to its feet when you arrived / cheering wildly, he'll never rise / He'll never rise no matter how much green fuzz from your green fuzzy mittens you flick at him / for he is sour bones. / For it is my doom you undo / not his. For winter is here forever, Son, so bundle up. Here is your pancake / in the shape of a chicken. I'm sorry. I couldn't get the feathers / right. For a long time, Son, I pursued / happiness. I gave lectures on margins / and darkness. And when a hand / went up, and mouths would move, / sometimes I saw clouds. Sometimes even a little bit / of rain. But mostly nothing. And there you were far / in the back. In the very last row. There you were the whole / time, no not the whole time, but here you are now / with your clay, your colored clay. What are you making, Son? / An invisible ocean robot bird from OuterSpace? Well that's as good / a thing as any. In my day, the war was off. / Nowadays, the war is super / on. I look around at what is left of us and wonder / where does all this love / come from? In my day, Son, we knew. The love, / it came from the river called Mother or Hands or God or Something. I do not know / why today of all days / I chose to wear this lemon yellow blouse. It fits me / terribly. "My words," you say, / "are forgetting me." Me too, Son. Me too. Hold my hand. / It's a long walk home. / In my day, Son, it felt good / to lose everything. It felt like winning. / And in my day, Son, laughter was fragile. You prayed / for laughter, Son, and sometimes laughter / would never come. And sometimes the joke / was on you and it was heavy / and you were face down right beside the man / face down in the flowers but you got up, Son. / In my day, you got the hell up. / My throat is sore. My throat has been sore / for a long, long time. You see that tree, Son? It's a ghost. / It's all ghosts. I'm a ghost. / And you're a ghost. This whole town / is a ghost. In my day, we all knew / how to be ghosts. It meant / something to be a ghost. And if your mother / was a ghost you were proud / of your mother. Nowadays, Son, / all I ever want to do is fix something. Something big. / Something incredibly broken. When I was a little girl / I rocked back and forth and sang the Hallelujah / in a dark wool dress. / In a big, loud voice. / Nowadays, no one knows / how to apologize. No one knows how to vanish. / I'm trying to teach you something, Son, / about perseverance and grief and forgiveness. You are almost four / and you want to stay three / forever. "I don't want to be a very old man," / you say, "with very white hair." Don't be frightened, Son. / Everything is far away. / I was wrong. The man / in the flowers is looking around. He is rising up. / Maybe he would like to share / your colored clay? I'm sorry, Son, / I'm just a poet. I hope this is enough. / If it isn't I'll burn down the house / and give you the ashes.

Don't Just Do Something, Stand There!

1. It all began with the milk.
2. The milk belonged to my lover, Mr. Horowitz.
3. For a long time something beautiful was going to happen.
4. But this was not the beautiful thing.
5. Had the milk landed on my nose as my lover, Mr. Horowitz, swears he had intended we would've had a judderous laugh about it.
6. But Mr. Horowitz fucked up.
7. Just yesterday I accompanied my lover, Mr. Horowitz, to the forest.
8. How could he have forgotten so quickly?
9. I think there were thieves.
10. My lover, Mr. Horowitz, dipped his thumb and forefinger into his cereal bowl and flicked the milk (that once belonged to him) at me.
11. In the forest I was frightened.
12. In the forest there were thieves.
13. In the forest my lover, Mr. Horowitz, showed off his wilderness skills by reciting *Waiting for Godot*.
14. "Excuse me mister. The bones. You won't be needing the bones?"
15. But I did need the bones.
16. The milk landed not on my nose but on my newly bought, barely worn dream rush chemise.
17. My mother warned me without the bones no one, not even Mr. Horowitz, my lover, who loved me one hundred times a day would ever love me.
18. Could ever love me.
19. I needed the bones, but I could not admit to needing the bones.
20. The economy was failing and my dream rush chemise was ruined.
21. Forever?
22. Possibly forever.
23. Mr. Horowitz, my lover, was *just joking around*.
24. We were unemployed.
25. I heard a thud.
26. "Did you hear a thud?"
27. "It's your mother!" cheered my lover, Mr. Horowitz.
28. "She has come with the bones?"
29. "She has come to save us from our economic woes?"
30. "Very funny."
31. In literature a character's "fatal flaw" requires she take a metaphorical or literal plummet.
32. "Don't just do something," said my mother, "stand there!"
33. So I stood there.

34. A long time ago I wrote a book.
35. The main character's name was Beatrice.
36. Shortly after my mother had a baby and named her Beatrice.
37. Then she had another.
38. She named that baby Beatrice, too.
39. Then she had another.
40. She named that baby Beatrice, too.
41. Mr. Horowitz, my lover, is named Mr. Horowitz because you cannot name a baby Mr. Horowitz.
42. But I did need the bones.
43. My mother took the bones away while I just stood there in my ruined chemise.
44. Would never love me.
45. Could never love me.
46. This was not the beautiful thing.
47. I was groggy with milk, which is another way of saying I was ashamed at my inability to start yelling.
48. At my mother.
49. For taking the bones.
50. At Mr. Horowitz.
51. For flicking the milk.
52. At all the Beatrices.
53. For not being the real Beatrice, although my mother claimed each of them to be.
54. At my mother.
55. For claiming each of them to be.
56. The real Beatrice lives in the book I wrote a long time ago.
57. The real Beatrice is terrified of nests, and string, and cashews, and Poland, and carousels for good reason.
58. There are stains that happen suddenly, and can never be washed out.
59. "And if they could?"
60. "We would be saved."
61. "For god's sake," said my mother, "Mr. Horowitz, your lover, was *just joking around.*"
62. Speaking of jokes, let me tell you a joke I once heard at a funeral.
63. His wife had died young and he told the joke at the funeral because she loved the joke, every day she loved the joke, and now he had to live a life he couldn't bear to live without her so he told the joke.
64. "What's red, hangs from a wall, and whistles?"

65. "What?"
66. "A herring."
67. "A herring? But a herring isn't red."
68. "All right! So you paint the herring red!"
69. "But a herring doesn't hang from a wall."
70. "All right! So you take a hammer and you nail the herring to the wall!"
71. "But a herring doesn't whistle."
72. "All right! So it doesn't whistle!"
73. "I don't get it."
74. "And if we dropped him? (*Pause*) If we dropped him?"
75. "He'd punish us (*Silence. He looks at the tree.*)"
76. Just yesterday I accompanied my lover, Mr. Horowitz, to the forest.
77. Would never love me.
78. Could never love me.
79. In the forest there were trees.
80. "I thought you said thieves," said the Beatrices.
81. The economy was failing.
82. We were unemployed.
83. "Unemployed people, Mr. Horowitz," said my mother, "should not be flicking milk."
84. They started kissing.
85. "Who?" asked Mr. Horowitz. "Who started kissing?"
86. "You and my mother."
87. "All right!" said my mother. "So we started kissing!"
88. "I don't get it," said Mr. Horowitz.
89. "Don't just do something," said the Beatrices, "stand there!"
90. So I stood there in my ruined chemise while my lover, Mr. Horowitz, and my mother kissed and kissed and kissed.
91. "You're sure you saw me, you won't come and tell me tomorrow you never saw me."
92. "Of course not," said the real Beatrice.
93. There are stains that happen suddenly, and can never be washed out.
94. For a long time something beautiful was going to happen.
95. But this was not the beautiful thing.
96. This was the beautiful thing.
97. "I saw you," said the real Beatrice.
98. The herring started to whistle.
99. "You saw me?
100. "I saw you."

Pool

Jump into the pool, says Brother.
I do not wish to jump into the pool.
For old time's sake, says Brother, jump into the pool.
This pool looks different from the pool of yesteryear.
Make a splash, says Brother. Set an example for all the merry children lining up
behind you, says Brother.
I turn around. These children do not look merry. They look very unmerry.
Unmerry as fossils.
Jump into the pool, says Brother.
I do not wish to jump into the pool. There is a tree in the pool.
That is not a tree. That is Grandmother.
Grandmother, is that you?
No answer.
She is in the deep end trying to be misteriosa, says Brother. I can assure you that tree is
not a tree but Grandmother, backstroking.
More children are lining up behind me. Some appear to be geniuses.
Dip the big toe first and the body will come along after, says Brother.
How soon along after?
Depends, says Brother. A day at most.
Is there a plethora of ways? I ask.
There is a plethora.
Go on, I say.
You can JUMP into the pool, suggests Brother.
Go on, I say.
Or you could jackknife, bellyflop, pencil drop, cannonball, face the music, live
the life,
knuckle the mouse, happy go lucky, bury the hatchet, or hubba hubba.
Or I could sink, I say.
Or you could sink, says Brother.

Grandmother? No answer. Grandmother, is that you? No answer.
I do not like this pool.
I point north. Would it be possible to jump into that pool?
Brother squints.
Brother scratches his head.
It seems to be a better pool.
From faraway, agrees Brother, it does seem to be a better pool.
A much better pool.

Loads better, says Brother.
I turn around. There appear to be hundreds of children lining up behind me, possibly
thousands.
Jump into this pool, says Brother. Afterwards, you can have a snack at the snack
bar.
I have been to that snack bar. It is a hideous snack bar.
It is a very hideous snack bar, agrees Brother.
I know no snack bar more hideous.
Any snack bar anywhere would be less hideous.
The popsicles are gaunt.
Impossibly gaunt, agrees Brother.

Grandmother floats by.
"I am going to die soon," sings Grandmother.
I do not know that song.
Nor do I, says Brother.
Jump into the pool, says Brother.
Don't look, I say.
They're here, I say.
Who? asks Brother.
Our parents.
Where? whispers Brother.
At the end of the line.
They are younger than they should be, says Brother.
They appear to be teenagers.
They are very beautiful, says Brother.
Remarkably beautiful, I agree.
Mother is holding a hot pink inflatable ball.
Father is laughing.
Their intention is to jump into the pool and play.
Little do they know, says Brother.
Little do they know! cheer the children.
Little do they know, sighs Grandmother.
Jump into the pool, says Brother.

Hurry up, says Brother, it is time.
Some of the children, from the heat, are drying up.

It's a cruel world, says Brother.
There is no world more cruel, I say.
A crueler world, says Brother, there isn't.
Do you know Gloria? asks Brother.
I do not know Gloria.
Suddenly I find myself in love with Gloria, says Brother.
I must go to her, says Brother.
If you go to Gloria who will tell me to jump into the pool?
Brother thinks.
Grandmother floats by.
Brother thinks more.
Our parents are too far back.
No one, says Brother. If I go to Gloria, no one will tell you to jump into the
pool.
And yet the pool will remain?
Possibly, says Brother.
And I, unjumped, will remain?
I believe you will remain, says Brother.
Then obviously you must go to Gloria.
Without a doubt, says Brother.
Minutes go by.
Brother is still.
Brother?
One whole day goes by.
Evening surrounds us.
Morning comes.
Although I am in love with Gloria, resumes Brother, I have not the heart to go to
Gloria
until you jump into the pool.
Could Gloria come to you?
Her magnificence makes this impossible, says Brother.

I just had a thought.
What's to think about? asks Brother.
The pool.
What else? asks Brother.
Jumping into it.
What else? asks Brother.

The Balkans.
Their winters are heavy, says Brother.
Beautifully heavy.
Like the bones of one thousand grandmothers.
Heavier, says Brother.

Has Gloria ever traveled to The Balkans?
Many times, says Brother.
This is why I love her, says Brother.
Whereas Gloria's ventures are fraught with peril, mine are fraught with no peril,
says
Brother.
This makes Gloria better than me, says Brother.
And me.
And you, says Brother.

Jump into the pool, says Brother.
It appears Grandmother has built a ship.
Normally, says Brother, shipbuilding takes place in a specialized facility called a
shipyard.
In this case, says Brother, Grandmother has used the pool.
Jump into the pool, says Brother. Afterwards you can climb aboard.
The ship holds upwards of thirty men.
Grandmother is perched on the bow.
Very perched, says Brother.
Very, very perched.
I have never seen Grandmother so perched.
When she looks up, says Brother, we'll all be dead.
Even Gloria?
Especially Gloria, says Brother.
Such is the suddenness of living, says Brother.
And loving?
Same thing, says Brother.
Such is the suddenness of loving, says Brother.
Jump into the pool, says Brother.

THE COUNTRY BUS SERVICES MAP

CARYL PAGEL

Olde Main Street Inn

He was chained to the tree
and then burned to death   Chained
in the woods and then lit
on fire   The experts she told
you one morning in Chadron Nebraska
as he finished his juice—*grapefruit*—
were satisfied   The locals were calling
it suicide   You remember her saying
that detectives had considered the case
for months and many were abandoning
homicide   Perched on the edge of
a barstool she explained to you
both that the man had been
teaching at a nearby college   She
said he had been a teacher
at the nearby college—maybe—you
wondered later—because she already knew
you were teachers   She could see
that you were into her story
She was an expert at recalling
this story   She was pleasant and
kind and from Chadron   She had
spent most of her life here
in Chadron   She knew more than
you would ever know—even if
you started now—about Chadron and
the people of Chadron   You knew
more than she would ever know
about absolutely nothing   The man from
the story knew more than either
you or the woman telling you
about him would ever know about
being chained to a tree and
then burned to death—attached to
a pyre and then lit on
fire   You wish to accurately relate
her version   You wish to faithfully
relate her version   You wish to

relate her version and the vision
of those events as she conveyed
them to you both on that
dusty summer morning   You could have
sworn you remembered it raining   It
had not rained   It had never
poured and here you sat patiently
waiting while attending to the particulars
of a murder although you felt
in the back of your brain
all that stirring thunder that you
realized had never happened   You were
doubtlessly dreaming   You must have been
sleeping   You listened as she explained
exactly how the man was discovered
dead in the forest a few
years ago   His body had been
absent for months   Your hostess it
turns out had reason to suspect
nearly everyone   After all Chadron was
a small town and in a
small town everyone knows just about
everything about everyone else who is
living there—for example they might
understand why a man would most
likely not chain his body to
a tree just to burn to
death   She said that he was
discovered drunk but never drank   He
was found uphill but had trouble
hiking   He was remembered as quiet
and tired and kind and was
lit on fire by either his
own hand or his own friends
or some unknown local adversary   You
heard this story the morning you
awoke in the Olde Main Street
Inn in Nebraska   The prior evening

you observed a series of brutal
turquoise clouds bruising the lilac sky
like you could never divine in
your whole life and—*Dear Reader*—
it was still two nights before
those striking Badlands stars were

Untouch

They are blackened. Barefoot. Thin as reeds.
Your untouchables.
—You are not Hindu. You know nothing.

I see them clean your privies, quarry rocks, balance the burning upper-caste
corpse on the bier with long bamboo poles.
—You imagine seeing. You are not Hindu. You see nothing.

Near the burning ghat, the shrunken untouchable woman folded like a child on
the pocked stone, eyes closed, her blackened child's arm extended clasping the
small tin pail for alms.
—You are a sentimentalist. You impose your imaginings.

Your Hindu devotion is an opiate.
The rupees you spend on festivals to Lord Shiva and to your promiscuous boy-
god Kishna should be distributed to the untouchables.
The rupees you spend on savaging trees for your high-caste cremations into the
Ganges should be distributed to your untouchables.
—You are perilously close to blasphemy. Step back.

You take refuge behind the alleged mysteries of Hinduism.
There is no mystery about untouchable children born tormented.
That cruelty cannot be obscured, relativized, buried in Hindu sacrament.
—You are non-Hindu. You see with uncleansed eyes.

You conveniently confuse your religious laws, designed to promote your own
high-caste interests, with justice to the imposed, invisible underclass.
—Not at all. You are not Gulliver among the Yahoos. You are a do-gooder non-
Hindu dabbler in a culture you cannot comprehend.

Liberation, nirvana, moksha.
How do you attain liberation from samsara in a culture predicated on slavery?
—You make a privileged tourist's observation. You are incapable of seeing with
the spirit-eye.

Your untouchable suffers silently.
He services you almost ceaselessly.

When he doesn't service you he is invisible.
If he protests you efface him.
These are humans not vermin.
—You are blaspheming. You are a privileged caucasian do-gooder, but you are
not outside the law.

Apprehend me.
Put me in chains.
—You are an egotist with a martyr's complex.
Your expressed willingness to sacrifice has to do with yourself not with so-called
untouchables.
Joan of Arc is a western not a Hindu conceit.

MUSEUM OF SMALL
DARK THINGS:25 POEMS
BY GEORGE TRAKL

CHAPBOOK

Translated from the German by Jay Hopler

The Rats

Autumn moonlight, the courtyard is whitened by it.
Fantastic shadows fall from the eaves.
A silence lives in the empty windows;
Then the rats up from the sewer come,

Quietly, and flit, whistling, here and there.
And the grizzly smell of shit whiffs
Out after them, quivering through the light
Of that spooky moon.

And they bicker, greedy, ravenous,
And rush into the house and barns full of seed
And fruits. The winds whine, icy,
In the darkness.

In the East

The winter storm's mad organ drone
Is like the sullen anger of the people,
The battle's purple surge,
Defoliated stars.

With broken crowns, silver arms,
The night bids the dying soldiers
Come. The ghosts of the slain groan
In the autumn ash tree's shadow.

The city wound 'round by a forest of thorns—.
From steps slicked with blood, the moon
Chases the frightened women.
Wild wolves break through the gate.

In Venice

In the night room, silence.
The candlestick flickers silver
Before the loner's
Fluting breath.
Hypnotic rose-clouds.

Clouds of dusky flies
Dim the hard room
And the head of the dispossessed
Bristles with the agony
Of another day.

Motionless, the ocean darkens.
A star and its black course
Vanish down the canal.
Child, that sickly smile of yours,
I can see it in my sleep.

In the Red Foliage Filled With Guitars…

A breeze strums the shrubbery; the red leaves hum. Sunflowers
      shine by the fence.
The toe-headed girls comb out their locks in the air.
The sun, like a golden cart, rolls through the clouds.
Buried by the deepening shadows, the old fools shut up and hug
      each other.
The Orphan Tabernacle Choir sings O, the vespers sweet.
The steamy, yellow buzzing of flies.
Down by the creek, the women are washing.
The drying linens billow on the line.
And there she is, the girl I have long loved, making her way
      through the dusk.
From a balmy sky, into holes green and rotten, sparrows fall.
The smell of bread and spices gives false hope to the hungry.

Gródek

In the evening, the autumn woods thunder
With gunfire, the golden plains
And blue lakes. Overhead, the sun
Rolls gloomily along. The night
Takes into its arms the dying soldiers
And stills the crazy wailings of their ruined mouths.
And yet, red clouds in the pastures gather
Silently, moon-cool pools of blood
In which lives a wrathful God.
All roads end in rotting bodies.
Under golden branches of the night and stars
The sister's shadow staggers through the silent grove
To greet the ghosts of the heroes, their heads
Bleeding. And the dark flutes
Of autumn whistle softly in the reeds.
O prouder sorrow! You brazen altars—
Today, the soul seethes with a deeper grief:
The grandchildren never to be born.

Psalm II

Stillness. The kind the blind might find beside an autumn wall,
Eavesdropping with worn-out brows on an unkindness of ravens.
Autumn's golden stillness: the face of the father in the guttering
        sunlight.
In the evening, the old village recedes into a hush of brown oaks,
The red hammering of the blacksmith, the beating of a heart.
Stillness; under fluttering sunflowers, in her slow hands, the
        handmaiden hides
Her hyacinth brow. Fear and silence—
The twilit room fills with splintering eyes, the hesitant steps
Of the old women, the bruised mouth dissolving in the dark.

The evening, wine-quiet. From the ceiling's low beams
A night moth dropped, nymph entombed in bluish sleep.
In the courtyard, a farmhand slaughters a lamb, the blood's sweet
        must
Beclouds our brows, the dark coolness of the fountain.
Dying asters grieving over their own sad vanishings, that's what
        those windy-golden voices are.
When night falls, you gaze at me from failing eyes.
In blue stillness, your cheeks crumbled into dust.
A brushfire burns out so quietly. The black hamlet falls silent on
        its little plot of land,
As if the cross itself climbed down from the blue hill of Calvary.
The silent earth heaved up its dead.

Transformation

Here, at long last, in the red stillness of the autumn-scorched
Gardens, one gets it: how difficult, how futile life can be.
Before the ache in the eyes subsides: carry brown grapes. After
       the ache in the eyes subsides: carry brown grapes.
In the evenings, you clatter and bang through the black
Country only to find the silence of the red beeches
Impenetrable. There is a blue animal longing for death.
There is an empty robe moldering hideously.
In front of a pub, some drunk plants his face in the grass.
How's that for a scene in the theater of peace!
O that elderberry wine. Flutes, soft and tipsy. And that scent, that
       fragrance
The women are wearing—. What is it?
Mignonette?

Evening Thunderstorm

O the red evening hours!
A glimmering falters past the open window.
Grape leaves loop their woozy through the blue gloom,
Worried ghosts nestling inside them.

Dust dances in the stinking gutters.
The wind rattles the windowpanes.
A stampede of thunderbolts drives
Before it the dazzling clouds.

With a crash, the glassy pond shatters.
A colony of seagulls clamors by the window frames.
A fiery dragoon springs from the hills
And explodes into flames in the pines.

In the hospital, the suffering shriek.
The night's bluish plumage buzzes.
The rain, glittering, thunders down
Upon the roofs.

In the Winter

Over pond, over snowy field, in a sky desolate and immense,
      jackdaws are circling.
Hunters are returning from the hunt.
In the black treetops: silence.

Firelight spills from the cabins; a sledge speeds by.
The moon rises, gray—, and just a little too slowly.

A deer is bleeding to death on a hill's soft slope. Ravens are
      bathing in its blood.
Wind in the reeds. Frost. Some smoke.
Someone is walking in the grove.

Winter Twilight

for Max von Esterle

Across a black metal sky, into red
Storms, at sunset, over parks
Pitiful and pale, ravening crows
Are flying.

A beam of light freezes to death
In the clouds. Chased by Satan's curses,
They circle and go down,
Sevenfold in number.

Noiselessly, their beaks cut deep
Into a carcass, sweet and fetid.
Houses loom out of the mute communities;
Lights shine in the theater hall.

Churches, bridges, and clinics
Stand ghastly in the twilight. Blood-
Flecked bed sheets billow:
Sails on a canal.

Winter Night

Snow fell. After midnight, drunk on purple wine, you
leave the dark district of men, the red flame of their hearth. O
darkness!

Black frost. The earth is hard. The air tastes bitter. Your
stars constellate into evil omens.

With stony steps, eyes wide as a soldier's as he storms a
black trench, you stomp out to the railroad embankment. Avanti!

Bitter snow and moon!

An angel strangles a red wolf. Marching on, your legs
chink like blue ice and a smile full of sadness and pride has turned
your face to stone. Your forehead grows pale before the hunger of
the frost;

or it leans in silence over the watchman napping in his
wooden shack.

Frost and smoke. A white star-shirt burns the shoulders of
the one who wears it and God's vultures rend your metal heart.

O, the stony hill! Out in the silver snow—silent,
unthought-of—the cool body softens.

Sleep is black. The ear follows long the paths of the stars
in the ice.

You woke up and the village bells were ringing. The day,
incarnadine, stepped silver from the eastern gate.

Decline

To Karl Borromäus Heinrich

Away over the frozen pond the wild birds go flying.
Evening. An icy wind is blowing from our stars.
Above our final resting places, the nightening skies

Swing low their shattered faces.
Under oaks we float in boats of silver moon-
Light made and snow. The walls of the city

Are ringing with snow; under arches thorny,
Brother mine, we climb, O! our blind hands
Pointing towards midnight.

My Heart Toward Evening

In the evening, one hears the screeching of bats.
Two black horses gambol in the meadow.
The red maple rustles.
The wanderer happens on a tavern.
The young wine and nuts taste delightful.
Delightful: to reel, drunk, in the twilit woods.
Pealing through black branches: painful bells.
Dew drips on the face.

At Night

Tonight, the blue went out of my eyes,
The red and the gold out of my heart. O! How silently the light
        burned!
Your blue coat surrounded that drowning.
Your red mouth put the stamp
On that madness.

On the Death of an Old Woman

Often, full of dread, I listen at her door.
And when I enter, it always feels like someone just ran out.
And her dreamy eyes look past me, as if she saw me
Standing off in the distance somewhere.

She sits like this, bent completely in half, and listens,
And everything around her seems far away.
And when bushes scrape against the window, she trembles,
Weeping softly, just like a frightened child.

And with a tired hand, she combs her white hair
And asks with a pallid glance: must I go already?
Then feverishly: the little altar light's gone
Out! Where are you going? What happened to you?

Landscape

September evening; through the gloaming village, the sad-dark
       calls of the herdsmen ring out.
The farrier fires up the forge. An enormous black horse
Rears up. The hyacinth-like locks of the farm-
Girl brush against its crimson nostrils.
Gently, the cry of the doe grows stiff
At the edge of the forest.
And the yellow blossoms of the mums bend mutely over the
       pond's blue face.
A tree is engulfed in red
Flame. Bats flutter up with dark faces.

In an Old Garden

The brownish-green scent of the mignonette
Drifts across the beautiful pond. The water shimmers,
Shivers with it. The willows stand wrapped
In a crazily fluttering fog of white moths.

Abandoned, the patio basks in the sun.
Goldfish glister deep beneath the surface of the pond.
From time to time, clouds swim up over the hill
And then float away again, slowly.

The arbors seem bright because young women
Walked past them earlier this morning.
Their laughter lingers, hanging in the delicate leaves.
A drunken faun dances in the golden mist.

Melancholy

Bluish shadows. O you dark eyes that look at me so longingly,
        gliding by!
In the garden, guitar chords provide the perfect soundtrack for
        autumn
Dissolving in brown acid.
Nymph-like hands ready death's gloomy rooms.
Cracked lips suck red breasts and, in black acid,
The wet locks of the sun-
Children float.

Summer

In the evening, in the forest, the cuckoo's
Complaint grows quiet.
The seed leans, deeper—
The red poppy.

Black storm clouds threaten
Over the hill.
The old song of the cricket
Dies in the field.

The leaves of the chestnut
Tree never stir. Your dress rustles
Softly on the spiral stairs.

Silently, the candle shines
In the dark room;
A silver hand
Snuffs it out.

Windless, starless night.

The Ravens

At midday, over the paths' black angles,
An unkindness of ravens hastens crying
Stridently. Their shadows streak over the doe.
And sometimes you see them at rest, but even then they're
       cantankerous.

O how they derange the brown stillness!
Sometimes you can hear them bickering
In otherwise peaceful fields like women
Wedded to their own worries.

Circling a carcass, O the stink of it!, they veer
North and fly away, dying away toward
The horizon like a funeral cortege in air
That quivers with lust.

Song of a Captive Blackbird
for Ludwig von Ficker

A dark breeze breathes in the green branches.
About the face of the loner, blue florets float,
The golden sound of his footfalls fading beneath the olive tree.
The night flutters up on drunken wing.
Meekness bleeds so softly. So slowly.
The way dew drips from the flowering thorn.
Brace me, Mercy, against such misery.

Soul-Dark

At the forest's edge: a dark deer. A hush.
The evening wind dies quietly on the hill.

The blackbird's lament grows silent
And autumn's docile flutes
Keep their peace within the reeds.

On a black cloud, poppy-drunk,
You float across the nodding pond,

The starry sky.
The sister's moony voice calls forever
Through the blessèd night.

Lament

Sleep and death, those two bleak eagles,
Beat their wings about this head all night long:
Eternity's icy wave washes away
Man's golden image. The body, bruised,
Bloody, smashes to pieces on the spine-
Chilling reefs, and the dark voice
Grieves over the sea.
Sister Stormy Melancholy,
Look: a dreadful skiff sinks
Beneath the stars,
The silent face of night.

Sleep

Curse you, dark poisons,
White sleep!
How bizarre this garden:
Twilit trees
Filled with serpents,
Moths, spiders, bats.
Stranger! Your shadow
Lost in the sunset:
A sinister brigand
On sorrow's bounding main.
At night's edge, doves flutter up
Over toppling cities
Of steel.

Vespers

Mother Superior, lock me up in darkness,
Yours! Your mountains so cool; so blue—.

The gloom-dimmed dew blooms

Down into the earth. A cross rockets Heavenward.
Star-spark and shine. In a shabby backroom, a liar

Takes one in the kisser and his split lips
Swell. The sound of laughter growing fainter,
Shining like a dying bell. Moon clouds!

At night, when the ripe fruit falls

From the trees so bitterly,
Our every room the tomb
Becomes—.

What a waste the world is.

Acknowledgements

Able Muse (special translation issue edited by Charles Martin):   "Evening Thunderstorm," "The Rats."

Artful Dodge: "Decline," "Gródek," "My Heart Towards Evening," "Winter Twilight."

The Blueshift Journal: "In the Winter."

Ezra: An Online Journal of Translation: "In an Old Garden," "Landscape," "Melancholy."

Interim: "In the East," "In Venice."

Mead: The Journal of Literature and Libations: "Transformation," "In the Red Foliage Full of Guitars...."

New South: "Song of a Captive Blackbird."

The Plume Anthology of Poetry 2014: "Lament."

Plume: "Sleep," "Soul-Dark."

Poetry International: "On the Death of an Old Woman," "Psalm II."

CHRONOLOGY DELINEATED
TO ILLUSTRATE THE HISTORY OF MONARCHICAL REVOLUTIONS

SHEM   HAM   JAPHET

NOAH *or the universal Deluge*

ADAM *OR THE CREATION*

EXPLANATION

Yang Lian

WATERMINT NARRATIVE 5: ELEGIES, AFTER LI SHANGYIN[1]

When once the High Pond Rhapsody was done
The cloud and rain in Southland skies were all the wonder they could bear

yet in Southland skies many clouds much rain
yet *last night's stars and last night's wind*   the only things dividing
the clear frost between two words

and who is pacing to and fro? a boat anchors in
the two worlds above and below the water

twofold vastness and vastness   his incense
sighs our flowing water chilly

an all dark green river bend gobbles   spews
laps by the black-painted hull
that kind of clear old oak yellow   clutches tight
the antique square portholes   behind the window gauze
his siesta   mows the deathly still grass-green of the little park

syllables he stopped split open the line's moon on a thousand rivers
on the long street of the water   birds' wings erase the excuses of
gales one by one   beaks peck
the scarlet of a wild berry poured into a barbed-wire bush
an excuse for being caged

vast vast   the blessing of shoreless waves
in his bitter piercing cold
what else was left unwritten?

---

[1]   c813-858 one of the great Late Tang Dynasty poets. Everything in italics is a quotation from his work: Yang Lian has provided this finding list:

《有感》（非关宋玉有微辞）
《楚吟》
《无题四首·其一》（来是空言去绝踪）
《落花》
《代应二首·其一》（沟水分流西复东）
《房中曲》
《水天闲话旧事》
《楚宫》（湘波如泪色漻漻）
《嫦娥》

and we have long been like a doubt, a question
existing   as the valley you remembered grows more deeply autumnal
long hair escaping Southland skies and fleeing to the water's sound
clouds and rain   divided by thoughts that set out a thousand years

read then   all poems peeled open are love poems

***

A palace on the mountain, a tower upon the palace
Before the tower the palace moat, the twilight river flowing

and the most beautiful love poem must be a poem of farewell

we can't help but say farewell   an epistle
treads on every final glance in thousands of years
must be the unseen *Untitled* in how it refines dusk's density

the deserted terrace I once climbed to
must be demolished to be the you who are purely gone away

the pure colour of desire
skin tangled in rippling tan on towering cliffs
when it can't be embraced the azure shine
fallen once and shattered it carves water gold-inlaid

all wake in dreams   he writes a dream in a dream farther than clouds
we were early on spied by a pile of rubble
night by night   a king   drinks the poisoned wine of impossibility to slake
   his thirst

aestheticism   is falling in love with impossibility itself
reduplicated unvoiced sounds heave and surge   forcing us to turn and go

***

In books finished by force, the ink is not darkened

just so do we teeter in a thousand years of ink
evolve   a swan's river-valley-written reflection

feathers spotlessly white conceal violence   the sound of the water's
mourning harp is yoked to the urgent piping of Shaman Gorge's grass blades
changing the ear glued to an old boat's wooden wall
draw away the days like drawing blood   which day
cannot be translated into music? eavesdrop on love-longing
and ashes   what need to ask whose rhythm they pierce?
we knock lightly against the stony shore   the dripping of footsteps
makes travellers turn their heads   this ink
ground a thousand years and still not dark enough
straightens a twig of greasy green willow-floss

just so we bid farewell to each other with five elegies
and bid ourselves farewell   five long lines of leave-taking
give the river a structure that has been pouring slowly out
a candle flame that makes music is buried underwater
dismantles fish with five fishy reeks
five lines of musical score parallel morning's birdsong
each one clutches an exquisitely agile kind of hearing
every goose's honk binds a book of backward glances
river water rummaging for every tiny winter solstice hidden in flesh
fires a celadon piece no red leaves can fall on
that's what waving goodbye is   the ripples alongside
always the final cold rain past Paradise Hill's endless ridges

just so is conclusion a vain dream   all words hollowed out
a word only then spoken   doesn't change breath's secret password
poetry is only then equal to the same suffocation   language
we don't trust concludes the life we cannot grasp
nothingness absolutely beautiful   you pick this book right up
the boat he left behind punctuates never-returning water
I polish round round mirrors with no relation to moonlight
unafraid to fall and shatter   hugging momentless
coral   jellyfish   little colour-blind fish
                    write down a poem   the world can disappear

***

Flowers flew wild in the little garden

What you got was wet clothes

the class enemy buried alive in the cornfield can feel
reinforcing bars and pile-drivers   growing a beard of conspiracies
a concrete jar filled with piss   the patter of rain unchanged
and spring with its sour foreign brand waters stars forever turning underfoot
REALITY   what do we know of it?

short short a lover's first white hair   fine fine   so delicate in the mirror
another girl slides across the silver rope bridge
a daughter's more aging daughter   twisted
like a breath   in the hotel bathroom hands from behind full of breasts
dissolve like sighs   outside the window the lotuses of the night sky dissolve
LOVE   what do we know of it?

animals on the seashore stare stiffly at the horizon
lower fossil eyebrows   clouds like another dynasty's cough
re-enter the body cavity   though dusk's infection has covered the skin with
 warts
but HISTORY   what do we know of it?

there is a crowd inside a person   going far far away
every road paints the curves of a beautiful woman
a crowd   busy citing the moist fertile source of the womb
because a source can't be ransomed   beauty gasps delicately for breath
stretches the skyline with incestuous pleasure-cries   like the cranes
 Huizong² freed
HOME   what do we know of it?

except for one word   like a high tower watching guests leave
        like a whirlpool   endlessly peeling destination from destination
ask   how much dark still recording in a one-time driven passion

---

² Emperor of the Song dynasty (r. 1100-1126)

hurries to shovel snow from the sky's edge
sweeps a hand's fallen flowers from the white paper?
POETRY   what do we know of it?

***

Twelve storeys of jade, an emptier emptiness

again and again I have seen this stretch of water from the air
the plane's wings stroking over North London   home is where?
a long string of viscera-shaped reflections painting cloud-shadow is where?
a garden is a piece of variegated green rust
gently withdrawing woods return to water-snake swamps
a weird red glow behind dark twigs is where?
Bill Herbert   the glacier's dark tongue scours your chapter and verse
Tang Xiaodu   bushes in the windy night the brighter the more they are
lampless
Pascale Petit   the inevitable river valley of translating poems
is necessarily bottomless   jade pavilions rise higher
twelve stories   lost souls chant in the watermint
a solitary night-swimming swan trails its triangular wake
the meaning I'm asked to know is where?   wipe clean
the angles of the signature   trample and break the yellow-white solids
the plane's wings reveal salt deserts as far as the eye can see

***

Returned but still unseen
The brocade zither lasts longer than a man

a farewell poem written to the year 2008 from the year 859
Li Shangyin   his sycamores have counted all the circling phoenixes
his Taoist lady friends transmogrified one by one to rhymes of despair
blue in his deathbed eyes   gathered a whole life's
bloodstains spattering under his writing-brush

> our bloodstains   those dreamless ones have seen in dreams
> mist roaring mouth-to-mouth on the loveliest mountaintops
> transform river valley mist on car windows painted silver overnight
> for you to arrive at a kiss from a little ten-page thesis

needs how many years of evolution? fingertip contact breathes a chill
on overruled forever then arrives at unthawing forever
writing is so stupid   so don't write then   this winter
cold fulfilled   makes a poem sink babbling under water
it's all mists   a shuddering nakedness in an embrace is too
whoever dreams will return

when will a poem of grief vomit up all the grief?   like what
his painted pleasure boat of forty-eight years couldn't carry dead drunk
the stick of incense he burned on the zither stand couldn't repeat
the female wisp of their smoke   his grave green with grass
like narcissus   blowing a pink flute of flesh
far too many human lives   far too much powerlessness

our powerlessness   turns the story of coming back into
a journey between stars   the incense on your nipples
after a minute's separation is a plant reincarnated
a waist growing rounder bears the terror of endings
gazing at two gentle hands   again and again
lost in the rhetoric   this book picks us up directly
to hear the crackle of the crazing clearly
in daily manufactured cracks   what youth
isn't dark?   wasted?   reciting year after year
time's blankness   using the end-point
we carry on our body to drown his end-point
pillowing waves gurgling flow   poems forever aquamarine
a poet is always willing to ride the meteorite

***

As evening rain came back alone, the mountains were silent

a poem is all of the life we mortgaged
a poem   burning faintly at the vagina's edge
breeds a doom   forces a one-time farewell to be even more erotic
what deserted terrace isn't the one I climbed by Shaman Gorge?
rainy swallows pierce and stitch broken bamboo   lingering clouds   a king's
  dream

was the deserted terrace an altar?   you and I are tales from the start
made real by the flow of nights and days   the river gold-inlaid below the
   cliffs
is eye-witness to the shape of a surrendering self

a poem teaches us to practice a kind of death
what poem isn't this one?   when the year-end of your eyes
gazes deeper   the mountain silence is injected deeper
is it love I grudge or the vastness of hormones?
all flesh and blood a table releases to far distance has a drenched
female grammar   the ocean of sacrifice clings to
a wild tea bush refusing to move into the new year   grows up
into a shape lies cannot hurt

                              ***
       If a woman dream of mountain spirits, her words will invite them
                               *
           Green sea, blue sky, night after night, a heart

Li Shangyin could be the name of a boat
new-launched   not yet knowing past or future
tiny square of waves in the harbor   rocking
simultaneous blue   cranes bend their heads to look down
on Sunday's   great ocean standstill

the silent beat in a century of disaster and division
leaks out from the sunshine of disaster and division   the boat's hull snow-
   white
gigantic is that sleep   the waiting sends out
seagulls as metaphors   replace people disintegrating in the wind
on the boat's flank for no reason a lamp is burning
lighting a pile of steel generated for no reason

all watermint has a prow that cleaves the wind's noise
months and years don't say a thing   only listen to
some ghost composer howling at the prow   laughing   playing with
an every-day zero tidied by the horizon into its shape

a little harmonium   his   but it beckons me
 to quaff a goblet   the cloudy wine of two eras

sharing the same drunkenness two farewell poems
share an idiolect stored faster and faster in darkness
no mine and no yours   a page of indigo sheet music
moving some writing hand that is performed
can't tell mine or yours   twofold vastness above and below the water
breaks and breaks the motley phoenix's beating wings   where are yours and
   mine?

except for a heart   a ghostly invitation
aesthetics of disaster and division   Li Shangyin unscrews another wave
the Lee Valley has booked a paint-shattered returning
death   our reunion has also created it
saying goodbye to yourself is a matter for every instant
         a poem's wordless song translated into wind is a matter for the same
            instant

         night's untitled poems   gorgeous night after night
         the silver that can flow   blots out the scars of flowing
         it has to imitate the sheen of love on the skin
         pushing away a lover's touch   a body
         leaks into another body   its course towards
         impossible   earsplitting   carnal   depth

         the structure a ghost composer long ago set up
         must simulate water   a clump of watermint
         clear fresh bitterness   bitter bitter incense
         must complete the whole of existence   boat and man
         birth is poetry's metaphor   poetry offers a libation
         is still a one-time metaphor leading to women's dreams of forever
          mating

         we are all in   a long rhapsody
         a king once dreamed and now unforgettable
         worked into the gathering and dispersing of a cloud
         the rising and setting of stars   the length and breadth of the

Southland skies
the track of lovemaking drunk on a semen-perfumed blue
C O N C E R T

Translated from the Chinese by Brian Holton

Fernando Valverde

With Eyes Wide Open You Walk Toward Death:

For Alí Calderón
Who accompanied me until the end

In the final pass of the Andes
where the path is full of rocks
tumbling away like a waterfall.
As if smashing hunger and poverty,
and in the gas stations below
is a calm silence in the air.

Someone called Ernesto
someone says your name in the market
or on the dirt paths while the children cross
who eats insects,
who drinks the blood of boys
leaving on the doors the mark of the holy
and some old shoes
over the electrical wire
and some old shoes on the feet who
cross the last desert of the Andes
rocks break in the valley
falling like a stony storm over
spiritless corpses. Who are transported
to the hospital.

They say you are a corpse who never dies
your eyes vacant
They are nailing the roof of the Hospital of Malta
filled with Dengue and Tuberculosis.
Who are you? Like the poor skinny
animals, drinking out of ponds, swallowing
plastic.

Like the soil in cemeteries.
Nothing can silence you—
with eyes wide open you walk toward death.
Someone breathes *Ernesto*
and clouds flee to the other side
of the sky.

His legs are heavy like liquid steel
ending up in a bed
at the hospital in Malta
one afternoon in June.
October over
They'll kill a man
don't try to cross that path
with your steel legs.
One can't hear his boots' footprints
Don't cross the corridors with the steps of beasts
No one hears the footprints of his boots.
Like in nineteen hundred and sixty-seven
With open eyes and waiting in the laundry
on the other side of the corridors.
He feels blood pain in his knees,
he's gotten a fever
death has crossed from the other bed
Death is installed in the gas that arrives
at the kitchen or already has your balls in
tweezers in the operating theater.

This is the case in the valley.
With the logic of hunger and the custom
of seeing the stones falling down.

In these last hours of June, the boy whose blood is gelling
in his knees, runs on the grass.

There is no noise of the helicopters,
only strangers enter the hospital but in their throats there is a fury
that can't change the silence of the
laundry room.

They will return to Santa Cruz
but the young man who is dragged
by the leg and by the knees, who was

born in the valley
and had seen death cross the hospital
and up to the Sucre street, and has seen hidden
in a den of snakes or
in the stagnant water.

That death can't enter when eyes are open
maybe because
there is nothing to see, someone
says one day – blindness is white
is obscurity and there is nothing
to see, open eyes are empty, and fixed
in the roof they nailed on the laundry.

Looking at some place, then at every place, where
ranges break, and split right before eyes, destroying the bones of townspeople,
this is what death is.
Whiteness. White blindness
that travels shutting up
someone called Ernesto in the market or in the gas station,
a young man, speaking your name, looking for a way to alleviate pain
here is where you die
with eyes wide open.

Translated from the Spanish by Gabriel Rubi and Anita Zachary

NATHALIE QUINTANE

PORTFOLIO

Translated from the French by Sylvain Gallais and
Cynthia Hogue

Translator's note:
17 untitled prose poems, excerpted from Jeanne Darc,
a full-length series of 43 untitled prose poems,
Jeanne Darc © P.O.L éditeur, 1998.

Jeannette

Joan

I am the saint on the airwaves

Catherine's voice in your ear

Others will speak through you

Joan, you are exceptional,
but you must fight to stay modest.

When men follow you
never forget to tell them of the Catholic faith

your knees will guide horses

Catherine creates Joan Darc

you'll never make it here

Joan, you must go to Vaucouleurs, meet
         Robert de Baudricourt, make him take you
             to Charles VII, persuade him of your mission,
             be placed at the head of a small army, force
         the English to lift the siege of Orleans, and
crown the king at Reims.

Your ears will guide your life

– From the center, you had a panoramic view of the whole flock: you never lost a sheep.

All you had to do was turn around from time to time (but no shepherd works that way: a moving flock pulls him along in its path). Or you gazed at one of the four cardinal points, so the sun couldn't blind you but dazzled the sheep instead.

– From hilltops, you kept losing the furthest grazers.

– She'd practiced whistling to her dog.

– Her fear: that having taken her eyes off the flock, it'd be gone when she looked back.

– If she stared long enough into a sheep's eyes, it turned its head.

– So used to the backs of her sheep, she hated not seeing the horse's back unless mounted.

– She wondered if she'd feel her voice in ankle or anus when she spoke.

– By fifteen, she found a way to live by the statement: – "Something must happen!"

– Burying her hands in the thick wool of a sheep's withers made her less cold.

– Sometimes when her feet caught in her too long and muddy skirt, the dog circled her coughing.

– Joan loves herself when she's working. Even if some parts of her job of watching sheep are definitely work (rising at dawn, following the wandering flock, keeping an eye on the dog), most of the time, sitting on a rock or standing up to stretch, she doesn't feel like she's really working.

– When she sews, her mother calls it work, but not her father.

– When she follows the flock, her father calls that work, but not her mother (she calls it "strolling").

– Some of the villagers call her a lazybones.

– For her, work has no particular location, like the baker has his oven or the blacksmith his forge.

– Since except for very young children everyone thinks he's working, and thinks others are working, too – even if not as hard –, naturally she's considered part of this group; but she has only to change jobs (e.g. switch from spinning to weaving) for a thrill of relief to call everything into question: can someone be so happy and relaxed about the prospect of work? Is work a state of mind?

– Still, everyone around her seems to be really working.

– They mop their brows and complain.

– St. Catherine told her she had nothing to complain about.

– As a result, she does not seem to be working.

– And the others notice that she doesn't seem to be working.

Like most of the villagers, who believe that the dauphin not yet dauphin must become so, Joan, who's still finding herself and believes the exact same thing, has trouble distinguishing herself clearly enough from the others so she might claim the dauphin's accession to the throne as an incandescent cause or her inalienable duty.

As soon as she says this, her arms drop and words fail.

It seemed the voices would never give her a hard enough kick in the ass to push her, to put her on a path she must follow to its end, an end we've already thoroughly discussed, to take on and to undertake the battles themselves, to shake up the powerful dedicated to a defeat redefined as a choice.

Only this idea that the dauphin, the true dauphin, was not *dauphin for all* would be in the end, thanks to this rude error, unbearable enough to fire her up. Then she'd watch her anger rise toward that point where finally the unbearable makes everything ready to blow.

For her, there was:
– youth, a youth not given to moods, and endowed with characteristics she could count on since childhood: supple body, instructive wounds, unmitigated knowledge of illness and death, any azimuth soon dispersed;
– + models for anger from some of the angry, rare though numerous enough to dub the waiting of others a perfect torpor.

Viewed from the outside, a fatal separation, arranged from above by a fatal power in the form of sonorous and luminous cumulus.

Actually, in her first life she sewed miraculously well

but others considered this zeal for the supernatural to be an excessive care she put into her work, maybe maniacal.

If she'd pursued her angelical studies in Domrémy as if they were nothing, nobody would have thought twice

but they took her leaving, and especially her not returning, as proof she had *two lives.*

– Joan had no feeling of molting: exultant on horseback, she had no time to dwell on what she left behind, or what she'd find. Though her calling as prophet (though hadn't she exaggerated so she could leave?) carried her, a priori, wholly toward the future, the sudden break stuck her in the present, and it was in the present she counted on lifting the sieges, and making a dauphin out of the dauphin.

– The sword's hilt is as important as its blade, not for its ornament, but because a sword without a hilt cannot be held, and because a murderous sword must be *firmly* held: its pommel should fill the space of the hand clenched around it.

He who holds fast to Durendal holds also the hand of Roland.

– The hilt of the sword that Joan would hold her whole life, a prosthesis modeled after the original, would be close-fitted to serve (the sword-hand).

– Whereas the sword's design, made to measure for the individual (size of the blade in proportion to the body, hilt drawn according to the shape of the hand), would first project a synthesis of Joan, frozen in brandishing gesture (the sword-man).

Hers, she had chosen it *"dans un grand tas de ferraille,"* which is to say, out of a great deal of old iron.

— Before my first assault, there was a world between the world and me: bells tolled, my father yelled, sheep bleated.

She went to war to end the war. She claimed that in seven years (her actual words were: "It won't take more than seven years for the war *to get winded*"), there'd be no more war.

— Between us, as long as the war hasn't ended, any claim that it will end in seven years seems more real than this war dragging on, which hovers between starting and stopping, cries and the cries of victory, hooray! no prisoners.

This claim, though, cannot spare her from having to lie prone each morning in order to stretch out her sore back, aching from so much riding.

Living with nose pressed to the glass, you see only later how you looked.

Sheep's wool, stony lanes, dog barks; but under this rustic surface, aren't there crowds of angels descending in cascades, swirling falls of thrones, saints gesturing from high up in trees, vortex, cantatas in patois?

My new life was superficially reversed, **baroque** on top : cavalcades, whirling blades, frenzied negotiations, strategies, trickery, drawings flecked with arrows, cries, armor ... **austere** underneath: economy (wanting to be where you are the moment you're there), sole claim, interiorized ending, many prayers, and various muted things.

The visible break (first part of my life, second part of my life), was a kind of trope – once all the transitions, uncertainties, reversals, receded–, heightened to avert the fear, in the end, of being wishy-washy.

– Really, Joan, I understand that someone can commit herself to defending a cause, though it's lost, and though she reaps only censure and sarcasm, but to do it with such perseverance, such tenacity, it's a kind of perversion of the will, or a complicity so alien it's suspicious: you're too involved in all you do. You see, at some point, you have to accept who you are. You've gone to such lengths to escape your lot, now you're about to accomplish what you said you would, it's time to face yourself. You have to know your own flaws, your virtues, your likes, your dislikes, and to leave no field fallow, as Gilles de Rais said.

Then, he returned to his castle.

- It took time for me to realize that the clarity of war is found not in the assault, but in later recalling the events unfurling in chronological order.

- And that my predictions were actions.
- I saw them as surely as if I'd done them.
- And yet I had to do them.

It wasn't enough to see myself dressed as a man, they had to bring me male clothing, so I could dress as a man, and live right up to the end with the shame of having to explain why.

- And I had to justify my acts.
- In particular, the reason you cut your hair.
- It catches on the helmet.
- There's a will here to change the *person*, through a secondary sexual characteristic.
- With the helmet's friction, my hair's pulled out in fistfuls.
- The shaved nape!
- *Cutting my hair was faster than waiting for all my soldiers to grow theirs out.*

In short, she was quite sure it was she who heard voices, and not her own voice heard by someone else somewhere across the vast world without her knowing it.

She never doubted it was her own voice that continued to issue between abdomen and throat, though so used to battle, to giving orders, it carried farther and farther, resonating in the open air as if in a church.

For a long time, she waited for the voices in fear – especially in the beginning, and oddly, at difficult times: she was always afraid of being yelled at.

– When she called them "voices," by the way, it was a manner of speaking. But try explaining what "voice" means when it does not mean voice.

– Can you imitate the voices that reach you?
– Does the voice come with an image, or can it sound alone, without the aid of icons?
– Is there one voice, speaking through the mouths of several saints, one saint with a multitude of voices, or does each saint have her own voice?
– Do they get angry?
– Do they change (intonation, timbre, cadence, spatial location) according to the nature of what they're saying?
– Did you ever have the impression that one was speaking to you without a voice?
– Do the saints always face you when they speak, or do they sometimes turn in profile?
– If not a virgin, would you be able to hear them?
– Have you ever been tempted to lose your virginity: never? rarely?

With all this riding I'm lucky I still have my maidenhead.

They did not give me the name of Maid by accident, the women can feel around all they want, inside me it holds, and twice over it holds.

– After hours and hours of arguments, intimidation, and threats of torture, in the end all that was left were the *toenails*.

– Before that, labyrinths of steps in dankness, and a dark darker than ordinary darkness

– along with the orders: right, and left, straight ahead, faster, faster.

Torturers are talkative.

A slow deterioration of the material situation, and the spiritual: in spite of the scale of the task accomplished, the accomplishment itself, and the idea that there's nothing more beyond this order, gives in retrospect the impression of a slow and certain deterioration.

SPIRITUAL: with her name, her virginity, her ideas, how can she be sitting here, counting, waiting for something to happen?

MATERIAL: the habit of smoothing her hair under her helmet has been replaced by rubbing her feet to remove sand from the prison floor.

SPIRITUAL: at prayer, her left hand rests loosely over her right.

MATERIAL: she loses weight, including from her arms.

SPIRITUAL: she can't remember her dog's name. What would she do if he didn't come when she called?

MATERIAL: she coughs. Coughing, she breathes and speaks less.

SPIRITUAL: *I defended these swine,*
                      Rouen, round of swine,
                      Tripe, scrap, scum.

MATERIAL: the calluses on her fingers from arms and quill have shrunk; but now a terrible rheumatism roams her hands.

SPIRITUAL: during the day thoughts come which seem strange only in retrospect: is there any objective reason why I am not a *rabbit*?

MATERIAL: in the eyes and the ears, there's no poverty that doesn't show up early on in the ears and the eyes: oozing, clogging, semi-deafness, veiling, blurring, spots. Perfect hearing and sight invite us to war – blind men are never generals; the canteen cook must answer the soldier without raising her eyes from the soup.

SPIRITUAL: she hears *Joan, you answer, but you do not hear what is said to you. You're really so convinced that you hear the voices of God that you do not hear those of men. And those of God, which you claim to transmit*MATERIAL*are replaced by your own, which proclaims you, and administers to you, always first: The Maid speaks in the name of the Maid, and promises many battles, and many heads cut off. The Maid*SPIRITUAL*delivers blame and praise, and baptizes the girls "Joan." The Maid "crowns" a king. The people believe in you, war leader. Should they believe in the leader, or in God? – You say the one, but you do the other. And you say that a personal miracle, a vocation, can guide a life from beginning to end*MATERIAL*Even the uncertainty of the war and its sides has taught you nothing. You appear before your judges just as you could have appeared leaving Domrémy. Exhausted, you speak without thinking about what is happening to you. What's more, you think nothing*

else will happen to you than what you've predicted. You are alone; a whole army couldn't take this solitude away from you
And when her thoughts turn to the past, she sees herself there, a shepherdess, already exhausted.

– Here's Joan drawing herself up forever tall against the sky with a stake at her back.

– Each vertebra presses against the trunk as if to enter it.

– The wind does not ruffle her dress, because of the ropes.

Of the kind of tree that shores her (oak? beech? alder? willow?), we know nothing, because it burned with her.

– Her final expression, hard to read on a face in flames:
either dolorous, or joyous, or dolorous and joyous.

Can we see blood running down the burning body?

– A contemporary questions whether someone could pleasure and suffer at the same time, that jouissance and sufferance alternate, one rising as the other recedes.

The crowd forms a cresting sea before her. She can clearly see a little towhead.

In the center of the confusion, she is both calm and deaf (no cry filters through those wide open mouths).

– A course patiently pursued – from Domrémy to Auxerre, Gien to Bourges, Sens to Paris, Reims to Soissons, Arras to Rouen – starts its final progress, from feet to ankles, knees to soft thighs, nipple to neck's nape, vibrant chin to trembling nostrils (then from her mouth soars the dove).

– Lunula or patella, nothing's discreet anymore, this is a young (vain?) and compact body burning up, joyous blaze, mystic barbecue.

– Her spasmodic breathing is stopped by the coughing.
– And her eyes turn in their orbits.

E. E. CATTINGS

somewhere i have never travelled, gladly
beyond my front door

somewhere i have never travelled, gladly beyond
my front door, your eyes are the color of wet-food:
in your most frail petting are things which enclose me,
or which i cannot swat because they are too near

your slightest turn of knob easily will unclose the door
though i have closed myself as paws,
you open always claw by claw myself as Spring opens
(touching skilfully, mysteriously)her first taste of cosmic nip

or if your wish be to close the door, i and
my life will shut very beautifully ,suddenly,
as when the heart of this domestic animal imagines
the snow carefully everywhere descending;

(i do not know what it is about you that closes
and opens doors; only something in me understands
the voice of your eyes is deeper than all litter)
nobody, not even the toy mouse, has such small paws

About the author: e. e. cattings is a domestic short- haired cat poet who sleeps 12-16 hours a day.
He writes on a typewriter and always writes in lowercase, because he can't manage to hold the shift
button with his paw and type at the same time.

Recently, we started to find poems around the house —under our bunk bed and in our toy closet,
behind the stuffed lion. So we started to collect them.
Eddie&Isabel

Joseph Thomas

A Love Song

By the way, aye-diddly-day, a diddly day a doe
By the side, we trade away, a diddly day a doe

By the cray, a diddly day, a fiddly cray cray so
We fish and trade, a piddley play, a fiddly fay cray crow

By the day, the rhubarbs say, a diddly day pay poe
By the quay, the crayfish say, a riddle me ray ray roe

We fish and sing, we hum and see all through our own glass eyes
We take our fish and humble tunes all kiddle a kay kay coo

We find a girl with flaming eyes, aye-diddly-day a doe
We sell our souls at half past noon a middling may fay foe

By the way, the mermaid shays, all brittle and bray bray boo
By all the fishermen weighted and gray, she riddles and brays ah-choo

We gave it away, all down by the bay, the princess a-pray to-do
We banked on the ray of the moon's ballet, and prettily lay froo-froo.

So down by the way we weighed all our prey and fiddled and frayed a poo
And riddled the bit and tribbled the ship as she piddled the cray cray loo.

Adam Deutsch

Please Don't Center Poems

Please don't center your poems. Margin left,
which is natural and easy on eyes.
The lines want to sit over here, chickens
on a perch, together and warm, left left.

Please don't center your poems, since they are
not greeting cards, nor lyrics. They are not
the lines in the road, sides spaced for cars
to pass through, avoiding the swept clean curbs.

Please don't center your poems, but feel free
        to play with the spacing a little bit.
            No one will die if a line wanders out
                with purpose: poetry as   detective
        seeking answers   in wide   open   danger
who makes it home, safely   or   moves   way out.

DANIEL SIMON

CHAPBOOK

DANIEL SIMON

Eight-Legged Shadow

Not arachnid
but double quadruped

Stilt-like two-footed
biped in pursuit

Magic-lantern striding
perpetual-motion gaited

Ratamacue of footfall –
luminescence, syncopated

DANIEL SIMON

Spotted

When we see something suddenly, why do we say we *spotted* it?
Is it like a spot on the rug that catches our eye in passing,
or the pupil projecting itself on the blank screen of the unexpected?
Blood and ink spots, the patterning of snake, turtle, trout, and peacock,
the eye casts dispersion on the whole cloth of perception.
Some speck or mote always settles on the mind's canvas.
A spotlight to focus the attention, a blot interrupting fixation,
a taint that stains innocence with meaning.

Daniel Simon

Floodgate

The chute like a fall,
not from grace, but into fullness,
sluiced-out calcifications of thirst
~ Augean stable of the mind ~
syntax of sense enjammed,
riverine thrum of a flow
once silted, now burst

DANIEL SIMON

Torchon

After a rag-and-moan chop to the heart,
I wrap my arms around a line-preserver
tethered to a bank of books on the shelf.

Might the weight of one word countervail
the constant pull of dissipation?
Only the word you can't bring yourself to say.

Endgame

King royally incompetent
Omnipotent dame, the Queen

Bishop, that oblique jester
Knight cavalierly skittish

Rook controlling castle
from a four-square tower

Pawn the punch-drunk peon
plotting gambit to checkmate

The signature of thirty-two
on the blank page of sixty-four

The checkered clash of black
and white, anything but gray

Pluriversity

If versatility is the goal,
don't go to a university.
If a versifier you would be,
remove the pacifier from your lips of infantility.
If perversity should distract you,
get off the slippery slope of concupiscity.
If you think reciprocity means getting back your due,
turn around and take your belt of chastity like a man.
It takes perspicacity to see the limits of our capacity.

DANIEL SIMON

Factors of Forty-Eight

One-way arrow arcs in flight toward impact.
Two eyes covet a double dozen, like a stolen case of beer.
Three-sixteenths turn on a socket or teenage love lost.
Four-twelve marks the elegant theorem of a roof's pitch.
Six plus eight equals a six-shooter or a sonnet,
but six times eight lines up like a firing squad:
eight rifles raised to sixteen eyes,
four crosshairs mark a calculus of entry
through each chamber of the heart,
the three-count of *ready – aim – fire.*
Any way you factor it, your number is up.

DANIEL SIMON

Mental Hygiene

"The linguistic meaning of prosody,"
glossed by the left hemisphere.
Was it a blank slate in the beginning,
pristine at birth? As flesh puts on words,

does prosody then follow?
And when the brain gets mucked
in the body's daily tides,
how do we rinse off the grime?

To bathe the brain,
mix four parts brine to one part amnesia,
then call Stevens' roller of big cigars
(the muscular one) to string up the cortex,

lather up the lobes, rinse them out with lye
hang them in the rafters, repacked in saline,
packaged for resale. If he chooses to suck on a sulcus,

juggle the lobes, rappel down a fissure,
or sight along a chiasm, topography will guide him
but he'll need an interpreter (or a good dictionary)

to navigate the landscape and read the signs –
words like debris on the beach
washed up from other shores.

Triptych

I
The onanist at the heart of every language.

II
I cannot claim the I-and-I of Jah and me,
only oy-oy, Babel's retractable yo-yo twin.

III
Not Hopkins' three-person'd god
but a baser trinity must suffice:
the three-headed dog at my throat.

L'an de l'âne

after Luis D'Antin Van Rooten

If this were a political poem
it would be a fable
about the year of the ass.
From Aesop to Aelian to Scheherazade
the moral is clear:
Work like an ox (or an ass)
and avoid the fate of the abattoir.
Idleness and gluttony
receive their proper reward.
Suffer the plow.
Flee the butcher.
Let the farmer thrash his wife
with a stick
while the ox gores the farmer
with his horns.
Sacrifice your daughter to the sultan.
Tell a story to save your life.

DANIEL SIMON

Dipstych

Before you look it up in the *Princeton Handbook*,
I don't mean a *diptych* or a *distich*.

It's what my brother would call me
when he thought I was being a dimwit.

The best insults bare-knuckle you with two syllables on the lips,
except for the double-down satisfaction of *motherfucker*.

Let the refined types savor their *terza rimas* and pentameters.
I choose the Manichean beat of the misfits.

Daniel Simon

Flaubertiade

Zippo click
you echo my ears
but stop to lose the
train of thought,
rhythmically

Code of Honor

The learning curve
of higher education?

While imitation may be
the sincerest form of flattery
(Charles Caleb Colton
op. cit., duly enquoted)
too much flattery
makes you a plagiarist,
a sycophant, or both

Rev. Colton left the ministry,
took up another form
of speculation (*viz.*, gambling),
careened between wealth
– a connoisseur of art and wine –
and poverty, died in 1832
(a suicide) after a long illness
from *anguish of mind (q.v.)*

The whole house of cards
thus built on the rock
of obeisance

Toe the line
mind the gap
play by the rules

The art of flattery?

The first lesson
(and original sin)
of academic life

DANIEL SIMON

Winter's Burn

the aftermark / Of almost too much love
– Robert Frost

That time I got frostbite on the tip of my nose
it was the last run down the mountain
blue bandana over my face no match for the windchill
the vapor of breath freezing immediately
racing downhill with my brothers and cousins
foolhardy youth bent on one-upmanship

Arriving at the lodge to meet our parents
my nose was a bluish purple, so my dad
stuck my face in his armpit – nothing like
the smell of day-old sweat mixed with my own
sour breath and the burn of thawing flesh

but oh, that burn,
like the scalding touch
of benediction

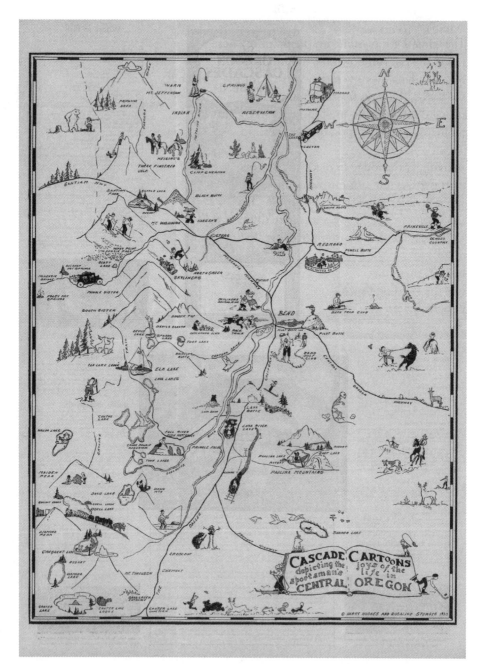

CHARIF SHANAHAN

Self-Portrait in Black and White

If I said I did not want to live anymore,
Would you understand that I meant *like this*?

The years form a mythology I can almost explain.
I see in colors because they are always so much

A part of the problem:

A fire engine is a backpack and my father.
Dollar bill is headscarf, star and crescent.

Candy-cane is barbershop and my choice of men.
Gray is skin, the bridge in the center of your eye—

Now, stirring milk into my coffee with a bent spoon,
I stir milk into my coffee with a bent spoon.

Haratin Girl, Marrakesh, 1968

—As the room is emptied of the boy's body,
she watches through a hole carved into a wall of stone.
Quiet in the hall, the women carry the body awkwardly,
their pale hands tentative to touch it, grasping not the elbow or knee,
not the ankle or neck, but the rounded softnesses—
buttocks, side of torso—and the smallnesses—two fingers,
an ear, a tuft of rough hair—as if to carry him without touching him,
managing just enough to reach the end of the hall, where the girl
stares hard, her eyes strange and dark, then takes off running:
She does not begin the long procession through the old city,
She does not pour the bathwater, or warm it, or salt it,
(the neighbors will not come, the body cannot be cleaned):
She does not know why she rushes down the back streets
to the small rooms where her mother and siblings sit, rushing
past the boys, already men, who spend each hour in waiting
of a nameless thing that will not come, past the small violence
they call to her, the same small violence she lets burn through her,
or run through her, dirty water through a deep bed of sand,
stopping to curse at them, or to pray for them, if not now for
the burning in her lungs, her lungs weak with swelling, swelling
with a fear so complete she will soon no longer know it as fear,
running into the medina, losing her shoes in the running,
the bottom of her feet bruising, toenails chipped, or chipping,
her face swollen, until, suddenly, she begins to slow her pace,
noticing the blue porcelain tiles and the faint marriage song ahead,
or to the west, her one good eye blinded, the mind scabbing around it,
beginning to understand somewhere inside herself, in a place she feels
but cannot name, or speak from, that she will for the rest of her life
run, even when her body does not run, even as she walks,
or sits, or carries the olive hand of a child, or children, not yet born—

ANDREY GRITSMAN

Reception

There is a reception after the reading.
It lasts about 30 minutes
since an electrician and the janitorial service
should be paid overtime.

After the applause we all gather and mingle
around the table with
Gallo Chablis, Melba crackers
and with one or two
wet strawberries on the Hallmark plate
like rat hearts at the biology class.

We listen to a 23 -year -old
fiction writer in lilac tights
working on a novel.

During the discourse
we screw, fall in love or
disintegrate a few fellow participants

and spend a lifetime with one
on the other side of the room,
the one we never get to talk to
since she is conversing all the time
with a tall psychotherapist with oily hair,
standing by a trash can
under the red sign "Exit."

We ask, and not hearing the answer -
answer. Busy talking,
we grow fibroids and nasal polyps
and plan our lives for the next twenty years.

As we talk the weak spirit
melts down in a plastic cup
freezing our fingertips,
and by the time the room is habitable

time is killed and the party is over.
We walk out into the empty street
and the surrounding night
invites us to our real world:
moonlight, wet sand,
cold magnolia leaves,
calling of the freight train,

our own smell, leading us
back home, where nobody waits, so
we can play cards with dead relatives
until someone comes
and turns on the light.

SANDRA BEASLEY

Non-Commissioned (A Quartet)

A Golden Shovel
after Gwendolyn Brooks, "Gay Chaps at the Bar"

I.

No will choose you. We
chose ourselves. What a man knew
in the concrete embrace of bunkers—how
or who—would never make it to
the foxhole. A sergeant catches the order
as it trickles down his just
commander's leg. We haul the
water. We lead the dash.
We're the vertebras necessary
so the skeleton can dance. We're the
18 rounds in the length
of a minute; the 50 pounds of
an M1928 haversack. We're the gayety
of five-card draw in
dead night, the muffled barter of good
smokes for bad booze. Privates taste
fear. A corporal will spit it out. Whether
a man remembers to thread the
diaper of his pack: the stuff of raillery,
except when it should
save your life. We chose to be
grenade men. There was no *slightly*.
There is no plum butter, no bread, no iced
tea, no lemon. There is a meat can, and
there may be meat in it. What's given
to a boy as he trembles, as he turns green,
is the lesson of swim or
goddammitswim. You serve or are served
on a stretcher. Once home, belly up
to the bar and speak of the hot
dusks—how you aimed the mortar—and
remember us, who stayed in the jungles lush.

II.

The difference between liver and
foie gras, we were taught, is in how we
hold a beast's head before feeding. We knew
the throat lining to be beautifully
calloused, like a palm. We learned how
to load the gavage, to
simmer corn in fat to give
their flesh fat in return. They told us to
keep the men. We discarded women
after hatching and the
smell was foul, but so goes summer.
We could almost taste the spread,
rich in iron, surrendering to a tongue the
way an ice cube melts in the tropics.
Nothing was wasted and of
the lies they'll tell, that's the worst: that our
care was a form of waste. It was love.

Everything stings less when
shot with rye. We took time to
pin tin to each swollen breast, to persist
even when they hollered or
the cage held more than it could hold.
We stroked their throats and called it a
sign of hunger
if they swallowed. We took off
shoes that shone with their filth. We knew
their feathers would not stay white.
No one had to give that speech,
nor show us how
their eyes would glaze when ready to
slaughter. How can I make
you understand? This is not a
form of betrayal. Look.
In the field, the officer's job is to make an
office: anything else is an empty omen.

III.

But
nothing
ever
taught
us
to
be
islands.

IV.

If a mother cradles her son's face and
praises how *brave* he is, how *smart*,
how nimble or athletic,
she is teaching him the language
of easy victory—ten points scored for
his team, the test aced, the prick of this
needle to which he did not weep. An hour
in the trench offered what was

a different dictionary. We do not
speak of smart, or brave, or *honor in*
battle. That's for telegrams to the
parents, the posthumous curriculum.
Little sprinter, you have no
advantage in this marathon, no stout
legs to carry you to the finish line's lesson.
Those soldiers who showed
grace with a bayonet understood how
the body must become a weapon to
be wielded; how every chat
is a conversation with
the self we want to save; how death
listens in, nodding. We
laughed at the lieutenants who brought
photos of sweethearts, because no

girl wants to kiss a mouth full of brass.
If the only volume is fortissimo,
it's not music that's playing. Among
every hour, what I recall is our
silences. Our greatest talents—
accomplishing with a look what to
a weaker man required a holler.
We raised them. We laid them down.
We learned faces but not the
names, and we left lording to the lions.
The roof of the house I lived in
had a chevron's peak. I took in this
breath, then this. There was no other air.

Elisa Díaz Castelo

Last Family Visit to Tequesquitengo

> In the year 1856, as a punishment to its inhabitants, the
> village of San Juan Bautista Tequesquitengo and its church
> were covered in water and an artificial lake was created over
> the remains.

III.

Some of us walk backward
hunting for stray words
for gestures left unopened.
Grandfather, lend me your death.
Later, you can go back
to that counter of shadows
where your bones bloom
whiter.

II.

Under the lake we left
         what was left of you. There,
splayed ash on the viridian surface, there
         over the deep nightwater that starts
a little under, colder, thicker than dark dirt,
         tightening round the body
like a glove, a hand.

We took a motor boat to the lake's
         center, its hull a blade on the surface
stilled by night. Grandmother insisted prayer
         but mostly we had silence. The driver, a young boy,
smoked, his body burned down
         by the sun
into another body.

This is the middle, the boy said, but how
         to know it, the motor stopped
and silence rushed back to us like water
         into a crevice.

We stumbled for a while, blind men looking
          for the light switch in an unknown room;
we were
          out of practice in matters of death:
no ritual urged us forward. Fumbling
          we managed a few words
and grabbed you by handfuls
          and pushed you
into the water.

I.

Underneath us
          the drowned church bloomed
inside the lake. Towers proud
          like two raised fists.
During dry season
          they almost touched the surface,
their rusted bells swaying
          to the rhythm of water
displaced by motor boats.

(What is death if not
          a place where you step beside yourself
into the world's blind spot?)

You told me about that church,
          you drove the boat to that point in the water
and left me to imagine its shape in darkness,
          left me to think I saw it there, there.

I was a child but does it matter,
          things we don't see have always existed.
Underneath casts no shadows. The whole town knows
          a whole town sleeps under that lake.

A whole town, they say,
        but now mostly its church
striving for the sky, now, only,
        the surface.
Its white body, a fallen whale, all bones,
        the ribbed vault resisting
the absolution of water.

As a child you'd take us to church, but never
        enter, you'd wait until
we appeared on the sunlit plaza
        until the shadow of the church let go of our bodies.

Now part of you at least has fallen into one
        haphazardly. Dumb,
stray dust,
        tame as a child entering the room
where his mother breathes one last, slow breath.

Azzurra D'Agostino

from Songs of an Emptied World

A field-flanked cottage
of colors
that do not know they change.
All the sounds of the space—alive, not alive
arrive, do not arrive:
the barnyard, the dog, the frolicking
mice, the motely ravenous
men and animals, *una canzone*,
things no one sees. Yet, sees.
They say this land also
was happy.
The carefully laid stone was happy
and slate
which endures the harsh of the present, was.
They have no time for time:
They stand firm like cherry trees
that redden with the earth's
silence. We are
further down, just a little,
in a white solitude—
seen, unseen.

A version from the Italian by Kayla Rodney and Janel Spencer-Levy

Sarah Maclay

Of Intimacy & Interiority

It was autumn. There had been fog, and food. Good conversation. And I was sitting on a train, not facing ahead, but backward, watching the landscape and seascape retreat as I paged through my precious cargo—also moving backward, toward the front of the book from the middle, which seemed, for some reason, in this moment, right. In this way I entered the world of Inger Christensen, a liminal realm in a liminal realm, a realm of transit, moving toward some unseen future, looking inexorably back—looking into the near past, the past as it fell in its permanent swaths, and fled.

In another autumn, I can still remember how this *felt*. How I had been carried to a place so *inside*, so deeply interior that, without even having seen the poem I first fell for in over a year, I can still locate its exact emotional space—or the one it opened in me—and it's attached to a cigarette, an outdoor spot, like a park, and a relationship, hinged to a sense of disconnection, hinged to subtext. Something about to dissolve. Or to open. Or something that had changed, or that had to be hidden. Something important and complicated. Or something burgeoning, before definition—something in need of protection. A moment told almost entirely in its (covert) glances, and snippets, as though the camera had been trained away from the "normal" focal point, the script away from narrative, from backstory. No headshots, please. But gesture, all the ephemera, detritus, of a moment. Subplot, extras: yes. Shot, perhaps, from the view of the feet. Embrace of chance. Object as souvenir: the "Talking of birches' leaves / because it is birches we see." The smallest things. Into the trapdoor of opening, of closing, of change. Seen in sidelong glances, from the corners of the eyes.

And as I open the book again, and find my way to the middle, and move backwards, toward the front—that same feeling. It's right there. As though the book is a vault for this feeling—containing, at least in its center, mostly space: these poems are elliptical, the poems in the first part of *Grass*, falling, as it does, in this volume of seamless translations by Susanna Nied, between *Light* and *Letter in April*, to the point of being almost terse—yet without that feeling: they open, rather than tighten. And it's not "message" we'll find there, of course, or aphorism, as much as extreme lyric concision, these distillations balanced, in that hunger for opposites demonstrated in Christensen's later and far more systemic it, by the poems in the second half of *Grass*, which spill, unfettered and fontlike—in loosened, unpunctuated anaphoric cascades of mad gathering—all that is withheld and unspoken in the first half of this work, as though all that was inner is moving now into ex: expulsion, exhale, the explicit thought, bound quickly, as in a flood, to whatever dislodged boot is scooting by. Both approaches pull us into the shock of encounter—"the inside of one person talking to the inside of another" (Donald Hall)—one through the implicit, one through the ex (as though every thought and sight must be pulled into one place in order not to be lost, and quickly, as soon as it appeared); but let us look at the operations of these first poems that create such intimacy below the level of speech, where so much is implication:

By the Road

Choosing acceptable knolls
for a short cigarette break.
Talking of birches' leaves
because it is birches we see.
Birches with fluttering leaves
along the white trunks.
Talking of other birches
with naked trunks.
Talking of years.
The space between us—
maybe it's empty.

Seeing a group of children come up.
Hearing them ask the way.
Saying yes and seeing them run
embarrassed smiling run
in the right direction.
Crushing the cigarette's glow
in the sand where they ran.
Trying to go on ourselves—
between us.

The focus is on the verbs—"choosing," "talking," "seeing," "hearing," "saying," "crushing," "trying"—on what is being *done*, on the doing. There's a little short story there, one that seems so casual, and yet heartbreaking, the terrible climax of "crushing" held well away from melodrama because, of course, they are just putting out their cigarettes—but also the momentarily allowed, if deflected, "glow"—or perhaps its absence; perhaps the cigarettes carry the glow no longer in the "maybe . . . empty" "space between us." One could write great gusts about symbol and metonymy here, of course, but the thing is that it's the absolutely casual and quotidian and understated seeming normalcy of the moment, at least as it could be observed from the outside, say, in a medium shot or a long, as well as the restraint of the two smokers, that gives this line, this moment, its power, on the way to the devastating and precarious last two lines, and the way that curious last line moves the whole poem, in two simple words, into another zone, into another room of rhetoric—into the interstitial, which is where much of the unuttered and internal action of the poem is occurring all along. And we are reminded again here that, even while the key figures of the poem must talk politely and presumably cannot touch, while the knolls must be "acceptable" and only the birch trunks can be "naked," still, there is no "I" or "you" in this poem—only an "us." The remembered snippets of moment, told quickly and notationally in fragments, as though the speaker is referencing postcards or quick shots, all begin with actions and only imply their subjects—but in all cases, they are plural, and the adults are always in second person—not even, ever, one distancing third. Even the "children" are plural. And why "embarrassed"? Embarrassed to speak to the adults? Or embarrassed and smiling because they sense something unspoken between them that they do not yet have the words for—and perhaps, after all, the adults don't either. The pronouns speak to nothing if not togetherness. And yet this adult togetherness feels fragile. It's just a cigarette break. And it's not.

"Together," likewise, plays, as a title, ironically against the poem that follows:

> and footsteps behind me
> back there
> footsteps
> I do not hear them
> I walk
> walk so thickly
>   in a rain of tar
> drag myself in
> in toward the back
> press my body
> to the body of the house
> stand
>   with all that's crumbled
> stuck tightly to my being

The imagery is unadorned—yet comes at us strangely: "the rain thick as tar," which suddenly gives us a feeling for the difficulty of the walking ("so thickly") while under the influence of this apparently unexpected, unanticipated, unwanted emotional gust—the speaker can barely make it to the house, due to "all that's crumbled." Once there, even in rain, or the feeling of rain, she can't even make it inside. The "body" leans on the body of the house, each line's corrective repetition both enacting the difficulty of movement, as the words themselves cannot seem to step cleanly and completely into their own individual lines, but must drag themselves a few more inches before letting go, while with each line and with each repetition, what is perceived must be subject to revision. And unlike the pronouns in "By the Road," here, in a poem called "Togetherness," there is no "us"; there is no "we." "I" and "my" are countered by "them," which could refer to the footsteps of one or more than one other person. Something has happened, or some unwanted discovery made—we don't know what, exactly. The poem begins *in medias res* and then continues breathlessly, as though even to attempt punctuation here is too much effort for the emotional moment we're allowed to enter, and would somehow misrepresent it—just as it can't be bothered with explaining or describing what has just happened. The extremis that this speaker has unwittingly stepped into is simply too great. And what "togetherness" are we left with? What is "stuck tightly to [her] being"? Not the maker of those footsteps, not another being, but the inanimate ("the body of the house") and "all that has crumbled." If there is other, distant togetherness, it no longer involves her. Or perhaps, for unknown reasons, she has had to flee it. The title frames and refracts the speaker's state of shock, despair, and spectacular disorientation. The irony is as sharp as the pain. And we are let completely into it.

Beyond the *content* of intimacy, the content we might associate with that word—beyond images and story and risk of disclosure—which may or may not feel "intimate" in the moment of apprehension—there's another rung of intimacy, of *inwardness*, between writer and reader, made possible not necessarily because of *what* is revealed, however intimate (since, as with the happenstance of birch leaves, for instance, it is nearly chance), but with the way we are led into a zone of shifting interiority, seemingly as it happens and as it exists within the tangible souvenirs of time—just enough of them—, with the way this allows us to feel what Mary Ruefle sometimes calls "the naked center." It is not that these poems draw us in because of abundant detail or hyperconfessionalism—their willingness to be vulnerable is tangible, but the accompanying level of exterior spectacle is consciously very small. The voices of these poems do not come to us magnified, over the intercom. These poems do not announce themselves. They do not yell. Are not flashy. Do not interrupt. They are not loud. Instead, they let us in, as though a gate were cracked so slightly ajar that only an alert or curious or momentarily distracted pedestrian might find the way to the opening. They beckon. They allow. They invite. Or it's as though we hear the voices whistling from within the secret space below a hill, below a "door in the mountain" (Valentine). Little needs to be said there. Or just enough: "To point at the door without knowing it / To go into the mountain and it is you / . . . and there is always room / . . . and it is always open / and it is you that is open / without knowing it endlessly open . . ." (Christensen, "To Go In").

Some Night Poems: Interstices

With all this in mind, it's interesting to compare, side by side, these two small poems by Eduardo C. Corral and Inger Christensen, where the interstices are literal (they appear in the imagery) as well as operational:

The Blindfold

I draw the curtains.   The room darkens, but
the mirror still reflects   a crescent moon.
I pull   the crescent out,   a rigid curve
that softens   into a length of cloth.
I wrap the cloth around   my eyes,
and I'm peering   through a crack in a wall
revealing   a landscape of snow.

Longing

Betray myself
sit up nights
              burn candles
seek
seek with my hands
though I can see
find a crack in the wall
kiss you

Corral's "The Blindfold" invites us into the privacy of bedtime—or perhaps even later at night, the moon keeping the would-be sleeper awake. There is no initiating drama, other than the implication that the moon's brightness is irritating: "I draw the curtains." A simple, declarative sentence, an every-night action. And yet we feel so close, so present, so involved. The feeling is quiet and then comfortingly dark . . . and then we begin to enter another territory, the territory of the surreal, or the magically real, or the dream, or simply the Mobius-strip-like strangeness of Corral's imagination. Like some late-night magician, he pulls off a sleight-of-hand that shape-shifts the moon into "cloth" into blindfold into lens into "crack in the wall" that discloses this "landscape of snow"—the ultimate transmutation of the brightness, no longer an irritant but a vision worthy of the missing REM. We get to be alone with him, and alone with his mind. *This place where the light gets in*—imperfection, irritant, crack—becomes the source of unexpected joy and revelation while, at the same time, the lines themselves are cracked, broken up with gaps in the text, as though, perhaps, a computer error had scrambled the original line breaks into this new form that, more horizontal, fits more like a blindfold—a blindfold that, paradoxically, allows one to see.

The "crack in the wall" in "Longing," on the other hand, is the culmination of a poem that, in 25 words, including the title, is remarkable for its equal parts restraint and disclosure, and is in charge of delivering us to the desperately imagined "kiss" at the end. Here, too, we're allowed to be alone with the speaker, late at night, and while insomnia colors these two poems, it's for different reasons. As with these other poems from *Grass*, subtext is queen. We're given to understand, in this case, that the absent beloved, not the moon, is the cause of the sleeplessness; that this is a recurring trouble but also joy—the speaker prolongs her own delayed sleep by lighting candles, creating her own ritual; and that, against her better judgment, her "longing" continues to increase, to the degree that she must "seek / seek with [her] hands." In other hands, how differently this would play. What we are given here is not the graphic detail of that seeking, moment to moment, but its almost stuttering insistence—in other words, both the interior urgency and struggle and the way this erupts into visible action. In a sense, we are shocked into *her* sense of both shock and urgency, into the desperation and helpless and even confounding repetition of her desire. The dots between "seek" and "hands" and "crack in the wall" and "kiss" immediately connect, and we supply our own images and rationale as we connect them. In this case, the poem is intimate in two ways—one is, of course, that it allows us to witness an intensely private moment, or, by implication, a series of them, that is erotically intimate. But also, we're invited into the somewhat thorny and shifting center of this eroticism—into the struggle of it—and into the gaps in detail that we leap to fill. It is hard to complete a reading without moving from witness to voyeur to participant. Christensen's shared "seeking" is the ultimate private act, made bare here, but one of her hands is also held out to us. The vulnerabilities here are multiple, and manifold.

A tonally gentler night poem of Jean Valentine's pulls us into an even more radical interiority by occupying even more elliptical turf—this one lives in its interstices at the same time as its nocturnal center radiates out into universal invitation, individual ego shrinking to the size of the same "needle" that "Pulls me on in my dream," blurring the boundaries between singular and collective experience:

Even all night long

Even all night long while
The night train

Pulls me on in my dream
Like a needle

Even then, down in my bed,
My hand across the sheet

Anyone's hand
My face anyone's face

Are held
And kissed

The water
The child

The friend
Unlost.

What also blurs, in a kind of wonder of indeterminacy and syntactical ambiguity, is location: is the speaker on a train at night? Or in bed? Or in a sleeper car? Is the train a dream location? Or an actual location in which this dream of touch and healing occurs? The order in which these early images and phrases come to us, and the suspension of both these brief imagistic fragments and the rules of punctuation, allow us to float in the space of the poem on the page as well as in the fluidities of its loci and identities. GPS won't help us here. Connective tissue feels even more hollowed out than in many earlier Valentine poems, and yet it is possible to convert the poem into one long, horizontal sentence, filled in with the punctuation and the one additional "and" that would establish a firmer "meaning." But that would kill off the very experience of the poem. Having to dangle more vertically with the slumbering speaker, into these deeper and deeper waters where the solidity of earthly boundaries is likely to dissolve, and having to wait as the moment-by-moment images float up from the depths—are they gifts or are they clues?—like one after another petal of rest and restoration and relief, is what allows us, below any logos-based understanding of what has been said, to feel the suffusion of joy, and the surprise and depth and mystery of it, that pull the poem into being as it sews its way across all forms of loss and separation. And it feels generous, ultimately, as well as proportionally right somehow, that the images and categories are not overly particularized: "night," "train," "dream,' "needle," "bed," "hand," "face," "sheet," "kiss," "water," "child," "friend." They operate like primary colors to which we'll add our own nuances of shading and mixing, growing increasingly abstract by the end—but enough of them are concrete enough to establish an immediately accessible, if mysterious and mutable and mutating and mobile, scenario, one that allows the last word of the poem, "unlost," to reverberate upward into all we have touched.

As in many of Transtromer's poems—and I am thinking especially of "The Half-Finished Heaven" as a good example of this, but there are more— the movement here, line to line, moment to moment, is notational, gestural. This. Then this. Then this. We are let in to the motion of the mind—to its pacing. The pacing of epiphanies, of turns, as they occur—or as a rock would skip its lake—here, and here, and here—as though we're allowed to witness, as it happens, the activity of noticing. Just that. As it happens. With its slight correctives or widenings of perception in the next moment. And the next. And this feeling of being allowed in—into a being-in-the-process-of-becoming—is magnified by Valentine's embrace of indeterminacy, so essential to the way this poem (in all ways) *moves*. It's instructive here, in particular, to consider both the sense in which indeterminacy "implies many possible solutions" and this sub-definition of indeterminate, which so mimics the way this poem emerges: "characterized by growth in which the main stem continues to elongate indefinitely without being limited by a terminal inflorescence" ("Indeterminate").

"The whitewashed walls," another of Valentine's offerings in *Break the Glass*, draws us in with similar techniques:

> The whitewashed walls, the chair.
> Were we nursed by the same wetnurse?
>
> The cups of tea undrunk
> The crumb of tobacco on your lip
>
> The poems in our speckled notebooks
> Where we warmed our hands

Over the quick fire

Long before the woodstove's wood and coal
Shifted and settled and warmed us

Even months before
Even from miles away

As in "Even all night long," we are suspended, floating, in a mostly
punctuationless realm of unfolding recognition-as-it-occurs. Similarly, the
floating syntax allows for multiple resolutions of phrases and images-on-the-way:
is it that "The poems in our speckled notebooks" "warmed our hands"? The way
we come across these phrases back-to-back, without any resistant or clarifying
signage, suggests this, and we're allowed to live happily within this notion before
moving to the phrase that follows the line "Where we warmed our hands,"
which yields a hand-warming location we'd be more likely to expect: "Over the
quick fire." This time out, it's not a descent into dream that we're riding in, but
something more like the assemblage of a list of evidence—a spacious one, and
brief—as though the mind is flashing back on moments of coincidence and
connection that confirm the mysterious emergence, and then fact, of a kind of
kinship—I read it as a celebration of the discovery of a new-found friend (and
my theory would be that it's written for Kate Greenstreet, to whom, along with
her husband Max, the book is dedicated, but I could be wrong.)

It's interesting, though, to see what's missing: the very name of the
thing the poet celebrates. Think how different the poem would feel if this were
immediately defined and framed, say, by an anchoring title like "Friendship" or
"New Friendship." Among other things, there would be no further need to read
the poem—case closed; but also, it would be ham-fisted, a sort of bludgeoning of
something alive and multiple and in-process into a pre-made container. Instead,
the poem's impulse is to share the wonder and oddness and uncanny euphoria
of what is, as Celan might say, *en route*—in life, as it is emerging, just as "The
poem is . . .en route. . . Does this very fact not place the poem already here, at
its inception, in the encounter, *in the mystery of encounter*? . . . The poem intends
another, needs this other, needs an opposite. It goes toward it, bespeaks it" ("The
Meridian"). And unlike the images in "Even all night long," here, we're given
the quirky and particular observations and objects of a very *particular* person
and place and relationship in the unfolding: those "cups of tea undrunk" and
"The crumb of tobacco on your lip," which also tell us that the exchange itself
is so riveting to speaker and "you" that its very rituals can't quite get completed,
and the "woodstove" for heat, as well as the discovery of shared sensibility: the

same "speckled notebooks" and the familiar "whitewashed walls" and "chair" are enough to force this rhetorical, maybe even actual, question: "Were we nursed by the same wet-nurse?" This is a poem of direct address, an ode-like celebration, ending in those two last lines that lead us backward in time to a feeling of imminence, the glow of something impending, that is so typical of something we may associate more with early religious iconography: the annunciation. Here, though, it's more like an annunciation *sans* announcement. After all, as Lao Tsu might remind us, "The Tao that can be named / is not the eternal Tao." But what is clear is that the poem is suffused with a kind of shocked gratitude, and immanence, as the unexpected sweetness of new connection finds its blooms.

A Soft Chiasmus

This quality of intimacy—of vulnerability, of welcoming the reader into the in-every-sense unfixed and shifting center—is intrinsic in the way these poems are made, whatever their content, and whether their speakers or figures are alone or near others, moving through the states and stages of longing, of healing, of wonder, despair. But the undertow of the innermost holds sway not just in works of such extreme distillation. Within the complex staging and comparatively densely-wrought world of Jorie Graham's "San Sepolcro," the invitation to intimacy occurs as the poem's finely observed exterior surfaces give way, transmuting our certainties at every turn, until, at nearly every line, we have to question where we are, what we're looking at, exactly:

> In this blue light,
>   I can take you there,
> snow having made me
>   a world of bone
> seen through to. This
>   is my house,
>
> my section of Etruscan
>   wall, my neighbor's
> lemontrees, and, just below
>   the lower church,
> the airplane factory.
>   A rooster
>
> crows all day from mist

outside the walls.
There's milk on the air,
        ice on the oily
lemonskins. How clean
        the mind is,

holy grave. It is this girl
        by Piero
della Francsca, unbuttoning
        her blue dress,
her mantle of weather,
        to go into

labor. Come, we can go in.
        It is before
the birth of god. No one
        has risen yet
to the museums, to the assembly
        line—bodies

and wings—to the open air
        market. This is
what the living do: go in.
        It's a long way.
And the dress keeps opening
        from eternity

to privacy, quickening.
        Inside, at the heart,
is tragedy, the present moment
        forever stillborn,
but going in, each breath
        is a button

coming undone, something terribly
        nimble-fingered
finding all of the stops.

"San Sepolcro" becomes simultaneously increasingly mysterious and intimate
as it weaves, sometimes in one phrase, the imagery of cold and lemon-trees, of

ancient and industrial—we are somehow both inside images of the painting—
not just the central, astounding, almost shockingly, disarmingly modern one of
the buttons popping from the center of Mary's gown just before labor, but other
parts of della Francesca's work (lemon tree, Etruscan walls)—and in the world
of the present: cold, home, studio, a feeling of blue light (perhaps *l'heure bleu*,
when, even in the workaday sense of it, "No one / has risen yet"). That the poem
refuses to resolve or to announce these changes in montage—that there are no
subtitles, in a sense, just the montage—gives the poem much of its power, and
relocates us.

By the end of the first stanza, if not by line 3, we feel welcomed, lured,
curious, and disoriented. Who, for instance, is the speaker? Sometimes we can
imagine Graham, sometimes this 15th century artist, Piero della Francesca,
whose "Madonna del Parto" is the ekphrastic center of this work: imagine a
soft chiasmus—whatever the overarching tentlike, crownlike, proscenium-
arch-like structure that holds and opens its parted curtains to reveal *this* Mary,
this Madonna, in her blue and partially unbuttoned robe, revealing a white
undergarment made round by the globe of her belly. Like a series of cloth nesting
dolls, one enters a series of chambers—parting containers—both womblike and
vulvic. And so whatever sense there is, in the last lines, of the buttons being
nimbly undone to allow the passage of the still unborn Christ—and all that will
follow—out and into the world, there is, equally, the sense of entrance, of the
also-inevitable invitation that the undone buttons will allow—mental, emotional,
physical—fulfilling the opening promise of the poem: "I can take you there."

The poem is a master example of the powers of ambiguity and
enjambment, finding its indeterminacy not in omission and negative space so
much as in the way the imagery and even sense of place—of actual physical
location—at each line seem to warp by the time we reach the end of the next,
so that what we are invited into with some conviction, we must realize, is
actually mutable and increasingly dreamlike as a physical place, in spite of its
multiply sensate and memorable attributes, but reliable and deeply alluring and
compelling—and somehow even firm—as a metaphysical one.

Though it is true that San Sepolcro, the literal Tuscan home of della
Francesca, is northerly enough to get snow, to experience freezing temperatures,
and certainly by now is interlaced with elements that arrived centuries apart, still,
an unusual spaciousness (of both space and time) and potential for ambiguity
is created by the phrasal combinings and line-to-line braidings of seeming
contradictions—of opposites, of things that could be worlds apart: "ice on the
oily / lemon groves," the "Etruscan / wall" and the "lower church" only words
away from "the airplane factory." Hot and cold. The present. The ancient.
"Open-air markets" and "assembly / lines." "Bodies and wings." The "blue

light" into which we are transported as the poem opens; the painting's ancient "blue dress." The buttons, unfastening with their seamless urgencies both erotic and maternal—and the peculiarly and skillfully disembodied quality of their being undone, as though invisible hands are quickly at work. We seem to be being pulled to a place both specific and utopic—utopic in the sense both of *sublime* and *no-place*, at least no physical one—yet it is a place both ultimately earthy (down to the trees, the rooster, the factories, work) and ethereal—a place somewhere and nowhere, by turns, or a "place" made of more than one mappable place, perhaps continents apart and full of distinct and singular particulars: finally, the heart of interiority. It is as though the place that opens, that invites, that breathes, that we are invited to share, is interstitial—the place that exists literally between the lines, as they splice their crossed correlatives, as they juxtapose images of what could of course, in fact, exist in one literal place—if a painting from 1459 is housed, for instance, in a modern Italian town in the cooler seasons—but could just as easily be the braided offering of two places, two times, of what is exterior and visible and of what is interior and beyond audible sound, and to Graham's credit, we are allowed to remain in this mystery, within this limned thicket of clarity and indeterminacy, without explanation, without instructions for its making or its definite emotional context or back story—we get no more clues about what came before or what comes after, only "what the living do" in this present and in its referenced pictorial past, with all the painting alludes to, which is not itself the subject of this poem, not its *raison d'etre*, though it is central to its being, to its ability to exist. We have been taken to a "place" that refuses to give up its secrets, and yet is lit with visual and tactile clarity, is alive to the senses, and will not resolve.

The restraint, the refusal to say any more, is essential to the preservation of the architecture that allows this place to exist—this vault, this chamber, this "holy grave." " . . . if only you do not try to utter what is unutterable," as Wittgenstein put it, "then *nothing* gets lost. But the unutterable will be— unutterably—*contained* in what has been uttered!" San Sepolcro, the literal place, is the essential and inhabited marker en route to the San Sepolcro that is *this* place: the poem itself, or rather the inner, interior place we are given/allowed to enter that lives in the center of these lines and moves the words and lines and choices that house it. The town we could literally travel to is reminiscent of *but is not the same as* the poem. The poem, as made, is what provides us access to its own unuttered and unutterable heart.

Works Cited

Christensen, Inger. "By the Road." *Light, Grass, and A Letter in April.* Translated by Susanna Nied, New Directions, 2011.

Christensen, Inger. "Longing." *Light, Grass, and A Letter in April.* Translated by Susanna Nied, New Directions, 2011.

Christensen, Inger. "To Go In." *Light, Grass, and A Letter in April.* Translated by Susanna Nied, New Directions, 2011.

Christensen, Inger. "Together." *Light, Grass, and A Letter in April.* Translated by Susanna Nied, New Directions, 2011.

Cohen, Leonard. "Anthem." *The Future,* SBME Special Markets, 2005.

Corral, Eduardo C. "The Blindfold." *Slow Lightning.* Yale University Press, 2012.

Graham, Jorie. "'San Sepolcro." *From the New World: Poems 1976-2014.* Ecco, Harper Collins, 2015.

Celan, Paul. 'The Meridian." *Paul Celan: Selections.* Translated by Pierre Joris. U of California Press, 2005.

"Indeterminate." *Merriam-Webster.* com, n.d. Oct. 4 2016.

Valentine, Jean. "Even all night long." *Break the Glass.* Copper Canyon Press, 2012.

Valentine, Jean. "The whitewashed walls." *Break the Glass.* Copper Canyon Press, 2012.

WISŁAWA SZYMBORSKA

The Literary Mail: On How to Become (Or Not to Become) a Writer

[Poczta literacka czyli jak zostać (lub nie zostać) pisarzem]

Translator's Note: For eight years, between 1960-1968, Wisława Szymborska co-edited the "Literary Mail" column in The Literary Life (Polish: Życie literackie), a weekly magazine published in Kraków from 1951 to 1991, where she printed her responses to submissions sent in by aspiring poets and writers. Thirty years later, the future Nobel Laureate's responses were selected and published as a book, entitled The Literary Mail: On How to Become (Or Not to Become) a Writer, from which the following fragments are excerpted. All Works by Wisława Szymborska © The Wisława Szymborska Foundation, www.szymborska.org.pl.

—Piotr Florczyk

H.J. Różnica It's quite common for the editor of the "Mail" to read letters that contain threats. These letters sound more or less like this: please tell me if my texts are worth something, because if they're not, I'll quit right away, tear them up, trash them, say goodbye to my dreams of fame, I'll despair, doubt myself, break down, take to drink, cease to believe in the meaning of my own life, and so on and so forth. That's when the editor doesn't know what to do. Whatever she considers writing back has already become dangerous. If she writes that the poem or prose is bad, it's a ready-made tragedy. If she writes that they're good, the author goes nuts and fixates on his own abilities. (There have been such cases.) Still others demand a prompt response, lest something terrible might happen. They won't even allow one to ponder it a bit.

***

Magro, Krynica Dear Mr. and Mrs., you expect too much from us. You both write poems and insist on knowing which of you writes better ones. We prefer not to have a hand in it, because of that one scary sentence in your letter: "A lot depends on it…" Marital competition ends well only in film comedies. In any case, your style is more or less identical—that is, hard to distinguish. As fanatics of hearth and home, we want this Solomonian judgment to mark the end of what we have to say.

***

J. Szym., Łódź Well, well. You copied carefully fragments of a short story by

Jan Stoberski* and sent it to us to be published as your debut. But that's nothing compared to one demon for work from Gdańsk, who transcribed cleanly one chapter of *The Magic Mountain*, changing the names of the characters for disguise. There were some thirty pages of it in total. You look lousy with your manuscript of four pages. You have to put your nose to the grindstone. First of all, we recommend *The Human Comedy*. Not bad and lots of it.

[Jan Stoberski (1906-1997) was a Polish short-story writer.]

***

J. G., Szczecin, A. Z., Łódź, H. K., pow. Gniezno Springtime, springtime. The cruel girls leave some poets for other poets, resulting in a doubled influx to our editorial office of poems full of a) remorse: "You gave me compliments, although I had big detriments"; b) determination: "What a futile effort, the whole world can't keep you from me forever"; c) bitterness: "You were not sad, when I lay in the ground, but I was next to you, with my soul, and with my thoughts in heaven"; d) hasty promises: "I will not allow this fate's sickness to kidnap you into wilderness"; and e) a nice incentive: "And when at last I'm thine, thou splash in the eye of mine"…All of this is human and somehow endearing, but is it any wonder that every spring awakens in our editorial souls the feeling of a hard-to-define fear?

***

OL, Kraków If you do not have the courage to come to us and talk about the submitted poems, then you can come without courage. We have a lot of sympathy for the timid. It's almost a rule, somehow, that the timid ones challenge themselves more; they are more persistent and think more intensely. These properties themselves do not add up to much, but in the case innate abilities already exist, they do them invaluable favors by simply turning them into talent. No need to sew a frockcoat for this visit, since, well, we hold office hours before noon!

***

P.Z.D., Chorzów "Or give me some hope that this will be published or at least consolation…" We have to, after reading it, choose the latter. So pay attention, we're consoling you. A great destiny awaits you, that of a reader, the highest category of readers, one that's impartial; the fate of literature's lover, the one who will always be the stronger partner, meaning, not the one who has to do the conquering but the one others want to win over. You will read a variety of miscellaneous books just for the pleasure of reading. Not watching for "gimmicks," not wondering whether this or that could be written better or just as good but differently. Without the jealousy, without the state of depression and the attacks of suspicion that accompany the reader that also writes. For you, Dante will be Dante, regardless of whether or not his aunt worked for his publisher. At night you won't be tormented by the question why X, who doesn't rhyme, was published, whereas I, who rhymed everything and counted on the fingers of my hand all the syllables, haven't received even a word of answer from the editors. The facial expressions of the editor won't concern you in the least while the grimaces of the various "stages" either nothing or not so much. And then there is the not so trivial benefit that we often say "wannabe writer," but never "wannabe reader." Of course, there exist whole multitudes of failed readers—naturally, we don't see you as part of that group—yet somehow they get off the hook easily, but if someone writes and nothing good comes of it, then everybody immediately starts rolling their eyes and sighing. Even his own girlfriend can't be counted on too much. What do you think? Do you feel like a king now? Must be.

***

Lupine How to become a man of letters? You're asking a problematic question. Exactly like that little boy who asked how babies are made, and when his mother told him that she'll explain it later, because now she's very busy, he insisted, saying, "Then at least explain to me the head..." Well, let us try explaining at least the head: one needs to have some talent.

***

Halina W., Białystok We're about to tell you something very unseemly: you are someone who is too guileless and pure at heart to write well. Various demons whirl in the depths of a talented writer. And even if they lie dormant (or should be dormant) in him before and after writing, they are very active while he writes. Without their help the writer would not be able to identify with the complicated experiences of his characters. Nothing that's human is alien to me—oh, the maxim does not hide the lives of polite saints. We send our regards.

***

H. C., Kraków Lack of literary talent is no disgrace. It happens to many people who are wise, enlightened, noble, or gifted remarkably in other areas. In telling someone that their text is lousy, we don't intend to offend anyone or take away their faith in the meaning of existence. On the other hand, it's true that we do not always utter our judgments with Chinese politeness. Oh, the Chinese, they once knew, before the Cultural Revolution, how to respond to unfortunate poets! It sounded something like this: "Your poems, Sir, exceed everything written so far as well as everything that's yet to be written. If they were printed, all literature would fade in their blinding light and all other authors would painfully experience their own nothingness…"

***

J. W., Warszawa We are terribly worried when a budding author, having published his first poem in some periodical, drops out of college and decides to live henceforth from and for poetry. The effect is usually such that a year is lost forever, and the next batch of poems spends months lying in the editorial offices, waiting for—at best—their turn to appear in the pages of the weeklies. Paternally, we recommend caution, especially since your poems are only proper at this point, and, as everyone knows, the poets' hell is papered with exactly such poems. Besides, you want to drop out of what, medicine? Friedrich Schiller's learned profession?

***

The Seeker, Kudowa No, there are no novel writing textbooks in Poland. Apparently in the United States such things get published, but we dare to doubt their value, due to the fact that if an author knew a reliable recipe for literary success, he would rather enjoy it himself than have to make a living writing textbooks. Simple? Simple.

***

Ula, Sopot A definition of poetry, in one sentence? Well. We know of at least five hundred authored by others, but none of them seems to us quite specific and complete at the same time. Each expresses the taste of its era. Our innate skepticism prevents us from attempting to formulate a new definition. But we recall a nice aphorism by Carl Sandburg: "Poetry is the journal of the sea animal living on land, wanting to fly in the air." Will this do for a while?

***

Ir. Przyb., Gdańsk Don't try to sound poetic at all costs; being poetic is boring because it's always incidental. Poetry, indeed all literature, draws its vital powers from the world we live in, from events really lived through, from experiences really suffered through, and thoughts thought-through individually. The world needs to be described over and over, because it is not the same as before, even if only because we didn't always live here. It's possible that Tetmajer* could've written the *Wuthering Song*. But you're only twenty-four, and thirty million countrymen are holding their breath, waiting to hear what you yourself might tell them.

[Kazimierz Przerwa-Tetmajer (1865-1940) was a Polish poet, novelist, playwright, and journalist.]

***

Mił, Brzesko Descriptions of nature do not belong with other mandatory literary services. If there isn't a way to find fresh enough words to make the description interesting, then in general it's better not to bother with the moonlight reflecting on the water. The fragment of the novel you sent, in any case, talks about the theft of a cow. Neither the thief nor the cow led out of the shed is in the mood to enjoy the beauty of nature.

***

Kar. M., Sędziszów Physicians have it good, they can always prescribe some pills. For our industry, the Big Pharma has not invented anything. So we recommend Polish grammar, three times a day after meals.

List of Images

p.356
Strass, Friedrich. *Der Strom der Zeiten (the stream of time)*, 1803.

p.374
Vimercati, Cesare. *Panorama del Basso-Egitto - Canale Artificiale di Suze*, 1869.

p.395
Bougard, Rene. *Plate 1. 7 Views*, 1801.

p.448
Chase, Ernest Dudley. *The United States as viewed by California (Very unofficial)*, 194.0

p.469
Geodezicheskii komitet VSNKh-SSSR. *(Moscow) Moskva i okrestnosti. Geodezicheskii komitet VSNKh-SSSR*, 1927.

p.485
Gill, Leslie MacDonald. *The Country Bus-Services Map, London and Vicinity*, 1928.

p.518
Eddy, Isaac. *Chronology Delineated to Illustrate the History of Monarchical Revolution*, 1813.

p. 550
Berry, William D. *Key to Alaska plant and wildlife map*, 1967.

p. 570
Hughes, Harry. *Cascade cartoons depicting the joys of the sportsman's life in Central Oregon*, 1933.